Alexander of Aphrodisias
On Aristotle Metaphysics 2 & 3

Alexander of Aphrodisias
On Aristotle
Metaphysics 2 & 3

Translated by
William E. Dooley, S. J. &
Arthur Madigan S. J.

B L O O M S B U R Y
LONDON • NEW DELHI • NEW YORK • SYDNEY

Bloomsbury Academic
An imprint of Bloomsbury Publishing Plc

50 Bedford Square	1385 Broadway
London	New York
WC1B 3DP	NY 10018
UK	USA

www.bloomsbury.com

Bloomsbury is a registered trade mark of Bloomsbury Publishing Plc

First published in 1992 by Gerald Duckworth & Co. Ltd.
Paperback edition first published 2014

British Library Cataloguing-in-Publication Data
A catalogue record for this book is available from the British Library.

ISBN HB: 978-0-7156-2373-2
PB: 978-1-7809-3444-0
ePDF: 978-1-7809-3445-7

Library of Congress Cataloging-in-Publication Data
A catalog record for this book is available from the Library of Congress.

Acknowledgements
The present translations have been made possible by generous and imaginative
funding from the following resources: the National Endowment for the Humanities,
Division of Research Programs, an independent federal agency of the USA; the
Leverhulme Trust; the British Academy; the Jowett Copyright Trustees; the Royal
Society (UK); Centro Internazionale A. Beltrame di Storia della Spazio e del
Tempo (Padua); Mario Mignucci; Liverpool University. The editor wishes to thank
Ian Crystal and Paul Opperman for their help in preparing the volume for press.

Typeset by Derek Doyle & Associates, Mold, Clwyd.
Printed and bound by CPI Group (UK) Ltd, Croydon, CR0 4YY

Contents

Alexander of Aphrodisias

On Aristotle Metaphysics 2

translated by
William E. Dooley

Introduction

Book 2 of Aristotle's *Metaphysics*, known as Alpha Elatton (little a) in contrast to the much longer Book 1, Alpha Meizon (Big A), is an anomalous work. A long central chapter that argues against the possibility of infinite causes is framed by two short chapters that have the appearance of introductory statements on methodology, either that of metaphysics (ch. 1) or of physics (ch. 3). The fact that in some MSS the book opens with a dependent clause (see 138,24-8 and n. 11), and that the ancient editors of Aristotle's works identified Book 2 by the same letter of the alphabet as that assigned to Book 1, is evidence that in antiquity the two books were regarded as parts of the same treatise.

These anomalies have made Alpha Elatton the subject of a lengthy controversy,[1] the principal issues of which are expressed in Jaeger's evaluation: 'The postscript to the introductory book, the so-called little a, comes after big A simply because [the literary executors of Aristotle's works] did not know where else to put it. It is a remnant of notes taken at a lecture by Pasicles, a nephew of Aristotle's disciple Eudemus of Rhodes.'[2] This judgment raises three questions about Alpha Elatton: Whether it is an authentic work of Aristotle, whether it is a unified treatise, and what is its relation to and place within the rest of *Metaphysics*. Four studies presented at the ninth Symposium Aristotelicum (1981) and later published in the proceedings of that congress,[3] give the results of contemporary research on these questions. The problem of authenticity has been greatly clarified by G. Vuillemin-Diem's analysis of the scholia in codex E which are the basis for the tradition that Pasicles of Rhodes was the author of Alpha Elatton, an attribution that is no longer tenable.[4] The other studies, however, do not establish a consensus

---

[1] The conflicting theories are summarised by E. Berti in his contribution to the Symposium Aristotelicum (n. 3), *Status quaestionis*, 260-5.

[2] *Aristotle*, tr. by R. Robinson 2nd ed. (Oxford 1948), 169.

[3] *Zweifelhaftes im Corpus Aristotelicum*, Berlin 1983, 157-294. Specific references to the articles from this volume cited here are given in the Bibliography, section 2.

[4] G. Vuillemin-Diem, 'Anmerkungungen zum Pasikles-Bericht und zu Echtheitszweifeln am grösseren und kleineren Alpha in Handschriften und Kommentatoren', *Zweifelhaftes im Corpus Aristotelicum*, 157-92. On the supposed

with respect either to the unity of Alpha Elatton or to its function in relation to the *Metaphysics*. O. Gigon believes that despite their widely divergent contents, the three chapters of the book all show a close relationship to Alpha Meizon; they constitute a supplement (*Anhang*) to the latter made up of remnants left over after its final redaction and put together with some semblance of unity either by Aristotle or by one of his pupils.[5] T. Szlezák, however, rejects the supplement-hypothesis: the chapters of 'Book' Alpha Elatton are three fragments from Aristotle's *Nachlass*, written at different times and lacking any internal unity, that were added to the end of the roll that contained the text of Alpha Meizon. By contrast, Berti's application of the historical-genetic method of analysis to Alpha Elatton seems to reveal a coherence among its three chapters, all of which have affinities with the *Protrepticus* and other writings that belong to the period when Aristotle was a member of Plato's Academy. His analysis leads Berti to conclude that Alpha Elatton is an introductory work, though only a fragmentary one, not to theoretical philosophy in general, as some have argued, but to a course of lectures given when Aristotle had not yet distinguished physics from metaphysics.[6]

Alexander, for his part, unhesitatingly affirms that Alpha Elatton is the work of Aristotle on the internal evidence of its contents; but the incompleteness of the book and especially its final sentence lead him to conflicting theories about its place and function in relation to the *Metaphysics*. At one point he regards it as a separate book rightly placed between Alpha Meizon and Beta, but in his commentary on Alpha Elatton itself he vacillates: it may be simply a kind of appendage to Alpha Meizon, or, at the opposite extreme, a separate treatise, independent of the *Metaphysics*, intended as an introduction to physics or to theoretical philosophy as a whole, of which physics is the first part. At the outset of his commentary on Beta, Alexander still refers to Alpha Meizon and Elatton as separate books, but later in that commentary and in the Gamma- and Delta-commentaries the distinction is not maintained.[7] Despite these inconsistencies, however, Alexander's commentary on Alpha Elatton can be read as a unified and coherent whole.

---

authorship of Pasicles see also Berti, 293-4.

[5] For another version of the supplement-theory, see G. Reale, 'Book *a elatton* as an appendix of Book A', *The Concept of First Philosophy and the Unity of the Metaphysics of Aristotle*, tr. by R. Catan (Albany N.Y. 1980), 39-45.

[6] The unity of Alpha Elatton is also defended by Reale, op. cit. 44-5, and especially by J. Owens: it is '... a well organized, profoundly meditated and closely knit composition' that is well situated in its traditional place as a link between Alpha Meizon and Beta ('The present status of Alpha Elatton in the Aristotelian *Metaphysics*', *Archiv für Geschichte der Philosophie* 66, 1984, 148-69, 167 and 169).

[7] Specific references to the relevant passages are given in nn. 5 and 7 to the text.

The topic of the central chapter is of considerable interest. The impossibility of an infinity of causes or explanations is addressed by Aristotle in a number of places.[8] Philoponus was later to turn Aristotle's arguments against him by arguing that the ban on an infinity of causes ought to rule out an infinitely long chain of fathers and sons, and so exclude Aristotle's belief in the beginninglessness of the human race, and indeed of the physical universe.[9]

Alexander's interpretation would protect Aristotle from this charge in advance. An infinite chain of fathers and sons, to take Philoponus' example, would prove only the infinity of time, not in the relevant sense the infinity of causes (150,23-4). It is only a chain in which each cause was different *in kind* to which Aristotle would object.

The subject of infinite chains of cause or explanation remained important not only for cosmology (did the universe begin?), but also for theology (does the existence or the motion of the world, even if beginningless, point, after a finite number of steps, to a divine cause?) and for scientific method (is there an infinite regress of scientific explanations?).

The translation is made from the Greek text edited by Michael Hayduck (*CAG* 1). Departures from that text are given in the notes as they occur, and are listed consecutively under Textual Emendations. Greek terms of special importance are given in transliterated form at their first occurrence. Square brackets [ ] in the translation enclose words not found specifically in the Greek text that seem necessary to an adequate understanding of the thought.

It was my good fortune that the reader of the first draft of this translation was R. W. Sharples, whose detailed comments and suggestions led to extensive improvements. I am also grateful to the editor, Richard Sorabji, for his aid in clarifying the argument in chapter two of the commentary. I owe special thanks to my colleague at Marquette University, Professor Thomas Caldwell, SJ, without whom this work could not have been completed.

[8] See n. 62 in text.
[9] See n. 62 in text.

Textual Emendations

Alexander of Aphrodisias

On Aristotle Metaphysics 2

Translation

The Commentary of Alexander of Aphrodisias on [Book 2], Alpha Elatton, of the *Metaphysics* [of Aristotle][1]

[INTRODUCTION]

[Book 2] of the *Metaphysics*, Alpha Elatton, is the work of Aristotle so far as can be judged from the investigation (*theôria*)[2] [it pursues]; but if one is to base his opinion on the evidence of its beginning[3] and brevity, it seems to be a part of a book rather than a complete book. To the extent then that this book too contains some discussion about the principles (*arkhê*), it can be regarded as not inconsistent with [Book 1], Alpha Meizon, but as continuing the treatment of the principles and causes (*aition*) from the words with which Aristotle[4] concluded that book: 'Let us return again to the difficulties (*aporia*) one might raise in regard to these same matters; for as a result of having stated these, we may perhaps be better prepared to solve the difficulties that will occur later on' [993a25-7]. In the present book he seems to be following up this statement that he had previously made in Book 1, since he asks whether the principles and causes [continue] *ad infinitum*, and shows that they have a beginning, and that they do not progress to infinity.[5]

[1] 137,1. Title: omitted in LF. MS A gives only *to elatton a meta ta phusika* to which Hayduck prefixes *eis* (on). This is a truncated version of the title to Alexander's commentary on Alpha Meizon, from which the bracketed words are supplied.

[2] 137,3, *theôria* echoes Aristotle's *hê peri tês alêtheias theôria* (993a30), where *theôria* has the sense of *skepsis* (inquiry), *episkepsis* (investigation). See H. Bonitz, *Aristotelis Metaphysica Commentarius* (Bonn 1849; citations are to the reprint, Hildesheim 1960), 127; and cf. Alexander *in Metaph.* 1, 6,20, *hê tôn timiôtatôn zêtêsis te kai theôria*; 123,14, *hê peri tês phuseôs theôria*.

[3] 137,4. A reference to the fact that Alexander's text of Alpha Elatton began with a dependent clause; see 138,24-8 below.

[4] 137,7. Since Alexander almost never refers to Aristotle by name, 'Aristotle' has been supplied in the translation without brackets. In citing the text of Aristotle, Alexander uses present or past tense indiscriminately: 'he says' or 'he said'. For the sake of uniformity, the translation gives all such instances in the present tense except where the reference is clearly to a prior text.

[5] 137,9-10. The *altera recensio* (hereafter *alt. rec.*) suggests that this book might be simply a part of Alpha Meizon rather than an independent treatise, and later on Alexander thinks it possible that it is a kind of sequel (appendix?) to Book 1

On the other hand, the conclusion of this book does not seem to belong to the structure [of the *Metaphysics*], but to be a kind of introduction to the treatise on nature (*hê phusikê pragmateia*) – it is as if Aristotle ended it with the intention of speaking about nature

15   in what follows, and of inquiring what nature is. For he says, 'Hence we must first investigate what nature (*phusis*) is, for thus the subjects with which natural philosophy deals will also be made clear' [995a17-19]. But an inquiry of this sort is the province of the natural philospher (*phusikos*); for that reason Aristotle has given his account of nature in the lectures [entitled] *Physics*. Moreover, the beginning of Beta [Book 3] does not include the [promised]

138,1 discussion about nature that would make [Beta] appear to be the sequel to [the present book]; instead, Aristotle there enumerates and explains the difficulties that must first be raised in the present treatise, [the *Metaphysics*].[6] Hence it would seem that Beta rather than Alpha Elatton follows Alpha Meizon, since the beginning of Beta is consistent with the conclusion of Alpha Meizon; for in the latter Aristotle promises to deal with the difficulties that should be raised about matters relevant to the discovery of the causes, and

5   this is obviously what he does in Beta.[7]

(143,23-144,4), a view incompatible with his other suggestion that it is a preface.

[6] 137,18-138,2. Later, however, Alexander suggests a solution to this objection: Aristotle is not saying that an inquiry about nature should be undertaken at once, but is only distinguishing physics from metaphysics (169,26-30). In that case, there would be no discrepancy between the conclusion of Alpha Elatton and the beginning of Beta.

[7] 138,2-6. Cf. Alexander's commentary on *Metaph.* 993a24-6, the text quoted at 137,15-16: 'He is speaking about the difficulties raised in Beta; and for this reason one might think ... that Beta is the sequel to [Alpha Meizon]. This is not, however, the case, but in Alpha Elatton too he does in fact speak about the difficulties he here proposes to discuss. For when he says, "Let us return again to the difficulties one might raise in regard to these same matters", he means the questions and difficulties about the principles and causes that he also raises in Alpha Elatton, the book that follows this one' (*in Metaph.* 1, 136,12-17).

Thus at the end of his commentary on Alpha Meizon, Alexander clearly regards Alpha Elatton as a distinct treatise or book properly located between Alpha Meizon and Beta, a position that he states tentatively at the beginning of his commentary on Alpha Elatton; but in the continuation of this latter he suggests alternative possibilities: this book may be simply a continuation of Alpha Meizon (n. 5), or a preface either to the philosophy of nature or to theoretical philosophy – these last are first stated as distinct possibilities, but are finally reduced to the same position (169,19-26). In this latter case, Alpha Elatton does not belong to *Metaphysics*, but is an independent treatise. This ambiguity persists in his commentary on subsequent books: the distinction between the two Alphas is maintained at the beginning of the Beta-commentary (174,15-20, cf. 213,14) but later in that commentary Alexander refers to Alpha Meizon as 'the book prior to this one', i.e. Beta (184,16), so that he seems to be thinking of Elatton as either part of or appendage to Meizon. The two books are not distinguished at the beginning of the Gamma-commentary (237,3-238,3), although the text as reported by LF mentions the distinction (*alt. rec.* 237 ad 3 and 12), and refers to Gamma as 'Book 4' (238 ad 1), thus counting Alpha Elatton as a separate book. But the title of Delta calls Delta the fourth book of

In my opinion, however, the topics discussed in Alpha Elatton are certainly not completely foreign to the present treatise, but are like certain prolegomena stated with common reference to theoretical philosophy as a whole.[8] For Aristotle speaks first about what applies in common to theoretical philosophy as a whole, showing that in one sense this study is difficult and in another respect easy. His evidence for the first point is that [until his time] no one had treated the subject adequately, and for the second that, on the other hand, no one [who had spoken about it] had been completely mistaken. He also adds a fuller explanation of why this study is difficult, showing that the cause of the difficulty is within us; for our intellect (*nous*) is weak with respect to the knowledge of things that are clear in nature. In addition to the above points, he praises those who have dealt with [theoretical philosophy] in any way whatever, because he believes they have made no small contribution [to its advancement]. And after stating how theoretical philosophy differs from practical, and that knowledge (*gnôsis*) is the true goal[9] of theoretical inquiry, he shows that knowledge of the principles and causes contributes above all else to the theoretical knowledge of truth (*alêtheia*). For the first causes and principles exist in the most proper sense (*malista ésti*), and things that exist in this way are also supremely true, and are causes whereby the other things possess their being (*to einai*) and the truth that is in them.[10] And in this book he also shows, in a general and common way, that there are principles and causes of the things that exist (*ta onta*), thus refuting [the assertion] that the causes progress to infinity.

10

15

20

[CHAPTER 1]

993a20 The investigation of truth is in one respect difficult, in another easy. An indication of this is ...

25

This text is also written without *hoti* (because), thus: 'The investigation of truth.'[11] And this reading seems more clearly to be a beginning [of the book], whereas the one introduced by *hoti* is not a

Metaphysics (344,1), and this numeration is consistent with Alexander's own reference to Beta and Gamma as Books 2 and 3 (344,22-5). Hence the evidence from Alexander on the status of Alpha Elatton is not consistent.

[8] 138,7-9. At the very end of his commentary, Alexander repeats this view and amplifies it (169,22ff.).

[9] 138,17. Reading *to kurion tês theôrias telos*, LF.

[10] 138,19-21. Cf. '[The first principles and causes] are principles of being (*to on*) in virtue of which exists each of the things of which we predicate being (*to einai*)', in *Metaph.* 1, 9,9-11.

[11] 138,24-8. Alexander's comment makes it clear that he read *hoti hê peri tês alêtheias theôria* (*because* the investigation of truth), and not the text as printed in the lemma, which omits *hoti*. He has already referred to this point (137,4): if Alpha

beginning, but a sequel to something said before it.

What Aristotle calls 'the investigation of truth' is all theoretical philosophy.[12] His meaning is not that it alone has truth for its object, for both political and practical philosophy deal with the truth in them, and the arts too investigate the truth of things within their province, if art is indeed 'a capacity concerned with making, involving a true course of reasoning' [*EN* 1140a4]. But what Aristotle means is that theoretical philosophy alone has the knowledge of truth as its end, and of truth that is such in the most proper sense; for it is eternal truth that this philosophy investigates.

Having established theoretical philosophy as [the knowledge] most appropriate for us and by nature,[13] Aristotle says that this knowledge might be thought difficult in one respect, but easy in another. It is difficult because, although many [philosophers] have made the attempt, none has succeeded in producing a treatise worthy of the subject; and this failure of those who have dealt with it to give a satisfactory account of theoretical philosophy is sufficient evidence that its investigation is hard to discover and difficult [to pursue]. But as counter evidence that this subject is easy, he says that those who spoke on it did not go completely astray, but that each of them said something worth while about it. For if we were to examine carefully each of the philosophers [who treated it], we would find that almost without exception each of them has spoken to good effect; and if we could bring together into the same treatise the opinions of all these philosophers, it would be obvious that the [existing] body of doctrine (*theôria*) about theoretical philosophy is already important and extensive. Certainly every one of those who spoke about the principles, as Aristotle acknowledges in the preceding book, gave at least a partial account of them; and even

139,1

5

10

15

Elatton begins with an incomplete sentence, its status as a separate book is compromised.

[12] 138,28-9. Cf. 'It is Aristotle's practice to call theoretical philosophy "truth" ', *in Metaph.* 1, 60,29-30. In this context, *alêtheia* is not 'truth' in the epistemological sense, but ontological truth, the *reality* that things possess, a point which Alexander later develops at length in trying to explain how some things can be called more true than others (147,1ff.). On this point see Reale, op. cit. 40 and 58-9, n. 114.

[13] 139,5-6. Theoretical philosophy is the most appropriate form of knowledge *kata phusin* (by nature) because the objects with which it deals are immaterial and thus *per se* intelligible. But in view of Aristotle's distinction between things better known by nature and by the human intellect (e.g. *Metaph.* 1029b4ff., and Alexander *in Metaph.* 1, things completely removed from the senses 'are the most difficult that can be known to man' (11,9-10)), it might seem that theoretical philosophy cannot be a knowledge *malista hêmin oikeia* (most appropriate for us). The *alt. rec.* explains that it is such by comparison with productive and practical knowledge: 'for other animals too share in the latter, even though not in the same way [as man]; but man alone partakes in theoretical knowledge' (139 ad 1). But the more likely explanation is that we progress from that branch of theoretical philosophy that deals with natural objects to 'first philosophy' or metaphysics; cf. 169, 24ff. Cf. too 140, 2-4.

though they did not express themselves clearly, nevertheless he did say that all the principles had been spoken of in some way because one philosopher mentioned this principle, another that. 'Nor did all of them fail [to attain the truth]' [993b1]. This is equivalent to saying that not a single one of all these philosophers completely 20 missed [the truth]. Aristotle makes clear that this is what he means by adding, 'but each of them said something [true] about nature' [993b1-2]; for this statement agrees with the assertion that none of them [completely] missed [the truth]. – The term 'nature' occurring in the text is confirmation that this book, [Alpha Elatton], itself 140,1 precedes theoretical philosophy as a whole.[14]

I believe that in saying that most [philosophers] have made some contribution to theoretical philosophy and that none of them was completely in error, Aristotle shows that such theoretical inquiry is natural for us, while his statement that none of them treated this subject as it deserves points out its grandeur and difficulty – that its 5 investigation should not be considered a trivial undertaking. Pursue it we must, because it is natural to us; but not in any superficial fashion, because it is difficult. Thus his words might be understood as an exhortation to us: on the one hand, not to take this study lightly, in the belief it is altogether easy, but on the other hand not to abandon it as if it were altogether difficult.

993b4 So that, since this subject is like the door of which the 10
proverb says, 'Who could fail to hit it?' ...

The fact that all who spoke about [theoretical philosophy] said something worth while would be an indication that this subject is easy; this Aristotle shows by citing the proverb, 'Who could fail to hit a door?' This proverb refers to simple tasks involving nothing difficult or hard to discover; the figure is borrowed from archers 15 shooting at a target. For if the target before them is narrow, they do not find it easy to hit the mark, but if the target is broad, it is not difficult for them to hit it, and hence all of them shoot successfully. If

[14] 139,22-140,2. At 993b2, the text on which Alexander is here commenting, Aristotle himself seems to be using *phusis* in the transferred sense of the term he specifies at *Metaph.* 1015a11, that of *ousia*, 'reality' or 'being', so that it means the same as the preceding *alêtheia* (n. 12). Alexander's present statement could be best understood on the assumption that he too is taking *phusis* in this wide sense, as in his commentary on Book 1 he calls the Platonic Ideas *phuseis*, 'realities', (and cf. 160,8 below, the nature, i.e. reality, of the good) so that he means that Alpha Elatton, as an investigation of being in general, is a prelude to the whole study of metaphysics. But in his comment on Aristotle's statement at the end of this book ('we must first inquire what nature is'), where the interpretation of *phusis* suggested here would mediate the difficulty of that text he has already noted (137,12ff.), Alexander seems to understand *phusis* only in its more limited sense of nature as the object of natural philosophy (169,19ff.).

then everyone hits the easy target, [it follows that] a task which everyone performs successfully is an easy one.[15]

20   'But the fact that men are both capable of possessing [this] whole subject and incapable of possessing a part of it, reveals its difficulty'

141,1   [993b6-7].[16] The second of the statements Aristotle has just made does however indicate that this undertaking is difficult and formidable. This was his assertion that 'individually, [philosophers] contributed little or nothing to the truth' because, as individuals, they neither treated the whole subject nor dealt completely with any of its parts; for if they contributed nothing or little to the truth, they

5   would, in addition to failing to treat the whole subject, fail also with respect to its parts. [By their failure], then, they show the difficulty of this inquiry. However, the statement, 'The fact that men are both capable of possessing [this] whole subject and are incapable of possessing a part of it, reveals its difficulty', involves a certain inconsistency, for in saying this Aristotle seems to be contradicting what he said before.[17] For previously he asserted that each [philosopher] had made a contribution with reference to some part of the truth of the things that exist, but had failed in respect to the

10   whole; but here he seems to say that those who contributed to the truth were able to have the whole of it but not a part. In an attempt to avoid [this seeming inconsistency], certain [interpreters] say that the text has been reversed, and that the appropriate reading is: 'The fact that men cannot possess the whole subject, but only a part of it, reveals its difficulty'; for this statement agrees with what was said previously. Perhaps, however, it is better to understand the text in

15   the way we have just explained:[18] i.e. that the difficulty of this

[15] 140,19, *kai hou ... touto. hou* (which) might refer to the preceding *skopos* (target), so that *epitunkhanousi* would again mean 'hit the mark': 'If everyone hits a target that is easy, a target which everyone hits is an easy one', hardly an illuminating insight. But even if *touto*, neuter, can refer to *skopos*, it seems better to take *hou* as referring proleptically to *touto*, and to give *epitunkhanousi* the more general sense of 'succeed'. Then the statement has a real point: If all philosophers hit the broad target – i.e. said something relevant about truth – the implication is that an attempt at which everyone has some success – i.e. the pursuit of theoretical philosophy – is easy.

[16] 140,19-20, *holon te ekhein*. The modern text of *Metaphysics* has *holon ti ekhein*, a reading implied in the commentary at 141,17, and that is quoted at 141,22; thereafter it is assumed.

[17] 141,6. From this point to 141,30, Alexander struggles to find an acceptable explanation of Aristotle's *holon ti ekhein kai meros mê dunasthai*. Bonitz thinks the meaning is obvious in light of Alexander's own example of the archers: as they can easily hit a broad target but not the precise part of it at which they aim, so philosophers are not mistaken about truth in its widest sense, but do not achieve the specific truth they are seeking (op. cit. 128 ad 993b5). So too Ross, who translates, 'The fact that we can have a whole truth and not the particular part we aim at'. Bonitz points out that this interpretation seems in fact to be the one suggested by Alexander himself at 141,23-5 below.

[18] 141,14. A reference to the immediately preceding lines, 2-6, where however Alexander is explaining an earlier text.

subject is shown by the fact that [philosophers] could not comprehend it as a whole, and were equally unable to grasp even a part of it completely. Thus the statement is equivalent to saying that [philosophers] were unable to possess not only a whole subject but even a part of it. For to say that 'they contributed little or nothing to the subject' means that they did not possess either the whole truth or a complete part of it, since, if even a part is hard to understand, the whole is difficult. And [this interpretation would involve] the following transposition in the text: 'The fact that men are incapable of possessing a whole subject and a part of it',[19] as if Aristotle were saying that their inability to possess either the whole truth or a part of it reveals its difficulty. One could also understand 'that they could possess a whole but were unable to possess a part' to mean that the fact that all [philosophers] were able to arrive at some notion and consideration of the whole truth, but could give no accurate explanation of even a part of it, reveals its difficulty. [Another] possibility is that the words 'all [the philosophers] taken together' are missing from the text. [If these words are added], the meaning would be that the fact that all of them collectively were able to possess the whole truth, but that each of them was unable to possess a part of it, reveals its difficulty. This interpretation seems at least more consistent with the previous statement that 'individually, they contributed little or nothing to the truth, but from [the labors] of all of them taken together an extensive [body of doctrine] results' [993b2-3]. This statement can be considered equivalent to saying that [individual philosophers] could not possess both the whole subject and part of it, but were able to comprehend only a certain part of it.[20]

In saying that the investigation of the truth 'is in one respect difficult, in another respect easy', Aristotle does not mean that both these qualities apply to it in the same respect, [so that he would be saying it is difficult and easy at the same time].[21] What he means is

[19] 141,19-21. The transposition consists in moving *mê dunasthai* (to be unable) to the beginning of the sentence, so that it governs both *holon ti ekhein* (to have a whole) and not only *meros [ekhein]* (to have a part) as in the original version. It is not clear, from the present statement, that Alexander wishes to emend the text of Aristotle, but that point is made explicitly in the *alt. rec.* After noting the inconsistency that results from the accepted reading, MS L continues: 'But taken in a transposed form, the text will not appear to be at variance [with what has been said before]. It must be emended to read thus: "The fact that men cannot possess a whole truth, or even a part of it completely, reveals its difficulty." ' (140 ad 16)

[20] 141,29-30. If any meaning can be found in this statement, it may be that no single early philosopher knew truth as a whole, i.e. as a totality consisting of various parts each of which he would know both in itself and in its relation to the whole. Instead, each of them came to know only a particular part, one presumably not recognised in its relation to the whole.

[21] 141,32. The bracketed words are supplied from the *alt. rec.* (140 ad 16).

that both these impressions[22] and opinions are current, that sc. it is easy from one point of view but difficult from another. For because all [philosophers] contributed something to the truth, its investigation is not difficult, but because none of them succeeded in giving a
35 complete account of even part of the truth, its investigation is not easy.

993b7 Perhaps too, since there are two kinds of difficulty, [the cause of the present difficulty is not in things but in us].

Aristotle has shown that theoretical philosophy is easy in one
142,1 respect, difficult in another. He now distinguishes [two types] of difficulty, showing which of them applies to philosophy, and thus explains once more in what respect philosophy is difficult, in what respect easy. There are two kinds of difficulty. The first of these is by reference to the nature of the object being investigated, when it is of such a sort that its own nature makes it hard to investigate. The
5 second kind of difficulty results from the weakness of the one investigating an object; for something that is by its own nature an object quite open to investigation because of its simplicity[23] can be very difficult for us to investigate because of our weakness. It is under the latter kind of difficulty that Aristotle locates both the technique (*tekhnê*) of speculation and [theoretical] philosophy, [whose object is] truth. He might even be making this very difficulty the occasion for urging us [to study] such philosophy. For if the
10 objects that are intelligible and primary by their own nature are difficult for us to know because of the indolence of our intellect, clearly it behooves us to train our intellect, stimulating it [to concentrate on] these primary objects, so that things intelligible by their own nature might become easy for our intellect to know.

Aristotle uses the example of bats to show how some things are difficult [to know] not through their own nature but because of the weakness of those who seek to comprehend them. Full daylight makes it difficult for these creatures to see because of the weakness
15 of their eyes,[24] although such light is not only visible in the highest

---

[22] 141,32. Alexander's term is *phantasiai* (imaginings), which may suggest that the popular beliefs about metaphysics are merely the fanciful suppositions of those who do not really understand this subject.

[23] 142,6. Cf. 18 below, the simplest things are the most perspicuous; and ps.-Alexander *in Metaph.* 687,7ff.: What is actually existent forever 'is in the highest degree intelligible ... because it is simple and intelligible by its own nature. Indeed, composite things are intelligible when the intellect separates them from the [matter and motion] in which they are and contemplates them as if they were simple.'

[24] 142,14-15. On the bat-simile, see J. Owens, op. cit. 149, n. 2. He points out that it seems to have no allusion to *blinding*. Alexander's *empodizei to horan* might mean that daylight has this effect on bats, but a less radical interpretation is suggested by his use of the term *empodia* in the immediate sequence to describe the effect of

degree by its own nature, but is also the reason why [other] things that are seen can be seen. Hence, as the eyes of bats are related to light, so in our case (he says) our intellect stands in relation to objects that are by nature most perspicuous – those sc. that are most simple, and such are the [first] principles. Our intellect is related in this way to the most perspicuous of existing things because it has not been set apart and separated [from the body], but exists [in union] with sense perception (*aisthêsis*) and the affective (*pathêtikê*) powers of the soul (*psukhê*), all of which are a hindrance to the intellect's proper activity (*energeia*). For our continuous activity directed towards sensible objects (*ta aisthêta*) interferes with the activities that are separate from sense perception.[25] Now if this is the reason why knowledge of the truth is difficult, Aristotle's previous statement is valid: 'knowledge of the truth is in one respect difficult, in another easy' – difficult, that is, for us but easy because of the nature of truth itself. And those [subsequent] remarks too would be made to establish this fact, that truth has both these aspects, and this for no other reason than that truth is by its own nature easy to know, but difficult for us to know because of our weakness.

993b11 It is right that we should be grateful not only to those with whose opinions we agree, [but also to those who expressed themselves more superficially.]

Aristotle has said that theoretical philosophy is in one respect difficult and in another respect easy; further that none [of the philosophers] who dealt with it spoke adequately about it. Now he says that we should not for this reason simply dismiss them, but should be grateful to them for having been of no small benefit to those who came after them. At the same time, he uses the example of these men to confirm that theoretical studies are worthy of our most serious efforts. For he thinks it right that we be grateful not only to those who expressed such opinions as we ourselves might find useful and adopt as our own because we think them correctly

---

sensation and feelings on the ability of the intellect to perform its proper activity. They are hindrances but not complete barriers to this function. For a detailed analysis of Aristotle's text and its implications, see Berti, op. cit. 267-72.

[25] 142,19-23. Asclepius makes an interesting comment on these lines: 'As Alexander says, we are not able to lay hold of intelligible objects since our intellect is weak with respect to knowledge of things clear by nature, because it is involved in sensation and imagination; but if it were ever to be separated, he says, it will lay hold of them. Hence even he recognises, willy-nilly, that our soul is separable from the body' (*Asclepii in Metaphysicorum Libros A-Z Commentaria* ed. Michael Hayduck, Berlin 1892 (*Commentaria in Aristotelem Graeca*, 6.2)), 114,36-115,2. The gibe is in response to Alexander's statement in his *de Anima* that the soul cannot be separated from the body and exist independently (Bruns 17,9).

stated, but also to the earlier thinkers, though they seem to have
spoken very superficially about these matters. The reason he gives
is that even these men have helped us in some way to discover what
we are seeking. 'For they developed before us the habitual capacity
[for thinking]' [993b14]; he means the power (*dunamis*) of our soul
15 whereby we are able to investigate matters of this sort (this is the
power of our intellect). This power [the early philosophers]
'developed' by sharpening it, as it were, and stimulating it by their
inquiries,26 inasmuch as they showed us the way and directed us
towards making our own investigations into these matters and led
us to the idea that speculation about the subjects with which they
concerned themselves is [an activity] proper for us.

This remark might also be Aristotle's way of urging us to [study]
20 all the theories (*doxa*) on these matters that have been proposed by
[earlier philosophers], since a ready familiarity with such theories
will make us more adept at discovering the truth. For how could we
possibly be grateful to these philosophers, as Aristotle prescribes, if
we had not first made a recension of their theories? From the
present text it would seem that this book, [Alpha Elatton], is in
some way a continuation of [Alpha Meizon], the book positioned
before it. For in the latter Aristotle reviewed the opinions about the
144,1 first principles expressed by the [philosophers] who preceded him,
and took issue with them on certain points. In this book he says that
the fact that we criticise the opinions of some of these philosophers
does not warrant our simply dismissing them as if they had been of
no help to us in [advancing] the present inquiry, but that we owe
some thanks even to those whose statements seem trivial; for we
5 have received some benefit from them too, because we have been
trained beforehand in the habitual capacity [for thinking].27

That those who in any way originated a discipline have their
value, and not only those who brought it to a more advanced state,
Aristotle makes clear by the example of Timotheus and Phrynis.
The former was reputed to be the best of lyric poets, whereas the

---

26 143,14, *hexin*. Bonitz notes (op. cit. 129 ad 993b17) that the term is used
proleptically in Aristotle's text: 'They formed our *hexis* by practice', as Ross translates
(*Aristotle's Metaphysics*, a revised text with introduction and commentary, 2 vols,
Oxford 1924, reprinted 1948; I, 215 ad 4). Bonitz further observes that Aristotle uses
hexis in the sense he assigns to this term at *Metaph.* 1022b10, i.e. that of *diathesis*
(disposition), the habitual state which a natural power (*dunamis*) (in this case that of
the soul's capacity for intellection) develops through its continual exercise. The stages
are neatly marked in Alexander's commentary.

27 144,5, *proêskêthêmen gar tên hexin*, lit. 'for *we* developed the habitual capacity
beforehand'. Alexander regards the developed capacity of the human intellect to
pursue metaphysical thinking as a collective inheritance that a later generation of
philosophers has received from earlier thinkers. Thus he can say that *we* developed
this capacity in the sense that, when we undertake theoretical investigation, we have
already been trained in its methodology by the efforts of those who preceded us.

latter, older than Timotheus, was not his equal in the poetic art. It was from Timotheus that [we received] the art of lyric poetry, but from Phrynis the fact that Timotheus came to be so excellent a poet,   10 for he would never have produced works of such artistry had not Phrynis preceded him and made the first attempts. And as with poetry, so too in the case of correct speculation about the truth: for from some [philosophers] we possess certain opinions which we may rightly adopt because of their exceptional content; but other philosophers were responsible for the fact that these later thinkers were able to discover and to enunciate [truths] of this sort.

993b19 It is also right that philosophy should be called   15 knowledge of the truth.

Aristotle has previously applied the term 'truth' to theoretical philosophy, and now confirms that this designation is legitimate; for he says that 'philosophy' means properly its theoretical part, as he makes clear by his next statement: 'for the end of theoretical   145,1 knowledge is truth' [993b20-1]. And this is especially the case with that knowledge that has for its object the first principles and causes, which [exist] in complete separation from sense perception and in virtue of their own nature, the knowledge that Aristotle calls 'wisdom' (*sophia*). He confirms his statement in this way. Since the end of theoretical philosophy is truth, and every scientific discipline (*methodos*) derives its specific character and existence from its end   5 and goal, it is fitting that theoretical philosophy should receive its name from truth, for truth is its end.

He also shows that it is fitting that theoretical philosophy should receive its name from truth by his reference to the practical sciences, for the end of practical science is action (*praxis*), and not knowledge of the truth [involved] in things to be done. For even in cases in which practical men do examine the truth in the subject   10 [with which they are dealing],[28] they are not looking to the truth of anything eternal. Aristotle adds this remark in the belief that truth in the proper and fullest sense is that which deals with eternal things, not the truth involved in things to be done. Surely practical men are not concerned with truth of the former sort, but with truth that applies to a particular action[29] at a particular time, and they

---

[28] 145,10, *pôs ekhei to hupokeimenon alêtheias*, lit. 'how the subject stands in relation to truth'. Alexander thus expands Aristotle's *pôs ekhei*, 'how things are'. On *aïdiou*, see n. 32.

[29] 145,13, *tini*. Aristotle's text has *pros ti*, which Alexander reports as a variant reading, 21ff. below. *tini* might also be taken as masculine, in the sense that the truth found in a particular action is such for a particular person.

refer their consideration to action.[30] For the nature of things to be
15 done is such that they are not always [done in the same way] nor
universally, but that they vary both according to the age of those who
perform them and according to the circumstances in which they
happen [to be done] and according to the relationship [of the agent] to
those toward whom they are directed. Indeed, even those inquiries
concerned with the virtues (*aretê*) and with the activities in accordance with these, which are not pursued solely for the sake of
theoretical knowledge, are in the practical [sphere] and deal with
particulars; for it is to particulars that these inquiries are referred.[31]

In saying, '[they do not look to] what is eternal'[32] [993b22], Aristotle
20 points out that in practical matters the end is not truth or scientific
knowledge (*epistêmê*), for the theoretical sciences deal with eternal
ojects. In certain manuscripts this reading occurs: '[practical men] do
not consider the cause in itself, but what is relative and in the
present.'[33] If the text is read thus, Aristotle would be saying that
practical men do not consider the cause that is such in the proper
sense and in itself (*kath' hauto*), the one that is cause of the fact that
things are true without qualification, but [the cause that explains
why] something is true in relation to a particular thing, at this
25 particular time. For this is the kind of truth [found] in things that are
to be done, and is the cause [that explains them] as actions.[34]

---

[30] 145,13-14, *epi tên praxin tên anaphoran tês theôrias poioumenoi*, lit. 'making the
referral of *theôria* to action'. This might suggest that practical men simply substitute
action for thought. But that interpretation is at variance with the context, according
to which action involves a cognitive element, reflection on the circumstances in which
it is performed. Thus *theôria* here does not have its technical sense of theoretical
knowledge whose end is truth, but the more general sense of looking to or considering
particulars, as Aristotle himself uses the verb *theôrein* of what is relative and
temporal (993b23). It is in this sense that Alexander says that practical men consider
(*theôrousin*) the cause of a truth that is such here and now (24-5 below).

[31] 145,16-19. Cf. *in Metaph.* 1: 'those very actions associated with the virtues,
which seem of all actions the ones to be chosen for their own sake, have obviously a
reference to something else' (2,4).

[32] 145,19, *ouk aïdion* (not eternal) shows, as does *ou peri aïdiou* at 10 above, that
Alexander read *ou to aïdion ... theôrousin hoi praktikoi* (practical men do not consider
the eternal) at *Metaph.* 993b22. Ross retains this reading, but Jaeger prints *to aition
kath' hauto* (the cause in itself), which Alexander next reports as a variant reading.

[33] 145,21-2. Here Alexander reads *pros ti* for *tini* (13 above). Bonitz interprets *pros
ti* of the specific end to which a particular action is directed (op. cit. 129 ad 993b22).
Ross however translates, 'what is relative', and this sense better fits the context.

[34] 145,26. Alexander's point seems to be that the factor that determines ('the
cause') whether a specific action is good or bad ('the truth') is to be found in the
particular circumstances in which the action is performed rather than in theoretical
considerations about moral principles. Thus if the question is whether one should pay
a debt, the moral pragmatist does not speculate about the nature of justice, but
considers such factors as the amount of money involved, the financial
circumstances and personal relationship of the two parties, etc.

993b23 But we do not know the truth without its cause.

This statement is equivalent to saying that it is indeed impossible to know the truth without its cause, so that if practical men do not base their knowledge of the actions before them on the cause that is such in the proper sense, neither do they consider the real truth in these actions. [Interpreted] thus, the statement might be a continuation of the second version of the text. But if it is taken independently, it might be intended to show that one who devotes himself to the truth must have a theoretical knowledge of the causes.

Aristotle has shown that he considers the inquiry he is now pursuing to be a theoretical investigation of the truth; further, that this inquiry is wisdom or theoretical philosophy. To this he adds that it is impossible for those who are ignorant of the cause to know the truth, teaching us, by this remark and by what he next says, that knowledge of the causes is a necessity for one who seriously concerns himself with truth, as he also said at the beginning of the *Physics*; and in the *Posterior Analytics* he showed that scientific knowledge is knowledge through a cause; and in the first book of the present treatise too he pointed out that knowledge of anything in the proper sense depends on the knowledge of its causes.

Aristotle is not however saying that every truth is known from its cause, for in that case the causes would proceed to infinity and nothing at all could be known, as he will soon prove. But what is clear is that it is impossible to know the truth of things having causes without [knowledge of] their cause. Now there are some things that can be known apart from a cause, for the things that have no causes are of this sort, such as the primary [realities] and the [first] principles, of which there are no causes. Either therefore Aristotle is speaking in abbreviated fashion, so that he omits what he said in the lectures [entitled] *Physics*: 'things that have principles and causes' [184a11]; or his statement that 'we do not know [a truth without its cause]' [993b23-4] means that we do not have scientific knowledge, for scientific knowledge in the proper sense is knowledge through demonstration (*apodeixis*), but there is no demonstration of the [first] principles, and consequently no scientific knowledge of them. Or he may also be making this latter point[35] by what he goes

146,1

5

10

15

20

---

[35] 146,21. The reference of *toutou* (this) is vague, but Alexander seems to be thinking of the preceding assertion that the claim that a thing cannot be known without knowledge of its cause must be qualified, or of the specific application of this qualification to knowledge of the first principles. The latter interpretation seems more probable, for he has just spoken of the special status of that knowledge, and now suggests that the meaning of Aristotle's 'We do not know a truth without its cause' is to be found in his subsequent statements, which distinguish in effect between truths of the first order and secondary truths that are such only in virtue of the higher truths. Cf. the *alt. rec.*: 'Only the philosophy called theoretical in its own right is capable of knowing truth of this sort', i.e. the first and most simple cause, 'and its

on to say, for the statement, 'so that what causes things that come
after it to be true is more true' [993b26-7], has this implication. And
[he may also be asserting this when he says], 'The principles of
things that exist forever must be most true, for they are not [merely]
sometimes true, nor is any other thing the cause of their being, but
25   they are [the cause of being] for the other things' [993b28-30].

147,1   **993b24 A thing has a quality in a greater degree than other
         things if in virtue of it the same quality belongs to the other
         things too.**

Aristotle has said that it is impossible to know the truth of things
having causes without the knowledge of their causes, and has thus
shown that knowledge of the cause is a necessity for theoretical
5   philosophy. This necessity he now proves in another way from the
fact that one who philosophises about the truth must know the
things that are true in the greatest degree; but it is the eternal
causes that are true in the greatest degree, for they are causes of the
truth of the things that exist because of them. Now that which is
cause of the fact that other things too are true is true in the greatest
degree, but the [first] principles are causes of the truth that is in the
10   things that exist because of them.[36] For each of the things that exist
participates (*metekhein*) in truth to the extent that it participates in
being (*to einai*), for what is false is certainly not-being.[37] Hence
eternal things are beings in the greatest degree, and knowledge of
them is the greatest degree of truth[38] – if it is indeed [philosophic]
knowledge.[39]

object is in the first instance this truth, but secondarily the truth in those things that
have their being from it as from a cause that is really and primarily true' (146).
   [36] 147,8. Reading *di' auta* for *di' autên*.
   [37] 147,11, *to pseudos mê on*. This truncated version of *Metaph*. 1011b26, *to legein ...
to mê on einai pseudos* (to say that what is not is, is false) is difficult to translate. In
light of Aristotle's text, *on* is most probably participial: 'What is false is a non-being
[thing].' But to avoid this awkward statement, we may take *mê on* as substantive,
'not-being', as the term is used by Alexander in his discussion of the Eleatics in Book
1 (44,13 and 45,1).
   [38] 147,11-148,1. On this passage see C. Genequand, 'L'objet de la métaphysique
selon Alexandre d'Aphrodisias', *Museum Helveticum* 36, 1979, 53.
   [39] 147,12, *ei ge epistêmê*. Here and at 148,17, where the expression recurs,
Alexander has in mind Aristotle's statement that philosophy is rightly called
epistêmê tês alêtheias (993b19-20). Hence *epistêmê* in his text is used in its general
sense of knowledge, but because it is preceded by *gnôsis*, it cannot be translated
simply as 'knowledge'. Since in Aristotle's text the point is that *philosophy* is a special
form of *epistêmê*, the term 'philosophic knowledge' seems appropriate to what
Alexander intends. Book Beta of *Metaphysics* does of course provide authority for
calling first philosophy a 'science', especially in relation to the particular sciences, the
truth of which is dependent on the truth of the first principles, and Alexander often
speaks of it in this way. Thus in his commentary on Book 1, in a passage very similar
to 148,2-17, he says: 'For the knowledge of the most sovereign things is the most

But if eternal things are beings in the greatest degree, the causes of their existing eternally are beings of a yet higher order, for because they are causes of those eternal things they are beings to a greater degree than these – beings indeed of the most exalted kind.[40] Aristotle explains the reason for this when he says, 'A thing has a quality in a greater degree than other things if in virtue of it the same quality belongs to the other things too.' For that through which things are the kind of thing they are, and in virtue of which they have the same name and nature (*sunônumos*)[41] as one another – e.g. hot things – [must itself possess that quality in a greater degree].[42] For it is necessary not only that these things should have the same nature as one another, but also that the cause of their being such should also have the same nature as they; for a thing will itself be[43] in the greatest degree what [other things are] when it is the first thing of this sort. Thus, e.g., the cause of the fact that hot things are hot will be hot in the greatest degree if it is itself the first hot thing; it is in this way that fire is the cause of heat in things that are hot. For Aristotle makes this point clear by saying, 'that in virtue of which [the same quality belongs to the other things too]', since something can cause other things to be the kind of thing they are without itself being of that kind – rubbing, for instance, is the cause of heat in things, but is not the cause of their heat in the sense

15

20

25

excellent of the sciences, but the knowledge of the principles ... is knowledge of the most sovereign things ...; therefore the knowledge of the principles is the most excellent of the sciences' (131,16-20).

[40] 147,12-14. This statement appears confused because by *ta aïdia* (eternal things) here and at 11 above, Alexander means the heavenly bodies and other entities that he will later (148,24-6) specify. These are to be distinguished from their causes, the first principles: although at one place he includes both effects and causes under the term *ta aïdia* (149,10), he states the distinction clearly at 148,2-5. A further confusion results from his describing the heavenly bodies as *malista onta* (beings of the highest order), as they might be in comparison with terrestrial substances, but then saying that their causes are *mallon onta* (beings to a greater degree), so that they too must be called *malista onta*, a terminological confusion that also occurs in designating what things are *malista alêthê* (true to the greatest degree).

In reading the present passage (147,12-148,13) it is important to keep in mind the point made in n. 12: *alêthês* (true) does not have an epistemological but an ontological sense. The exposition is controlled throughout by the principle enunciated at 148,18, 'truth follows being'; so that things are 'true' to the extent that they participate in being (147,10-11).

[41] 147,17. Those things are *sunônuma* that share not only their name but also their nature, in contrast to *homônuma*, which have only their name in common. In the sequel of this passage, *sunônumos* is translated simply as 'having the same nature', since the identity of names is not relevant to the argument.

[42] 147,18, *ekeino malista thermon*. These words are omitted in the translation. They are an intrusion of a specific instance into the general statement, which is completed by the addition of the bracketed portion.

[43] 147,20. Grammatically, the subject of *estai* (will be) should be the preceding *aition*, but it seems tautological to say that a cause will have a nature in the highest degree if it is the first thing of that sort.

that it is hot in the greatest degree. But fire, since it is the cause of
heat in hot things because it is itself also hot, is for this reason hot in
the greatest degree.

[So too], then, the causes of things that are beings in the greatest
degree, since they are themselves beings, are beings to an even
greater degree than the former because they are their causes, and
148,1   they are even more true; for we posited that each thing participates
in truth to the extent that it participates in being (*to on*). Inasmuch
therefore as I call 'eternal' both the things that exist forever and
their causes, to this extent the former are called 'true' in the same
way (*sunônumôs*) with reference both to one another and to their
causes; but inasmuch as causes of the being of certain things are
5   beings to a greater degree [than their effects], to this extent among
eternal things the causes are more true than [the things they cause].
Consequently, the knowledge that is in the greatest degree directed
toward truth must be knowledge that deals with causes of the things
that [are true].[44] For if the things that are forever beings, those that
are the object of theoretical knowledge, are forever true because
they exist forever, then certainly among these things too the causes
are true to a greater degree than their effects, since the former are
prior and the latter posterior – not of course in time (both of them
10   are eternal) but by nature; for the cause is by nature prior to the
things of which it is the cause.

There is nothing paradoxical in saying that [one] true thing
differs from [another] true thing, if it is indeed the case that truth
depends on being and that the objects known have different [degrees
of] being, since some of them are objects of scientific knowledge,[45]
others of opinion; for as Aristotle will say in what follows, matter
(*hulê*) must necessarily belong to things that are in motion.[46] For
not all beings can be known scientifically, although [all] beings are
15   true, but truth is the knowledge of being (*to on*) as it is in reference

----

[44] 148,6, *toioutôn* must be taken with *tôn*, 'things of this sort', i.e. true. The
argument is that the first causes are pre-eminently true because they are the source
of the truth found in other things. The following lines reinforce this point.

[45] 148,12-13, *epistêta*. Alexander somethimes uses this term of things that can be
known in general, but also of those that are known demonstratively (see n. 67 to my
translation of his commentary on Book 1). Here the contrast with *doxasta* indicates
the latter, more technical sense. The same contrast is found at 164,20 below.

[46] 148,12-13. The reference is to *Metaph.* 994b25, *tên hulên kinoumenên noein
anankê*, where however there is a textual problem. See 164,15ff. below, and the notes
to that section. But it is difficult to understand the implication here that material
things subject to motion can be the objects only of opinion and not of scientific
knowledge, for that would be to deny the possibility of a true philosophy of nature (cf.
in Metaph. 1, 123,12-13: 'if movement is destroyed, the whole theoretical inquiry
about nature is also destroyed'). Perhaps Alexander is simply contrasting the
variable and contingent status of material substances with the immutability and
necessity of eternal things.

to each [particular] thing.[47] Truth does not have reference to things in themselves[48] (for the truth is not in things),[49] but it is the knowledge of the way in which [each thing] has being, to the extent that [it has being].[50] But if this is so, the knowledge of [being][51] as it is in the greatest degree is also the greatest degree of truth – if at least it too is [philosophic] knowledge.[52] Consequently, since truth follows being (*to on*), what is true in the greatest degree must follow that which is being in the greatest degree.[53]

---

[47] 148,14-15. The translation seems the most direct way in which to understand Alexander's paraphrase of Aristotle's *hekaston hôs ekhei tou einai, houtô kai tês alêtheias*, 'as each thing is in respect to being, so it is in respect to truth', a clearer statement that eliminates the problem of *kath' hekaston* in Alexander's text. The translation adopts this word order: *gnôsis tou ontos hôs ekhei kath' hekaston*, so that *hôs* = 'as', *tou ontos* is objective genetive after *gnôsis*, and *ekhei* is used absolutely with [*to on*] as subject. An attractive alternative is to order the words thus: *gnôsis hôs* [*ti*] *ekhei tou ontos kath' hekaston*, so that *hôs ekhei* is indirect question and *tou ontos* modal genitive after *ekhei*, lit. 'knowledge of how a thing stands in respect to being in each particular instance' (cf. *pôs ekhei to hupokeimenon alêtheias*, 145,10 above), whether sc. it is substance or accident, eternal or mutable substance.

[48] 148,15, *kat' auta*. I take this in the sense of *kath' hauta*. *auta* (plural) may be simply another instance of Alexander's often imprecise use of pronouns, or could be explained as a scribal error for *auto*. At any rate, *kat' auto* makes better sense as a sequel to the preceding clause: 'truth is not known in relation to the thing itself.'

[49] 148,15. By the parenthetical remark that truth is not in things, Alexander is reminding us in passing that truth exists formally in the intellect; cf. *Metaph.* 1027b25-7 and ps.-Alexander *in Metaph.* 457,32: 'Truth and falsity are not in things but in thought' (*dianoia*). He may also be thinking of Aristotle's treatment of truth and falsity in predication, on which he comments at 431ff. But in making this remark, Alexander seems to forget that 'truth' in the present discussion is ontological, not epistemological (n. 12); for in the ontological sense truth *is* in things as a consequence of their being, the very thesis now being argued. He might too have recalled his own statement in his commentary on Book 1, where, combining two texts of Aristotle, he says, 'as if things themselves and the truth in them were showing men the way' (32,6).

[50] 148,16, *kath' hoson ... alêtheia*, an all but unintelligible statement. The attempt at translation transposes and interpolates the text to read: *gnôsis hôs* [*hekaston*] *ekhei tou ontos kath' hoson* [*ekhei tou ontos*]. The whole sentence and its sequel would in fact make better sense if the present clause were simply excised, for it might well be a careless repetition of 14-15. A major difficulty is removed if we suppose that a scribe wrote *kath' hoson* for *kath' hekaston*.

[51] 148,17. *tou ontos* must be supplied before *hôs ekhei*, for only thus does the argument conclude. I take the first *malista* (in the greatest degree) as qualifying *hôs ekhei*, as in *ekhei kalôs*.

[52] 148,17, *ei ge epistêmê*. See n. 39 on the earlier occurrence of these words. By contrast with that text, *epistêmê* here means philosophic knowledge *proprie dicta*, Aristotle's first philosophy or wisdom.

[53] 148,18, *tôi onti hepetai to alêthes, verum sequitur ens*, as the formula passed into medieval scholastic terminology, where it was understood to mean that truth as intelligibility is one of the transcendental attributes of being, an intelligibility that varies in direct proportion to the degree of being. Being is truth, but under the formality of its relation to an intellect.

20   **993b28 Hence the principles of things that exist forever must be most true.**

This means that the knowledge of these principles is always the truest [form of] knowledge, for if being (*to on*) is true, eternal being is eternally true. That which is more true than the eternally true must of course be most true.[54] Such are the causes of the things that exist eternally – of our universe (*kosmos*),[55] for instance, and the

25   stars, or of the four [primary] bodies (*sôma*), whose eternity is that of their species (*kat' eidos*), or of the eternal realities in the case of the things that are particular and subject to generation, for they too are eternal.[56] For the causes of such [eternal] things will be forever true because they exist forever (for certainly the causes of eternal things cannot [fail to be] eternal); and because they are causes of eternal things that are forever true, they will be more true than

30   these things, and consequently truest of all.[57] For we posited that what is the cause of being (*to einai*) for things is also the cause of their being true; further, that this cause is most true because it exists eternally, and that nothing is cause of its being, but it [is cause of the being] of the other things.

149,1   After saying, 'So that what causes the things coming after it to be true is most true' [993b26-7],[58] Aristotle adds, 'Indeed, the principles of the things that exist forever must always be most true' [993b28], with the implication that the proposition, What is the cause of the being of things is also the cause of their being true, is conceded. And if that point is conceded, it follows that the principles

5   of the things that exist eternally are most true, for things more true than those that are always true are truest of all. By these statements Aristotle is pointing out how intimately truth is linked to being; hence he adds, 'So that as each thing is in regard to being,

---

54 148,23. 'The eternally true' are the things mentioned next. See n. 39.

55 148,24. In his commentary on Book 1, Alexander has an interesting discussion of how nature functions as a cause (103,5ff.). The eternity of the world is the basis for his argument.

56 148,26-7. What Alexander may mean is that the form, e.g., of man is eternal, but only in species. Cf. his (?) *Quaestio* 3.5, Bruns 88,13ff.: 'For the things that come to be are the individuals, Socrates, Plato, this horse, and it is not possible for any of them to return and come to be again. ... For such things remain forever as regards the species, which is not a thing that came to be ...' (translation of R.W. Sharples, *Bulletin of the Institute of Classical Studies* 26, 1979, 30). Owens however explains the eternity in this case as that of 'the principles of generation' (op. cit. 160, n. 33).

57 148,27-9. Alexander seems to be proving *idem per idem* because the middle term in the argument, being, is only implied, not expressed. Eternal things are true because of their eternal being; therefore their causes, which have a higher degree of being, must also have a higher degree of truth. This connection is spelled out in what follows.

58 148,32-149,1. As this text is quoted above (146,22), it has *aléthesteron*, adopted by Jaeger on the authority of Alexander, rather then the *aléthestaton* that appears here.

so it is in regard to truth' [993b30-1]. This statement is equivalent to saying, 'For as each thing possesses and participates in being, so it participates in truth.' 'For [these principles] are not [merely] sometimes true' [993b29], because they are eternal things, although 10 the other eternal things have at least this [quality of eternity] in common with their [causes]. But the statement, 'Nor is there any cause of their being, but they are [the cause of being] for the other things', is intended to show their superiority with respect to truth even among the eternal things.

[CHAPTER 2]

994a1 But it is obvious that there is a beginning,[59] and that the causes of the things that exist are not infinite, either as a series 15 or in their kinds.

Aristotle has said that theoretical philosophy is knowledge concerned with truth, the kind of knowledge that results from knowledge of the [first] causes;[60] further, that the [first] causes are true in the greatest degree. By these considerations he established the fact that knowledge of the [first] causes is a necessity for theoretical philosophy, speculating as it does about truth, since the causes of the being of eternal things are true in the greatest degree. As a necessary sequel to these previous assertions he now proves 20 that there are certain causes and that there *is* a beginning (*arkhê*) among them, i.e. a first cause, and that the causes do not proceed to infinity; for if they did, [not only] would the causes be unknowable, but (as he will show) there would not even be a cause at all.[61] By proving that the causes are not infinite (*apeiros*) he also proves there is [a cause] at the beginning, and that the causes can be known. 25

He says that the principles or causes cannot be infinite either [1] as a series or [2] in their kinds (*eidos*).[62] They would be infinite [1] as

---

[59] 149,14, *arkhê* may well mean a 'first principle' as Ross translates, but 'beginning' seems preferable in view of the sequence, and thus Alexander understands the term: 'There is a beginning among the causes, i.e. a first cause' (21-2 below); cf. 153,6.

[60] 149,16. Alexander says *epistêmê*, and his description of this kind of knowledge as *dia tês tôn aitiôn gnôseôs* might suggest that *epistêmê* has here its technical sense of scientific knowledge, but the proper description of demonstrative knowledge is to say that it is *dia gnôsin aitiôn* (146,11), so that here he means only that knowledge of the first causes is the subject-matter of metaphysics.

[61] 149,23, *tên arkhên*. Here and at 151,17 below, it seems best to take this adverbial accusative as enforcing the negative: 'not even to start with', although it could be argued that in the present context, explicitly concerned with the question of the beginning of a causal series, *tên arkhên* means 'at the beginning', a sense it clearly has at 25 below.

[62] 149,25ff. Aristotle also deals with the impossibility of an infinite regress in the

a series if, in the case of a cause taken from each kind of cause, one were, as he proceeded, to keep naming successively some other cause, so that in the case of the material (*hulikos*) cause, for instance, this particular thing would always have matter that possesses some other matter, and this latter would again have 30 another, and so on *ad infinitum*, [with the result that] there would be no ultimate matter which is no longer from matter. Aristotle himself gives this example: if the matter of flesh were to be earth, that of earth air, that of air fire, that of fire something else, and so on 150,1 *ad infinitum*.[63] And again in the case of the productive (*poiētikos*) cause, which Aristotle calls '[the cause] from which is the origin of movement' [994a5], [the process would proceed] in similar fashion, so that this particular thing would be the productive or moving cause of that particular thing, something else would in turn be cause of the former, and of this latter cause there would be still other causes in the same way, and so on *ad infinitum*. Again Aristotle 5 himself provides an example: If the moving cause of man were to be air, that of air the sun, that of the sun in turn strife, and that of strife something else again, and so on *ad infinitum*. And a similar explanation [would be given] in the case of the cause that has

---

Protrepticus, Ross, fr. 12; *Posterior Analytics* 1.19-23; *Physics* 7.1 and 8.5; *On Generation and Corruption* 2.5, 332b30-333a5; *Nic. Ethics* 1.2, 1094a20-1. For a discussion of Aristotle's argument see P. Brown, 'Infinite causal regression', *Philosophical Review* 75, 1966, 510-25. The argument against an infinite series of efficient causes has had a long subsequent history as a means of proving that 'it is necessary to posit some first efficient cause that everyone calls "God"' as Aquinas concludes his exposition of the so-called Second Way (*ST* I, qu.2, art.3c). See A. Kenny, *The Five Ways: St. Thomas Aquinas' proofs of God's existence*, New York 1969, 34-45.

Aristotle argues first that a series of causes cannot be infinite in the upward direction because, since there would then be no cause that is truly first, all causes in the series would also be effects, 'so that if there is no first, there is no cause at all' (994a3-19). Alexander's commentary on this argument extends from 150,30 to 152,32.

The Christian philosopher Philoponus, who rejected Aristotle's belief in the eternity of the universe, was later to turn Aristotle's argument against him: if it is impossible for there to be an actually infinite number of events, hence of the causes that produce them, then motion itself is not without a beginning, as Aristotle thought it to be (Simplicius *in Phys.* Diels 1178,7-35); nor could the succession of human generation extend through an infinite chain of fathers and sons, so that both the human race and the universe are finite, i.e. have a beginning (S. Pines, 'An Arabic summary of a lost work of John Philoponus', *Israel Oriental Studies* 2, 1972, 332-6). Alexander anticipates such an objection; see 150,23-6 below, and n. 66.

[63] 149,29-33. Note that the causes in such a series, although they are generically (*kat' eidos*) the same inasmuch as they are all material causes, are later described as 'different kinds of causes' (*kata to eidos diaphora*, 150,25; 151,2; 153,7; or *anomoeidês*, 152,1) inasmuch as they are different things. By contrast, causes that are 'of the same kind' (*homoeidês*, 151,3; 152,2) in the sense relevant to the argument are not only generically the same but are things of the same kind, as in the genus of productive cause every father in a chain of fathers and sons.

reference to the end and to the 'that for the sake of which', so that each of the ends given exists for the sake of another, and is referred to some other end, with the result that there is not any ultimate end for the sake of which the others exist while it itself exists for the sake of nothing else. Similarly too in the case of the formal (*eidikos*) cause, or, as he calls it, the essence [*to ti ên einai*], if, among formal causes too, there were [always] to be some other form of the forms that are assumed [as causes of a thing], as for instance the form of animal [*zôion*] would be soul, that of soul something else, e.g. intellect, that of intellect in turn something else.

Such then is the infinity of the causes taken as a series. But infinity with respect [2] to the kinds of cause [would result] if there were not the four kinds of causes that Aristotle himself enumerates, or some other definite number of them, but if the kinds of cause were to be infinite, as is the case with those who suppose that there are infinite differences of shape [*skhêma*] among the principles.[64] Aristotle proves that it is impossible for the causes to be infinite in either of these ways, establishing first that they cannot be infinite as a series. But one refuting the infinity of the causes as a series must not assume that the infinity in question is a temporal one,[65] and continue to assign in this way the cause of [whatever] comes to be from something.[66] For thus the process must necessarily go back *ad infinitum* because time (*khronos*) is infinite and the universe is eternal; for an assumption of this kind proves the infinity not of causes but of time. The infinity of the causes could however be proved if it were assumed that a different kind of cause precedes another

[64] 150,16. A reference to the Atomists, whose only principles were material, so that this is not really an instance of different *kinds* of cause. Asclepius gives the example of souls that are causes and infinite; each soul, presumably, would be of a different kind (op. cit. Hayduck 120,14).

[65] 150,20. On this point see R.W. Sharples, *Alexander of Aphrodisias on Fate*, London 1983, 157, and R. Sorabji, *Time, Creation and the Continuum*, London and Ithaca N.Y. 1983, 227 and ch. 20.

[66] 150,21, *kai houtôs ... lambanonta*, a clumsy way of stating the matter. Alexander means that if one supposes a *temporal* succession of events, he must in fact postulate an infinite series of causes, since the process has been going on eternally. What is peculiar in the statement is that the one who thus continues to assign causes should be the proponent of the infinity of causes, not (as here) the one refuting that position.
Alexander is defending Aristotle against the charge that in ruling out an infinity of causes he is compromising his own belief in the eternity of the universe. In an eternal universe, the *same* causes are at work in infinite time, so that, e.g., the chain of causation from fathers to sons is an infinite one. But in Alexander's explanation, an infinite chain of fathers and sons proves only the infinity of time, not an infinity of causes in the sense that Aristotle rejects, that is, a chain of causes that are different in *kind*. Cf. 152,1-2 and 153,10-13 below. On the permissibility of certain infinite causal chains see R. Sorabji, op. cit. 226-31.

cause *ad infinitum*,[67] but the assumption[68] of an uninterrupted generation (*genesis*) that takes place in infinite time proves that the same causes are at work.

> **994a11** For in the case of intermediate things, which have a last and a prior, the prior must be cause of the intermediates.

Aristotle uses the following general argument to prove that no kind of cause can be serially infinite. In those cases in which there are intermediates, so that there is a first and a last member[69] and members between these, the first of these members must necessarily be cause of the intermediate members coming after it – if, that is, these are so related that one of them is cause and the others effects.[70] Aristotle shows why this is so, confining his argument (*logos*) to [a series of] three members. (He says 'first' and 'last' not in the temporal sense, but to point out the difference in kind among the causes;[71] for among things that are of the same kind (*homoeidês*), none is prior to any other with respect to the nature proper [to all of them].)[72] If then we were to take three members thus related to each other [as first, last, and intermediate], and had to answer which of them is cause of the others, we would say the first. Certainly not the last, for the last is not cause of anything, since it has nothing after it; nor even the intermediate member, for this member, if it is a cause at all, can be cause only of

---

[67] 150,24-6. In the context of Alexander's whole interpretation, this hypothesis must be regarded as an impossible one. The only sense in which there can be an infinity of causes is the case in which the *same* causes operate in eternal time, as in successive generations of sons by fathers, all of whom are the same kind of cause. As Alexander says, this case proves the infinity of time, not of causes in the relevant sense. In the case in which successive causes are of *different* kinds, the chain of causes must be strictly finite; cf. 151,26-152,2.

[68] 150,26-7, *epei … deiknutai. lêpsis* (assumption) supplied as subject of *deiknutai*.

[69] 150,32. Ross translates *Metaph.* 994a11-13, 'For in the case of intermediates which have a last *term* and a *term* prior to them, the prior must be cause of the later *terms*' (italics added). But a more concrete substantive, such as Aristotle's 'parts' (994a18) seems appropriate to Alexander's commentary, for he thinks of the *things* making up a causal series: thus the three elements making up a series are not simply terms but *members* in a causal chain such as, e.g., grandfather, father and son.

[70] 150,33-4. This has the appearance of a *petitio principii*, because the argument supposedly proves that the first member in a series *is* cause and the subsequent ones effects. But Alexander wishes to exclude a sequence of purely random events which are first, intermediate and last only by chronological succession.

[71] 151,2. Alexander says only, 'the difference among causes', but his meaning is not that 'first' and 'last' describe different kinds of causes, but the different relationship found among the members of a series, the first of which is cause and the others effects.

[72] 151,3-4. The *alt. rec.* illustrates this point by the example of Sophroniscus and Socrates. Considered simply as men, they do not differ at all, although in point of time one of them is older, the other younger. But the significant difference is that one of them is father, the other son.

what comes after it; but the question was which of the members
under consideration is cause of the others. Now as the intermediate
member is related to the one after it, so the first member is related   10
to the intermediate member, so that this [first] member is not cause
of the one after it because it has something else as its cause,[73] for if
that [first member] did not exist, the second would not, but if the
second did not exist it would not be cause of the third. Therefore, it is
clear that the first member is cause of those that come after it.

After stating this argument involving [a series of] three members,
Aristotle says that it makes no difference, so far as the proof is
concerned, whether we assume one intermediate, or several, or an
infinite number of them, since the same argument applies in all   15
cases; for however many members are assumed, the first of them is
cause in the proper sense, but not some intermediate member or the
last. Not the last, because this is simply not a cause of anything, nor
yet any of the intermediates, because [each intermediate] needs
another thing for its being (*to einai*), i.e. that which is prior to it, and
if this other thing did not exist, [the intermediate member] would
not even be. Having postulated that the first member [in a series] is
in every case cause of the things coming after it, Aristotle goes on to   20
[a consideration of] the infinity that is said to be 'by series',[74] and
discovering that in an infinity of this kind nothing is first, he
concludes from this that there is not even a cause; for if [it is true
that] in every case what is first is cause, [then] among things
arranged in such a way that none of them is first but all are
intermediates, none of them is even a cause, not only not the first
but none of the intermediates either.[75]

[73] 151,10-11. This strange way of stating the matter obscures the sense. What he
means is that the first member in a series is not a cause as is the second, i.e. a cause
that is also an effect. It is cause in the primary sense of that which causes while itself
being caused by nothing. Relevant to the argument here are the texts from
Alexander's *Quaestiones* and from Philoponus discussed by R.W. Sharples, 'If what is
earlier, then of necessity what is later?', *Bulletin of the Institute of Classical Studies*
26, 1979, 27-44.

[74] 151,19ff. From 994a3 to the present point in the text (a19), Aristotle has in fact
been dealing with a serial or vertical infinity (in contrast to the horizontal infinity of
different kinds of causes), but with reference to a series considered from its last
member upwards, i.e. from effect to cause, and has argued (using, as Alexander has
noted, a general proof that applies to each kind of cause) that in an infinite series of
this sort all the members are simply effects. In the present section of his commentary
(151,20-152,32), Alexander explores the ramifications of this argument before taking
up Aristotle's refutation of serial infinity in the downward direction, i.e. from cause to
effect.

[75] 151,22-5, *ei gar en pasin ... tôn metaxu ti*, not one of Alexander's more lucid
statements. *oukhi tôn mesôn ti* (23) is omitted in the translation; it creates an
anacolouthon, and is repeated at 25 to correct the grammar. We are asked to imagine
things arranged indeed in a certain order (*taxis*) but in such a way that none of them
is first in line. *oude aition ti estin* really means 'nor is there even any cause' among
these things, a proper conclusion to both the sentence and the argument, but he goes

25   The phrase 'in this way' [994a17] is attached to the words 'but of [series] that are infinite in this way',[76] and is intended to indicate an actual (*kat' energeian*) infinity;[77] for among causes that are infinite

152,1   in this way none is first. [This statement] applies to what is different in kind, for in the case of things that are infinite but of the same kind, [each] one that is assumed in succession is cause in a similar way.[78] The words 'down to the present' [994a18] mean down to the last [member of the series], from which our inquiry into the causes begins.[79] For in the case of things in whose order (*taxis*) a prior and a

5   second member can be found, it is perhaps true to say that one member is cause of the other, even though not cause without qualification; for the prior member [is cause] of the one that comes after it. But [in a series] in which none of the intermediate members is prior to any other there is no cause at all.[80] Among infinite things, however, there is none that is prior to another, for (as Aristotle says)

---

on to say, 'not only is not the first among them' (which, *ex hypothesi*, none of them is) 'a cause, but none of the others either'.

[76] 151,25ff. Alexander now comments on two aspects of the final sentence of Aristotle's argument: 'But of [series] that are infinite in this way ... all the parts down to the present are alike intermediates, so that if there is no first there is no cause at all' (994a16-19). At 151,25 the translation adopts the reading of LF, *proskeitai de touton ton tropon têi lexei tôn de apeirôn*, for Hayduck's *to de touton ton tropon proskeimenon tois aitiois*. There is no mention of *aitia* in Aristotle's text.

[77] 151,26. Alexander explains actual and potential infinity at 166,9ff. below. His present reference to actual infinity is unexpected, because Aristotle does not mention a contrast with potential infinity.

[78] 152,1-2. The sense becomes clearer if we recognise that Alexander is distinguishing two types of infinity: an actual infinity that is impossible (one that involves different kinds of causes), and one that is merely an infinite chronological succession (the case of causes of the same kind). At 150,24 he has said that the causes could be proved to be infinite on the impossible assumption (see n. 67) that the causes in an infinite sequence are of different kinds, and at 153,5ff. below such a sequence is described: fire is the cause of water, water of earth, earth of something else, and so on *ad infinitum*. Here he points out that if there were (again *per impossibile*) an actually infinite series of this kind, none of the causes named would be first or a cause in the proper sense because (this next must be supplied from his later argument), tracing back from one cause to another, we could never arrive at a thing that has nothing prior to it, so that 'there is no first'. But, he adds, if the causes in the chain are of the same kind, they are infinite indeed but only in the permissible sense of a sequence that repeats itself in infinite time; this last is not stated explicitly but must be inferred from what Alexander has said at 150,19-27 (see n. 66). *homoiôs aition* (a cause in a similar way) at 152,2 echoes Aristotle's *mesa homoiôs* (alike intermediates, 994a18), but with a different emphasis: Alexander means that in the latter type of infinite succession, all causes are such in the same way. Asclepius, who quotes Alexander almost verbatim up to *homoiôs aition*, adds *hen de*, 'but one' (op. cit. Hayduck 121,4), apparently meaning that there is in effect only one cause, not an infinite number.

[79] 152,3, *mekhri tou eskhatou* (down to the last) is somewhat misleading, because it suggests a movement downwards rather than the upward progression that is now in question. But Alexander means that our inquiry begins with the effect now before us and works back to discover the cause, as he explains more fully at 17ff. below.

[80] 152,7. Reading *oude ti aition* for *tou hou aition*.

they are all equally intermediates. For if those things are prior that
are closer to the beginning [of a series] and to its first member, no
member is either closer to or more remote from the beginning among
things none of which is either a beginning or first. Hence the
intermediate members no longer have even an orderly arrangement,
and without [such an order] neither will any of them be prior, nor
will one of them be cause of another. And all the parts (*morion*) are
intermediates not only where things are infinite as a series, but in
the case of things that are infinite in any way whatever – if, e.g.,
something is infinite in size (*megethos*) or form[81] or time. For any
particular part selected from among all the things that are actually
infinite is intermediate; for if it were not intermediate it would be a
limit (*peras*), but if [these things] had a limit they would not be
infinite (*a-peiros*).[82]

Aristotle adds the words 'in similar fashion[83] down to the present'
because he was focusing his proof on causes that are infinite as a
series in the upward direction; for if we [begin] from some [effect]
present to us here and now[84] and look for its causes, all the causes
we discover are intermediate if the process continues upwards *ad
infinitum*. This kind of infinity of the causes does indeed prove that
none of them will even be a cause,[85] because the causes that precede
any [effect] we assume [as starting-point] cannot be traversed in the
upward direction, if they are in fact infinite; but in this way they
would not be causes at all. Aristotle, however, does not adopt this
line of proof; instead, by taking something as the last member and
setting a limit [to the series], he proves that it is impossible for there
to be any cause of this [last member] if the causes extend upwards

---

[81] 152,15, *kat' eidos*. This may be a throwaway phrase with no real sense, for it is
difficult to see how something could be infinite either in its substantial form or still
less in its species. Perhaps *eidos* here has reference to external appearance (cf. 155,20
below), hence 'stature', but that idea seems implicit to *megethos*.

[82] 152,16-17. That is, if any of a supposedly infinite number of things in a series is
not intermediate, it is either the first or last of them, and hence limits them to a fixed
number. The grammatical subject of *ekhoi* (17) is *meson*, but it is not the intermediate
that has a limit, but the series as a whole. Were it not for this final statement, *meson*
(16) might mean 'middle', for in an infinite series *every* member is the middle one
since every one has an equal, i.e. infinite, number of others on either side of it.
The passage that begins at 9 above and concludes here provides an explicit
argument for the principle that there is no ordering of prior and posterior in an
infinite sequence. On this point see Sharples, op. cit. 37 and note 142,44.

[83] 152,17, *homoiôs*. In Aristotle's text this adverb qualifies the preceding *mesa*: 'all
of the parts are alike intermediates', as Alexander takes it at 8 above. See also 152,2
and n. 78.

[84] 152,19, *apo tou enestôtos kai ontos nun*, lit. 'from the fixed point of time that now
exists', but the inquiry begins with the event or effect that is last to occur, and hence
is now present to us.

[85] 152,21-2, *mêde esesthai ti ek tôn aitiôn*, lit. 'that none of the causes will even *be*'.
But the point is not that no cause will exist, but that none of the supposed causes will
be *a cause*, as Alexander finally concludes.

ad infinitum. Indeed, it would not be possible to prove that there is no infinity of the causes in either an upward or a downward direction except by postulating a particular thing [beginning] from which we are to assign [causes] in either direction. Consequently, if there is no first member, there is simply no cause at all; for if all the things that are taken as causes are causes because they derive from
30   another the reason for their being of this sort,[86] but are not [causes] by their own nature, [then] if there is no first member, there will not be any cause at all, because none of the things taken as causes is such [i.e. a cause] by its own proper nature.

153,1   **994a19 But neither is it possible to proceed downwards to infinity, with the beginning above.**[87]

Aristotle has proved that the progression of the causes as a series does not proceed upwards *ad infinitum*, but that, if there is to be a cause at all, there must necessarily be something first and a
5   beginning. Now he proves in turn that the causes as a series cannot proceed downwards *ad infinitum* either, with a beginning of the causes and some first cause [above], so that every effect (*aitiaton*) would itself be in turn cause of another thing different in kind from those already generated. [This qualification is necessary], for if the [process] were such that what comes to be were again the same [kind of] thing as those produced before it, it would turn back on
10   itself [88] and the causes as a series would not proceed downwards *ad infinitum*, since things that are of the same kind have causes that are the same in kind. Aristotle clarifies this point by his example of matter, saying: 'so that water would proceed from fire, earth from water, and in this way some other genus would always be produced' [994a20-1] (he says 'genus' (*genos*) instead of 'kind' (*eidos*)).
The text in which Aristotle proves the preceding point is in fact

[86] 152,30. Taking *aitia* as predicate, and reading *toiauta* for *toiouton*.
[87] Aristotle next argues that the chain of causes cannot proceed to infinity in a downward direction. A comes from B either as the development of the perfect from the imperfect, as a man comes from a boy, or through the destruction of B, as air comes from water. The latter process is reversible, the former not, but in neither case can the series of causes be infinite (994a19-b6). Alexander's lengthy commentary on this argument extends from 153,13 to 157,37.
[88] 153,9, *anakamptoi an*. The notion of a reversal in the process of generation is an anticipation of Aristotle's argument that when one element comes from another, as water from air, air can in turn come to be from water as the process 'turns back', i.e. is reciprocal. This reversal is not really appropriate to the case to which Alexander here refers, that of a merely temporal infinity in which causes of the same kind continue to produce similar effects. Such generation is not reciprocal, for a son does not generate his father. But he does produce in his turn an offspring of the same kind as himself, so that in a chain of fathers and sons all fathers are causes of the same kind and all sons are effects of the same kind of cause.

obscure; what it says is, in summary, something like this. He first 15
postulates that there are two ways in which one thing is said to
come, or to have come, to be from another.[89] [1][90] A thing comes to
its complete state from something that is already coming to be and is
in process of being completed; in such cases, things advance to the
completion (*teleiotês*)[91] proper to them in virtue of a change
(*metabolê*) [taking place] within them; for in this way a man comes
to be from a boy, and this [type of] becoming (*genesis*) is by way of
growth (*auxêsis*). But one who knows scientifically also [comes to be] 20
from the learner, and this [type of becoming is] by way of alteration
(*alloiôsis*). Again, the thinker (*ho noôn*) [comes to be] from one who
is not thinking, a change that has reference to form, for it is a
completion.[92] The change of early morning into full day is also this
kind [of becoming], for the dawn reaches its completion and acquires
its proper form[93] by advancing towards daytime. Aristotle therefore

---

[89] 153,15-16. Alexander neatly distinguishes changes of the type later called
'accidental', in which one thing, while retaining its substantial nature, develops
either quantitatively or qualitatively (*alloiôsis*), and 'substantial' change, in which
one thing disappears and its substrate takes on a new substantial nature (*metabolê*).
In Aristotle's text, the two types are described together (994a20-b3). We get another
lengthy explanation of the two types from 155,20 to 157,27.

[90] 153,16. Alexander begins this lengthy explanation with ê (either), but the
correlative 'or' is never expressed. Instead the second type of change is introduced
(26) as an independent statement. It must be said that he is even more repetitious
than usual in explaining the comparatively simple point of how things come to be *ek
tinos* (from something), especially as the term is used of accidental change.

[91] 153,17-18. In what follows, *teleios* and its cognate forms are used in the two
senses noted in *Metaph.* 5, 1021bff., of what is complete and of what has a certain
excellence. The first meaning predominates here, so that *teleiotês* is usually
translated as 'completion, completed state'; but there are instances where 'perfection'
fits the context.

[92] 153,21. One who is actually thinking is completed 'with reference to his form', i.e.
his soul, because he has activated the soul's power (*dunamis*) for thinking, becoming
an actual rather than a merely potential thinker. In this context *teleiotês* might mean
'perfection', as in his commentary on Book 1 Alexander calls knowledge 'perfection of
the soul' (1,4). In the present context, *kat' eidos* could perhaps mean 'in accordance
with its species' in the sense that thinking is a specific perfection that all human
beings acquire; but since that is not the case with scientific knowledge, mentioned
just before, that sense seems unlikely here. That does, however, seem to be the
meaning of *kat' eidos* at 155,1 below; see n. 99.

[93] 153,23. In n. 81 I pointed out a difficulty in the use of *eidos*. That difficulty is
more acute here and at 155,20 below. In both cases *eidos* might mean external
appearance, an idea well suited to the example of the boy, whose *ateles eidos* is his
immature stature that is filled out as he attains the *teleion eidos* of full growth. But is
it possible to say that dawn, in becoming day, takes on the appearance proper to it? It
is dawn precisely because it *looks* murky (157,16). But on the other hand, how can it
be said that dawn or the boy take on the *form* of day and man respectively, the sense
of *eidos* adopted in the translation? Perhaps because Alexander has in mind the point
made later, that changes of this sort are all directed towards an *end*. This end is
contained from the beginning in the form of a thing: only analogically, of course, in
dawn with respect to day, but formally so in the case of real generation, in which
development from seed to complete plant or animal is predetermined by the form of

says that this type of becoming is 'from that which is coming to be'
25 [994a25], because it proceeds from something that has already come
to be and already exists but is incomplete and for this reason is
[still] coming to be. For progression towards the completed state
belongs to something that has already come to be and that exists.

But there is [2] a coming-to-be that is change from what does not
yet exist[94] to existing as this particular thing, as air is said to come
to be from water. And Aristotle says that this [type of] coming-to-be
is 'from the becoming' [994b1], because what comes to be in this way
154,1 does not come to be and reach its completed state [as] having
[already] come to be, or [as] already existing and in the process of
coming to be, but comes to be from the becoming itself, prior to
which it did not exist at all. Indeed, the change from [something's]
not being at all to its being this thing is coming-to-be in the proper
sense of that term, one that results from the perishing of what
5 already exists; for air comes to be from water not by the water's
becoming air, but from the perishing of water and from a change of
this sort.

Aristotle has distinguished two ways in which a thing changes
and comes to be 'from something' as from a cause and substrate
(*hupokeimenon*). (For he rejects [a meaning] that could also be
signified by the verbal formula 'to come to be from this thing'. This is
the sense in which [*from this*] means *after this*; thus it can be said
that the Olympian games came from the Isthmian games or, by
10 reversal, that they came after the Isthmian games, or that the
Isthmian came after the Olympian.[95] In the case of things that come
to be in this way, one of them is not said to come to be from the other
in the sense that this latter is a cause; hence Aristotle rejects this
meaning [of 'from something'] because his argument deals with
causes and the things that come to be from causes, but ['from
something' used in reference to] these games signifies only a
chronological order, for neither of them changes into the other nor
15 does one of them complete the other in any way.)

---

the thing that develops, so that the form is that towards which the whole process is
directed and in which it terminates.
    [94] 153,27. A slightly inaccurate statement, since the *terminus a quo*, water in the
example, does exist. He means, of course, that the *terminus ad quem* does not exist at
the beginning of the process.
    [95] 154,9ff. This discussion of the ways in which a thing is *ek tinos* (from something)
is based on *Metaph.* 5, 1023a26ff., especially b5-11. Cf. Alexander *de Fato*, Bruns
194,27ff., with Sharples' commentary on that text; and *in Metaph.* 1, 99,8ff. In the
present text, the reverse of the first statement is that the Isthmian games came after
the Olympian, as Alexander says at the end; but what he really means is that to say
that one set of games came *from* the other is equivalent to saying that one of them
came *after* the other. From a historical point of view it is not of course true to say that
the sequence can be reversed, but he is led to this inaccuracy by his insistence that
post hoc is not necessarily *propter hoc*.

Assuming then the two types [of becoming] described above, in which a particular thing comes to be in virtue of a change of some [subject or] substrate,[96] Aristotle proves that the progression cannot go on *ad infinitum* in either case. For he says that, on the one hand, things said to come to be from something through the perishing of this latter come to be 'from the becoming', not from what has already come to be and already exists. Things [involved in changes of the former kind] change back into one another, for as air comes to be 20 from water, so water also comes to be from air,[97] and this fact is obvious; hence air and water have the same substrate, i.e. the same matter. Clearly, however, things that change back into one another do not proceed *ad infinitum*, for they come back to the same point.[98] On the other hand, things that change from something that has already come to be, and that remains the same thing even while it is coming to be, do not change back into one another, but progress from intermediate stages to their state of completion. ([This is the case] whether the change is one of growth or alteration or of a specific 155,1

[96] 154,16, *hupokeimenon*. Alexander regularly uses this term in reference to substantial change (cf. 7 above), and in such cases 'substrate' properly describes the role of prime matter that underlies the change of one thing into another. But *hupokeimenon* can also mean 'subject', that of which something is predicated; and here it is used in that sense of an already existing thing that acquires some new perfection.

[97] 154,20. In addition to cases of simply reciprocal change such as that mentioned here, where A changes into B and B back into A, Alexander may also have in mind, in his numerous references to *anakamptein* in the following pages, *cyclical* changes in which A gives rise to B, B to C, C to D and D to A again. Aristotle's expression, *anakamptei eis allêla*, seems in fact to suggest a change involving more than two terms; cf. *GC* 337a4, 'For when Water is transformed into Air, Air into Fire, and Fire back into Water, we say the coming-to-be has completed the circle, because it reverts back (*anakamptei*) again to the beginning' (Revised Oxford Translation). (In his commentary on the present text of Alpha Elatton, Asclepius clearly thinks that Aristotle is referring to cyclical change: 'And these things', i.e. the elements, 'he says, come to be in a circular manner, and the straight line', i.e. a vertical line of causes going downwards, 'imitates a circle; for the fetus comes to be from a seed, then a youth, then a man, then a seed again' (op. cit. Hayduck 123,4-6.) On reciprocal and cyclical changes see Alexander (?) *Quaestio* 2.20, translated by R.W. Sharples, and the latter's commentary on this ('Alexander of Aphrodisias: problems about possibility II', *Bulletin of the Institute of Classical Studies* 30, 1983), 103-5 and 102. To accommodate instances of cyclical change we can perhaps say, in translating *anakamptein*, that the process of becoming 'bends back' on itself, or that the *things* involved 'change back' into one another.

[98] 154,22-3, *epi t'auton autois epanodos*. The reference of *t'auton* is vague. If B comes from A and is then reconverted into A, the state at the end of the reciprocal process is just what it was at the beginning. The sense might also be: 'they return to the same things [as they were to begin with].' Also possible is that *epi t'auton* echoes *t'auto to hupokeimenon* that immediately precedes. Change does not of course terminate in the substrate, prime matter, but an inaccuracy of this sort is not unusual in Alexander. In an eternal universe, cyclical or reciprocal changes of this sort do of course occur an infinite number of times, but that fact does not establish an infinite chain of causes extending to the present time because the causes at work, i.e. the elements, are limited in number; cf. 157,24-7.

perfection.)[99] On the one hand, then, we see that all things that come to be in this way – i.e. while their intermediate stages remain[100] and reach completion – have a particular end (*telos*) which is achieved, and that in no case does their progress towards
5   the perfection proper to them continue *ad infinitum*. On the other hand, we see that the coming-to-be of one thing through the perishing of another does reverse itself, for the perishing of one thing is the coming-to-be of the other. But if the process turns back on itself, the causes involved in this type of becoming do not, as a series, proceed *ad infinitum* in a downward direction. If then one thing is not cause of another *ad infinitum* in a series in the case of things that come to be either in the latter way or in the former, but
10   one thing comes to be from another only in these ways, one thing simply does not come to be from another *ad infinitum* in a series.

994a25 As we say that a man comes to be from a boy.

Aristotle has used examples to clarify the twofold sense in which a thing is said to change 'from something into something'. Taking up each of the examples,[101] he [now] explains how they come to be and
15   how they differ from one another. [1] Well, the things said to come to be as a man from a boy and the man of scientific knowledge from the learner have as their proper characteristic the fact that from something that already exists and is coming to be, and that, [as] an intermediate stage, is being completed, they change into what has come to be and is complete; for the man came to be from a boy who already existed, while that from which the man comes to be
20   remains; and it is the boy himself who comes to be and changes from

---

[99] 155,1, *eite tên kat' eidos teleiotêta* (or of a specific perfection). If Alexander is speaking precisely, he means some third type of change that is neither growth nor alteration, the two types mentioned just before and at 153,17-23 above. In that case, *teleiotês kat' eidos* is not a perfection acquired in virtue of, or in accordance with, the form, as at 153,21 (see n. 92), for all such perfections seem to be instances of *alloiôsis*. But what specific perfections are there that cannot be reduced to these two types? Perhaps Alexander would think that the ability of a mature male to produce seed that generates another man, or the development of a counter-rotating thumb, are human characteristics that are not simply the result of *auxêsis* (growth) in the individual. Perhaps too the fact that men are by nature social and political animals and hence organise themselves into societies under the rule of law might be thought a perfection of the species distinct from those acquired by individuals.

[100] 155,3, *hupomenontôn*. A slight inaccuracy: a boy does not remain a boy when he has become an adolescent, nor the latter a youth when he has reached man's estate; cf. 19-20 below for a similar inaccuracy. Alexander means that the original *subject* persists throughout the stages of its development.

[101] 155,14, *hekateron*, lit. 'each of the two', but Aristotle gives a number of examples. Alexander is really thinking of the two types of change that the examples illustrate. He deals with the first type of change from this point to 156,22, with the second type from 156,24 to 157,27.

his more imperfect form into the perfect form of the man.[102] In like manner, one who has mastered his subject[103] [comes to be] from one who is learning and moving towards perfection. Similar to his case is that of the thinker too, for his coming-to-be is a change in respect to the perfection of thinking; and thus the thing cognised (*to nooumenon*) is form and perfection of that which thinks, the intellect;[104] for everything that comes to be from something in this way comes to be while that from which it comes to be remains, being   25 preserved and changing into its completed state. After saying, 'as that which has come to be from that which is coming to be' [994a25], Aristotle adds, 'or as that which has been completed [from] that which is being completed'. The latter statement does not mean anything different than the former, but [merely] that the same thing can be said in both these ways. For what has come to be in this way has come to be from something already existing and [in process of] coming to be, and it has reached its completed state from that which is undergoing completion; for what comes to be is what is being   30 completed.

Having said that things that come to be in this way do so 'as from   156,1 that which is coming to be', Aristotle also shows that what comes to be is between what is and what is not. For[105] as becoming is between

102 155,20. See n. 93.

103 155,21, *ho memathêkôs*, lit. 'one who has completed the learning process'. This is Aristotle's *ho epistêmôn*, the man who possesses the developed capacity for scientific thinking. The expression here is very loose: the learner does not 'change into perfection', but into a person who has acquired the habitual capacity, a perfection.

104 155,23-4. A capsule version of the noetic theory that Alexander develops at length in his *de Anima*. The *eidos* (form) in this text later became the *species impressa* of medieval Aristotelians, the form abstracted from material things by the agent intellect that, united with the potential intellect, enables the latter to bring forth the *species expressa* or concept. It can be said not only, as here, that the thing known is form of the intellect, but that in knowing the intellect *becomes* the thing known. Thus Alexander: 'For the intellect makes even sensible objects intelligible to itself by separating them from matter and contemplating what it is that they are. Therefore the material intellect is actually none of the things that exist, but is potentially all of them. Before its act of thinking it is not actually any of its objects; but when it thinks something, it becomes the thing cognised, if in fact its thinking consists in its having the form that is known' (Bruns 84,19-24).

105 156,2-7. In this long and clumsy sentence, an extended paraphrase of *Metaph.* 994a27-8, Alexander gives a confused explanation of what is a direct and clear statement in the original. Aristotle is explaining the status of accidental change, that in which an existing subject comes to be in a new way; significantly he does not refer to this change as *genesis* (becoming). He compares it to substantial change, *genesis*, change from one thing to another thing; here the terminology is precise: *genesis* is between *to einai kai to mê einai* (being and not-being), whereas in accidental change the thing coming to be is between a *thing* that is and one that is not (*to on kai to mê on*), sc. in some qualified way. Alexander, however, obscures the distinction between the two types of change (4-5) and applies the term *genesis* to accidental change (6), saying that in this latter the thing coming to be is what exists and what does not exist in the absolute sense, an unwarranted addition to Aristotle's text and something that Alexander states in precisely the opposite way at 11-13 below. The distinction

being and not-being, since it is change from what is not to being, a
change which is neither what is not nor what already is[106] (for
5   change [comes about] through a becoming from a thing's not being to
its being), so too, in an analogous way, that which is coming to be, to
which the becoming belongs, is related to what is in the unqualified
sense (*haplôs*) and what is not in the unqualified sense, being
between them. This point could also be proved from the fact that
everything that comes to be seems to come to be by means of and
from some intermediary. For as things come to be in this way, i.e.
'from the becoming', which is between being and not-being, so too
10   that which comes to be 'from what is coming to be' itself comes to be
from some intermediary; for what is coming to be is between what
exists and what does not exist. For what is coming to be is between
what is and what is not. For in a way it already is and in a way it is
not, but neither does it exist in the unqualified sense (for what exists
[in this way] is already complete), nor does it not exist in the
unqualified sense; hence neither is it an intermediate of the
contradictory proposition (*antiphasis*),[107] for what exists in some
way is itself also a being.
15   To show how things that come to be from something in this way
come to their complete state 'from what is coming to be', Aristotle
adds the example of the learner. For the learner is one who is
becoming a man who knows scientifically; the latter comes to be in
this way because the learner is coming to be and, while remaining,
progresses towards scientific knowledge, which is perfection of the
learner; for the learner does not come to be in the absolute sense,
but becomes one who knows scientifically. Or [the act of] learning is
20   itself intermediate between knowing scientifically, which would be
being in the full sense, and complete ignorance, which would be
not-being in the unqualified sense.[108] Therefore, things that come to

---

between *to einai/to mê einai* and *to on/mê on* is also compromised (3-4). With this
caveat, it seems best to translate *genesis* throughout as 'becoming', despite its
ambivalent sense.

[106] 156,4. This strange remark is in keeping with the whole sentence. It is not the
change that is not-being and being, but the *termini a quo* and *ad quem* between which
it moves.

[107] 156,13-14. This is difficult. *metaxu* (between) implies a *pair* of contradictory
propositions, in this case 'It exists – it does not exist', and 'It is coming to be' would
seem to be precisely the intermediate between these. But Alexander seems to mean
that the single proposition, 'It does not exist', cannot be predicated as contradicting 'It
is coming to be'; such at least is the implication of the following explanatory clause. In
that case, of course, the proposition 'It is coming to be' is not *metaxu* two others.

[108] 156,19-21. This does not really contradict what he said at 12-13 above. There it
was the *subject* of accidental change that was said to be between being and not-being
in the qualified sense; here it is the *perfection* itself that the subject acquires that is
being described. *epistêmê*, the perfect form of knowledge, is to absolute being as
amathia, total ignorance, is to absolute not-being. The objection is of course that one
who does not possess scientific knowledge is not a complete ignoramus; he does know

be from another in this way come to be from that which is intermediate between what already exists and what does not exist.

994a30 On the other hand, [coming from something] as water comes from air involves the perishing of the other thing.

Aristotle now turns [2] to the second of the senses [of 'come to be from something'] that he has distinguished; he gives[109] as an example of this [type of change] the way in which water comes to be 25 from air. And he shows that [in this case a thing does not come to be from another] in the same way as one who knows scientifically comes from a learner, i.e. from an intermediate; for the coming-to-be of that which comes to be [in this second way] is said to come about as the other thing perishes, not remaining to be completed. 'Hence the former things do not change back into one another'[994a31-2], those sc. that come to be according to the first meaning of [coming to be from something]; these were things that [come to be] by way of 30 being completed. For these things do not reverse themselves, so that a man comes to be from a boy and a boy again from a man, because what is complete does not return to its imperfect state. Giving the reason for this fact, Aristotle says: 'For what comes to be does not come to be from the becoming but after the becoming' [994a32-b1], i.e. for what comes to be in this way does not come to be from the perishing of something else nor from the becoming itself, but from that which has already come to be; for having come to be is after the 35 becoming.[110] On the one hand, things coming to be through the perishing of the things from which they are said to come to be[111] have the becoming as the beginning of their existence, for their becoming is the change, i.e. the perishing of these [other] things; 157,1 [their beginning is not] things that remain and come to be. Things that are being completed, on the other hand, and that are said to come to be from something in this way do not come to be 'from the becoming', or from the first change,[112] but 'after the becoming'; for

---

some things, even though his knowledge is not demonstrative.

[109] 156,24. Reading *autos* for *auto*.

[110] 156,35. This seeming gibberish is Alexander's attempt to explain Aristotle's strange phrase 'after the becoming'. By *to gegonenai*, lit. 'the having come to be', he means the terminus of the process of becoming. We might translate in amplified form, 'For the end product of coming to be has been achieved only after the process of becoming has been completed.'

[111] 156,36. Reading *tôn ex hôn legetai gignesthi gignomena* for *tôn exôthen gignomena*.

[112] 157,3. *hê prôtê metabolê* might mean 'from the primary kind of change', i.e. substantial, but Alexander seems to be anticipating the example he gives, in which development from infant to complete man involves a number of changes.

what comes to be [in these cases] is that which has [finally] resulted
5   from the [process of] becoming: the new-born infant, for instance,
becomes boy and man as it develops, but the man does not come to be
from the becoming but from that which is coming to be and reaching
its completed state as a result of [the process of] becoming.[113]
Consequently, things that come to be in this way come to be not *from*
but *after* the becoming.

Having said that things being completed come to be after the
becoming, not from it, Aristotle adds that they come to be as full day
10 from daybreak; hence day comes to be from daybreak, but not
daybreak from day, for daybreak is incomplete. (By 'daybreak' he
means dawn.) But the Isthmian games do not come from the
Olympian in the same way as day comes from dawn, for in this case
one set of games merely comes after the other in chronological order,
whereas dawn becomes day as it changes and, although remaining,
15 as it is completed; for dawn is incomplete day because the full light of
day cannot yet be discerned in it, but it is still murky. He says,
'because [day comes] after [dawn]', [994b2] because dawn, as it comes
to be and is itself complete after [this process], becomes day.

Aristotle has said that things that come to be in this way do not
revert into one another, a point that is clear both from his examples
and for the reason he has stated. [Speaking now] about things said to
20 come to be from others through the perishing of the latter, those that
he had said come to be 'from the becoming', he says that they do
change back into one another. For as air [comes to be] from water, so
water comes to be from air, for neither of these is end (*telos*) of the
other; but all things of the kind that come to be from the becoming
have indeed a completed state peculiar to them but a common matter
that is capable of receiving [all] of them equally. But that things
25 coming to be in this way change back into one another is clear both
from direct evidence and from the fact that the specific differences of

---

[113] 157,4-7. Alexander seems to be involved in a contradiction, for after saying that
in accidental change things do not come to be 'from the becoming' (2-3), he says *to
gignomenon esti to ek tês geneseôs gegonos*, where *to gegonos* corresponds to the *to
gegonenai* at 156,35 (see n. 110). To resolve the problem we must assume that he is
using *genesis* in two senses: its proper one of the single movement found in
substantial change, and with reference to the whole *process* that characterises
accidental change, in which there is a succession of changes, e.g. from foetus to infant,
from infant to boy, etc. If *genesis* is understood thus, it is possible to say that the final
product of a lengthy development (*to gegonos*) comes *ek tês geneseôs*. The
interpolations in the translation attempt to convey this interpretation.

the [primary] bodies are not infinite, as they would be were one thing generated from another *ad infinitum* in this way.[114]

994b4 For things that are intermediate must have an end.

Aristotle means things that come to be not from the becoming, but from intermediates that already exist, as things that are being completed come to be; [his point is that] these intermediates, which are already beings of some sort, have an end. These things do not have a [process of] becoming that [extends] downwards *ad infinitum* because they have an end towards which they progress through the intermediates, whereas things [that come to be from the becoming do not proceed *ad infinitum* in a downward direction] because they change back into one another. He adds, 'for the perishing of one of them is the generation of the other' [994b6], something that was proved in the lectures [entitled] *Physics* [1.7]. The words 'for things that are intermediate must have an end' can be taken as equivalent to 'for in the case of things that are intermediate, there is an end of these intermediates'. 30

35

994b6 But at the same time, it is impossible for the first cause, being eternal, to perish, for since becoming is not infinite in the upward direction, the first thing from whose perishing something came to be is necessarily not eternal.[115] 158,1

Aristotle has proved in a general way, first, that it is impossible for the causes to be infinite in an upward direction, second, that this is also impossible in a downward direction. Now, taking each cause separately, he proves that none of them [can proceed] *ad infinitum*, and first that the material cause does not do so.[116] In formulating 5

---

[114] 157,24-7. Alexander gives no explicit proof that the specific differences are not infinite. It must proceed from the empirical evidence (*ek tês enargeias*) that the primary bodies are only four in number. But each difference, more accurately each form, causes a body of a particular kind with its own characteristics (*oikeia teleiotês*) to come into being. Therefore, if the forms were infinite, they would, given the infinite capacity of prime matter to receive new forms, produce an infinite succession of different bodies as one form was replaced by another in the process of change. It is less clear how the fact that the differences are not infinite proves that the primary bodies change back into one another. The argument is presumably that, given infinite differences, the pattern of change would not be constant but random, so that the destruction of one body would result in the emergence of ever new kinds of bodies, as in a Darwinian universe.

[115] Aristotle has just argued that a series of material causes cannot be infinite in a downward direction. Returning now to the possibility of an infinite regression upwards that had occupied him earlier (994a3-19; cf. n. 62), he shows that there must be an eternal ultimate material cause (994b6-9), an ultimate final cause (b9-16), and an ultimate formal cause or definition (b16-27).

[116] 158,5-7. Bonitz thinks Alexander wrong in saying that Aristotle is now

the proof that the causes cannot proceed upwards *ad infinitum* he
makes use of the fact that the primary substrate is eternal, for if it
came to be, there would be something prior to it from which it would
10 be generated [as] from a substrate, and thus it would no longer be
first.[117] But since this is not the case, the primary substrate is
eternal and ungenerated. Therefore, that from whose perishing
something comes to be is not the primary substrate. Therefore,
matter does not perish, but the same matter remains.

The words 'the first thing from whose perishing [something came
15 to be]'[118] are equivalent to 'that from which, as it perished in itself
and not in an accidental way, something came to be, is not eternal';
for matter does not perish in itself (because its accident, privation
(*sterêsis*), perishes in the generation of things that come to be out of
matter, for it is this accident that perishes in itself), but in itself
matter is imperishable. It would perish in itself if one thing were to
be generated from another *ad infinitum* and the same matter were
20 not to remain for all the things being generated.[119] And [thus]
Aristotle's statement would mean that to assert that one thing is

---

beginning a new line of argument about each kind of cause, for as he points out, the
first word in the sentence (*hama*, at the same time) indicates a close connection
between this sentence and what immediately precedes. Aristotle has just referred to
the *genesis* in which one thing perishes in the generation of another; from that he is
led to remark that the first material cause, i.e. prime matter, does *not* perish when
something comes to be from it, and that consequently the idea of a *genesis* in which
one thing perishes does not apply to prime matter (op. cit. 133 ad b6). Hence it is
prime matter that is at issue here, not, as Alexander says, the material cause
generally, although at 11 he draws the proper conclusion. Bonitz admits, however,
that Aristotle might seem to be arguing in a circle when he says, 'It is impossible for
the first cause, being eternal, to be destroyed', for as Ross says, 'eternalness so
obviously implies indestructibility' (*Aristotle's Metaphysics* I, 218 ad 6-9). In his
explanation, Alexander does in fact seem to be arguing circularly (159,1-5).
[117] 158,7-10. A substrate or subject (*hupokeimenon*) is that which underlies and
supports various properties, as substance is the subject of the accidents inhering in it.
In substantial change, one substrate disappears, and is succeeded by another; this is
the second type of change, which Aristotle has described as 'from the becoming'. But
the process cannot go back indefinitely; it terminates in the primary substrate or
ultimate subject, i.e. prime matter, which neither comes from something else nor
disappears as it takes on a succession of new substantial forms. See further n. 119.
[118] 158,14. The quotation is from the sentence given as the lemma at the beginning
of this section.
[119] 158,14-20. Prime matter is potentially all the things it can become through
receiving different material forms, but the fact that in itself it has actually none of
these forms constitutes a privation, the contrary of form (Aristotle *Phys.* 201a4 and
191a13). This privation, an accident (*Phys.* 190b27), is what ceases to be when matter
acquires a form, but matter itself, as the ultimate substrate, persists throughout all
changes. Unlike Alexander, Aristotle himself concedes that matter perishes in itself,
but only in the sense that when it has lost its privation it is no longer that which
contains the privation. 'In one sense, matter perishes and comes into being, but in
another sense it does not. For as that which contains [what perishes], it perishes in
itself (for what perishes, its privation, is within it), but as potentiality it is necessarily
imperishable and ungenerated' (*Phys.* 192a25-8).

matter of another in an infinite regression upwards[120] would be to say that the primary substrate, which must necessarily be eternal, perishes, if in fact it has nothing else as its substrate; for the causes do not proceed upwards *ad infinitum*.[121] [One who made the above assertion] would be saying, then, that this [primary substrate] perishes were he to deny that, remaining the same thing, it underlies whatever comes to be, but were to say [instead] that what comes after it [comes to be] through perishing of the substrate. For if [the primary substrate] were to perish as something comes to be from it, it would not be eternal.[122] For if the causes come to a halt in the upward direction, there must be something that initiates [the process of becoming] and is the first thing that comes to be from prime matter; but if prime matter were to perish [as that first thing] comes to be, motion (*kinêsis*) would not be eternal,[123] nor would [the matter] that underlies all things as primary be any longer either primary or eternal. Therefore, the material cause does not proceed upwards *ad infinitum*.

25

159,1

5

What Aristotle says here [944b6-9] is extremely compressed. For after saying, 'But at the same time it is impossible that the first cause, being eternal, should be destroyed', he adds, with the intention of showing that the first cause is eternal, 'since becoming is not infinite in an upward direction', but fails to say that for this reason the primary substrate is eternal.[124] Or it may be that having said, 'Things of this sort change back into one another, for the perishing of one of them is the becoming of the other' [994b5], he was attempting to confirm this statement by showing that the primary substrate, which is matter in the proper sense, is something eternal. For it would perish were it not to remain and be preserved in all the

10

---

[120] 158,21. The literal statement is 'that one thing is infinite matter of another in the upward direction', but the obvious meaning is that the process of tracing things back to ever more remote material causes goes on forever.

[121] 158,21-3. A strange argument. The proponent of infinity is assumed to argue that one thing comes from another as from a material cause *sine fine*, so that each successive thing that is generated has the one before it as its substrate. The refutation is that *because* the regression of causes upwards is not infinite (*quod erat demonstrandum*), a point will eventually be reached at which the cause supposedly first in the series has nothing from which it can come, hence nothing to support it, and is thus destroyed.

[122] 159,1. The text is corrupt at this point. The translation adopts Bonitz' conjecture: *ei gar phtharentos autou to ex autou egeneto, ouk aïdion.*

[123] 159,3. As Aristotle argues that it is, *Phys.* 8.1.

[124] 159,6ff. The passages quoted are again from the sentence given as the lemma at the beginning of this section. Ross says that the text of Aristotle with which Alexander finds difficulty is 'very obscure', and that the clause *epei ... einai* makes sense only if taken as elliptical; 'since becoming is not infinite in the upward direction [there must be an eternal first cause], but that which is the first thing by whose destruction something came to be cannot be eternal' (op. cit. 218, ad 6-9). Alexander thinks the ellipse is Aristotle's failure to identify 'the first cause' in his text with the primary substrate.

things that come to be, but if, [on the contrary], it were to perish as
the things generated from it come to be, and in this way again the
things [that come to be] from these latter; and thus the material
15   cause would proceed downwards *ad infinitum*.[125] But this is absurd,
for there must be some primary substrate (a point already proved),
and this must, while remaining imperishable, exist in all things that
come to be. Since then this is the case, the things that come to be
from it will change back into one another, so that the perishing of
one of them is the becoming of the other. For in whatever of the
things generated from it it exists, it will retain too the potentiality
20   (*dunamis*) of being able to come to be again in that form from which
it changed. [Thus] this primary matter will keep on changing into
the things that come to be [from it], but one thing does not really
become substrate for another *ad infinitum*, because the primary
matter changes into the contraries (*ta enantia*); and since it changes
into contraries, [the process of] becoming must turn back.[126] For it is
not the primary matter that perishes in the change that [terminates
in] the coming-to-be [of another thing], for then it would no longer be
25   eternal; but there is something else from which, as it perishes in
itself and in the first instance,[127] [another thing] comes to be. Book 1
of the *Physics* [1.7] showed that privation is the thing that [thus
perishes].

After proving, in respect to matter, that it is impossible for the
material causes to proceed downwards *ad infinitum*, Aristotle next
proves the same point in turn with reference to the final cause. He
says, 'Since that for the sake of which (*to hou heneka*) is an end, and
160,1   the kind of end that is not for the sake of something else'
[994b10-11]. This statement means the following. If there is
something for the sake of which, i.e. the final cause, what is cause in
this way does not proceed *ad infinitum*; for the final cause is that for
the sake of which the other things [are], but it itself [is] not for the

125 159,14, *kai palin houtô ta ex autôn*. Alexander is more compressed than
Aristotle. He apparently means that as things generated directly out of prime matter,
with the consequent destruction of the latter, become the source for other things, they
too are destroyed, and so on; but although prime matter does not persist throughout
the downward process of successive generations, there will always be some *proximate*
matter that enables the process to continue (cf. 15) because matter is, *ex hypothesi*,
infinite.

126 159,19-24. According to Aristotle, 'everything changes into contraries, e.g. from
hot to cold' (*Phys.* 205a6). Thus when matter is actually substrate of one contrary, it
retains the potentiality to acquire the other; so that coming-to-be does not involve an
infinite succession of new substrates but a series of reciprocal or cyclical changes
among the contraries, a process explained at 153,5-155,8 above. On the possibility for
contraries, see Alexander (?) *Quaestio* 2.20, cited in n. 97, and *Quaestio* 2.15,
translated and commented on by R.W. Sharples, 'Alexander of Aphrodisias: problems
about possibility I', *Bulletin of the Institute of Classical Studies* 29, 1982, 99-102.

127 159,26. Cf. 158,16-18 above, where prime matter is said to perish only in an
accidental way.

sake of anything, and this sort of cause is last. Consequently, if there is a last cause among the things that are generated naturally, and this is the final cause, it does not proceed downwards *ad* 5 *infinitum* – if it does so proceed, there *is* no final cause, or that for the sake of which, among the things that are generated naturally. But to deny that there is a cause of this sort among the things that are generated naturally is to eliminate completely from those things the nature of the good (*to agathon*); for that for the sake of which the other things come to be is the good. This point is clear from induction (*epagôgê*), 'for every art and every inquiry, and similarly 10 every action and choice, is thought to aim at some good', as Aristotle says at the beginning of the *Nicomachean Ethics*. And it is the supreme good at which all things aim.[128]

Consequently, the good is end among all things that come to be, whether through reason (*logos*) or nature, for no one attempts to do or make anything at all unless he is likely to bring his action to its end. Hence, if the goal of those who act is the end, i.e. the final cause, 15 nothing at all would come to be if this cause did not exist. Moreover, both reason (*nous*)[129] and nature will be eliminated as productive causes among the things that exist; for whatever comes to be through reason and nature comes to be for the sake of something, but if that for the sake of which things come to be through nature and reason did not exist, nothing would come to be either through reason or through nature.[130] Finally, as Aristotle says in the *Ethics* [1094a21], our desire (*orexis*) would be in vain if 20 there were not some end for all our actions, but one thing continued to be done for the sake of another *ad infinitum*.

994b13 And yet no one would attempt [to do anything if he were not likely to reach a limit].

He shows, by means of an obvious fact, that this kind of cause cannot be eliminated from the things that exist. Again, if each of the things that come to be has a definite (*hôrismenos*) end, the final 25

---

[128] 160,9-12. Cf. *in Metaph.* 1, 'All the things that are aim at the good, that good supreme among all goods, and the good is the first cause' (15,4).

[129] 160,16, *noun* echoes Aristotle's use of this term (994b14-15), where Ross rightly takes *nous* to mean 'reason', the more usual term for which is *logos*. Thus Alexander's *kata logon* (13 above) and *kata noun* (18-19 below) are parallel expressions.

[130] 160,16-19. Aristotle himself argues that the fact that a rational agent (*ho noun ekhôn*) acts with some purpose is proof that reason is present in the world; thus he has in mind only human actions and does not mention *phusis*, nature. Alexander, however, extends the principle of finality to the productive activity of nature, for although nature is an irrational power, it too acts for an end because its generative process terminates at a fixed point (*in Metaph.* 1, 103,37-104,2). Hence those who postulate an infinite series of final causes eliminate not only reason as a cause (*sic* Aristotle), but nature itself.

cause will not proceed *ad infinitum*. Once Aristotle has established the fact that there is a final cause, he substitutes the term 'limit' for 'end', showing in this way too that the causes do not proceed *ad infinitum*; for things that have a limit (*peras*) are not limitless (*a-peiros*).

994b16 But neither can the essence be reduced to another definition fuller in its formula.[131]

30   Aristotle proves that the formal cause too, i.e. the essence, does not proceed *ad infinitum*, [in such a way] that there is always another
161,1   definition (*horismos*) and some other form of whatever form or definition is assumed.[132] He clarifies this point by adding 'fuller in its formula'.[133] For the definition seems to exceed, by its verbal formula (*logos*), the thing defined, for the terms 'man' and 'rational mortal animal' are not equal as they are spoken – each thing that is defined occupies [only] the space of its name in comparison with the definition given of it.

5   In my opinion, the phrase 'fuller in its formula' has itself been added as an absurdity.[134] For if the one definition exceeds, by its verbal formula, the thing defined, the verbal formulae of which definitions [consist] would be multiplied *ad infinitum*, but this is absurd. Certainly it is not possible that for [every] definition given there should always be some other definition, so that if, e.g., the definition of animal is 'an animate substance capable of sensing',
10   there would then be in turn some other definition of this one, or of every [term] in this definition. For the farther [the definition] departs from the verbal formula proximate to man that defines him, the less will it give his form and define him, since the first and proximate verbal formula given is always the definition of the thing [itself], whereas the subsequent formula is no longer a definition of

---

[131] 160,29. Ross translates *logos* in Aristotle's text as 'expression'. Alexander however understands the term in its more technical sense of definition, more precisely of the verbal formula which expresses the definition.

[132] 160,30-166,1. On the relation of form to essence and of both of these to definition, cf. Alexander *in Metaph.* 1, 20,5ff.: 'Aristotle speaks of the substance with reference to the form, and rightly says that the substance of each thing is its form, since it is in virtue of its form that each thing is what it is. For this reason definitions too are formulated by reference to the form of the things defined, for he calls the definition ... "essence".' (See further n. 148.) Thus definition is the verbal formula that states the essence, hence the form, so that if we expand a thing's primary definition by succeeding definitions, we are in effect multiplying its forms.

[133] 161,2. Aristotle gives in fact two reasons for the statement: 994b18-20, on which Alexander comments from this point to 162,16; and b20-3, which Alexander takes up at 162,19.

[134] 161,5. Not as if Aristotle is saying something absurd, but that he is giving a reason for the infinity of the formal cause, presumably advanced by the proponents of infinite regress, that leads to the absurd conclusion stated at 6-7.

that thing, but rather of the definition given of it. In those cases, then, in which the first verbal formula given is not a definition, neither the 15 second nor the third nor any other [subsequent] formula would be [such], for each of these [later] formulae is a definition of the definition that precedes it, but not of the thing, because if the first formula given is not a definition of a thing, any formula given after the first would be far less a definition of that thing. For the first formula was given as [a definition] of the thing, but the second as [a 162,1 definition] of the formula given with reference to the thing, [so that] if the first formula is not [a definition] of the thing, neither will the second one be, [although] the latter too would have been capable of defining the thing had the first formula, of which the second was given [as definition], been a definition of that thing. For as a general rule, in [a series] in which there is no first there is no second either, since the second is second to some first; so that when there is no first 5 definition of something, there will not be a second one of it.

Aristotle's term 'the first [formula]' could also mean 'the last [formula]'; for the last verbal formula and the last cause and the last form, after which we no longer ask the question Why?, would be the definition in the proper sense; and if [this last formula] did not exist because [the process of defining] continues *ad infinitum*, none of the formulae that precede it would be [a definition].[135] Some [interpreters] have thought that in saying, 'fuller in its formula', Aristotle 10 means that something is always added to the first definition given, so that the second definition has a longer verbal formula than the one before it because of what has been added to it. Thus, e.g., if the first [definition given] of man were 'two-footed land animal', the next definition would in turn have added to it another of the differentiae mentioned above [151,2ff.],[136] such as 'rational' (*logikos*), and to this 15 [there would be added] yet another differentia, so that the first definition given would continue to be expanded *ad infinitum*.

994b20 Again, those who speak thus do away with knowledge, for it is impossible to have knowledge until one comes to the indivisible things.

[135] 162,6-10. This interpretation is reminiscent of a lengthy passage in Alexander's commentary on Book 1 in which he discusses the *eskhatos logos* (last formula) that answers the question, Why? There, however, the last formula is that reached by tracing *back* (or up) a series of formulae that define only incompletely to the ultimate formula that expresses the essence (20,7-21,36). Here, however, the last formula is the one reached as one proceeds *downwards* by adding new terms to the first formula. Because the process of thus expanding the first formula is, *ex hypothesi*, infinite, it is impossible to arrive at a last formula; and in default of this last one all the preceding formulae are invalid as definitions.

[136] 162,13-14, *allon de ... proskeimenên*. There is a textual problem here. The clause cannot be construed as it stands, although the general sense is clear enough.

By the 'indivisible things' Aristotle here means the things that
belong immediately, for, as he has said in the *Posterior Analytics*,
20 the sciences are from the things that belong proximately and
immediately.[137] But this would be impossible if there were to be
definitions of all the [terms] employed in the definition, and the
definition of the thing under consideration were to be inflated from
these [additional] definitions. In fact, what is shown, through the
definition, to belong to a thing is thought to belong to it immediately,
but if there were to be a definition of every definition *ad infinitum*,
25 there would always be some definition (*horos*)[138] intervening
between the cause through which an attribute is proved to belong to
a subject and the subject to which that attribute is proved to belong.
For it will never be possible to regard any attribute as belonging
immediately to a subject if there must always be a definition of every
[term] used [in the first definition], for 'animal' will not belong
163,1 immediately to 'man', but [only] because animal[139] is 'an animate

137 162,18-19. It is not clear what Aristotle himself means by *ta atoma* (the
indivisibles), a term that elsewhere means either individuals within a species (cf.
163,6 below) or indivisible species; Alexander's *nun* (now) may indicate his awareness
that the term is being used here in an unusual sense. Bonitz' explanation (op. cit.
134 ad b20) could apply either to the indemonstrable first premises or to essential
attributes. Ross says, '*ta atoma* must mean the most universal terms, those not
analysable into genus and differentia', a sense that, he says, 'seems to be without
parallel' (op. cit. I 219 ad b20). Alexander's interpretation is more complex. His
explanation here seems to be a clear reference to *Posterior Analytics* 1.2, so that he
would understand *ta atoma* as the immediate first principles of demonstration (so
Asclepius in his first interpretation of Aristotle's text, op. cit. Hayduck 131,5). But he
might also have in mind 1.6, which deals with the essential *attributes* (cf. 'it is obvious
that scientific demonstrations are concerned with essential attributes and *proceed
from them*', 75a29), and the notion of attribute is better suited to the sequence of
Alexander's explanation (thus Asclepius in his second interpretation of Aristotle's
text, where he is quoting Alexander, 131,33). For it is not the immediate premises
that belong to a thing, but the attributes or properties that are demonstrated to
belong to it by means of the appropriate definition; and definitions, as Asclepius says,
'derive their validity from the immediate premises' (129,17). Thus Alexander's
interpretation of *ta atoma* goes from the essential attributes, e.g. 'animal' in relation
to 'man', to the definitions through which such attributes are demonstrated, and
traces these definitions back to the indivisible and immediate premises (163,5 below).
138 162,25. It is difficult to decide, both here and at 163,4 below, whether *horos*
means 'term' or 'definition'. 'Term' would make good sense here. Alexander has just
said that a definition is generally assumed (*dokei*, 24) to reveal an essential attribute
of the thing defined. This attribute is expressed by a term: thus if the definition is
'man is animal' the term 'animal' expresses an essential attribute belonging
immediately to man. But if every definition gives rise to another, it becomes
necessary to say 'animal is substance'; thus the *term* 'substance' mediates between
man and animal, so that the latter term no longer expresses an immediate attribute
of man. However, the reference to demonstration through a cause that follows the
present text, and that to the immediate premises that follows *mesoi horoi* at 163,4,
indicate that by *horos* he means a definition that *intervenes* between the
indemonstrable first principles of demonstration and the essential attributes
demonstrated through them.
139 163,1. The text has *auton*, masculine, perhaps by attraction to the immediately

substance capable of sensing'. But again, the definition 'animate substance capable of sensing' will belong to animal in turn because of the definition proper to it, and similarly this latter [definition will belong to something else] because of its proper definition,[140] and so on *ad infinitum*; for the definitions given of definitions will always be intermediate definitions through which the attributes of which they are definitions belong to the thing defined. Therefore, the indivisible and immediate premises [*protasis*] will have been destroyed, and if they are destroyed so too is scientific knowledge and demonstration.[141]

Some [interpreters] have understood Aristotle's 'indivisible things' to mean particular things (*ta kath' hekasta*), and say that the sciences are in possession of their object at the moment when they discover that the [attributes] with which they deal apply to the particular instances peculiar to them. For one has scientific knowledge of the attributes of man at the moment when he applies his assertion [about them] to individual men. But it is not possible to arrive at particular instances if one assumes that the causes proceed downwards *ad infinitum*; for the particular instance is last [in a series], and it is impossible to reach this last member if the intervening causes are infinite. Understood in this way, the text is a general statement about all the causes rather than one restricted to the form, i.e. the definition.

994b21 And knowledge becomes impossible.

What Aristotle means is this. He has said that knowledge of actually infinite things is impossible, and that those who thus multiply either the definitions or the causes (for his argument is a general one applying to all things) destroy knowledge, if scientific knowledge of things is in fact from knowledge of their causes. He also said that infinite things are unknowable, [but] since infinite continua seem somehow to exist because of their infinite divisibility and [hence] not to be unknowable (for it is possible to think of the infinite divisibility of these continua), he next shows that infinity is not present in them in the same way as there is a progression *ad*

---

preceding *anthrôpos*. But, as we have noted, Alexander often uses pronouns loosely.

[140] 163,1-3. The sequence is not spelled out. It might continue: 'animate' is 'that which has a soul'; a 'soul' is the 'intrinsic principle of movement'; 'movement ... is'; etc.

[141] 163,5-6. The transition from definitions to the immediate premises of demonstration is abrupt. The *alt. rec.* states more clearly the connection between essential attributes, definitions, and the first premises: 'Definitions are formulated from the attributes that belong *per se* to things, and *per se* attributes are immediate premises; but if there were no immediate premises there would not be definitions either ... .'

infinitum in a series of causes. His words are, 'For how is it possible to
think things that are infinite in this way?' [994b22], i.e. that are
25   actually infinite. It is agreed that the line is divided *ad infinitum*
because the process of dividing it never stops, but surely we do not
think of it as [actually] divided into infinite parts – whenever we do
think of it, we bring the process of division to a halt by ceasing to cut
164,1   the line, and we apprehend the finite sections. For the division of the
line does somehow continue *ad infinitum*, and we do think in general
of [infinite] continua, but certainly not of the divisions of the line as
they are actually infinite, since the divisions of which we think we
always think of as finite. This is what Aristotle means in saying, 'It is
impossible for one to think if he does not come to a stop' [994b24], for it
5   is the finite divisions of which we think.

Hence one who is passing over a continuous, infinitely divisible,
line does not traverse it step by step, counting off the [successive]
divisions and actually apprehending these divisions to the full extent
that they could be cut off; for proceeding thus, he would never
traverse the line. (By 'one who is passing over the infinite line',
Aristotle means 'the line that is infinitely divisible'.) Rather, a person
traverses [an infinitely divisible line] by passing over the parts
10   collectively, because infinity is in the line only potentially, not
actually. But in the case of the causes, if there is one cause after
another *ad infinitum* in the downward direction, it will be impossible
for there to be knowledge of all the causes [in the series], [for] in their
totality they are actually infinite. If then the knowledge of the things
that exist depends on the knowledge of their causes, as was said
above, but the causes are unknowable because of their infinity, the
things of which they are causes are also unknowable.

15   **994b25** But it is also necessary to think of the matter that is in
motion.[142]

---

[142] 164,15. There is a problem with Aristotle's text; Alexander reports different
readings, and that given in the lemma is in fact offered as a variant at 24ff. below.
Ross prints: *kai tên holên ou kinoumenôi noein anankê*, 'the whole *line* must be
apprehended by something in us that does not move from part to part', thus
eliminating the reference to *hulê* (matter) and connecting this statement closely with
what precedes. Jaeger's text, *kai tên hulên en kinoumenôi noein anankê*, 'it is
necessary to think of matter in something that moves', is the reading found in
Alexander's commentary at 164,23. As for the interpretation of the statement, Bonitz
confesses himself thoroughly puzzled. He suggests, 'as a line is infinite because it can
be infinitely divided, a like infinity is found in matter, which can take on infinite
qualities. But one must always think about the matter that is in some one of the
things that are generated from it by motion and change (*en kinoumenôi*)' (op. cit. 134
ad b25). Ross comments, 'This is perhaps as much as can be made of the received text,
but it is obviously unsatisfactory' (op. cit. I, 219 ad 25-6). Understandably, then,
Alexander struggles to make sense of the various readings that he reports.

As an indication that the infinite is unknowable by its very nature, Aristotle adds a reference to matter, since matter seems by its definition to be infinite,[143] having no shape in virtue of its own proper nature nor any limit peculiar to it. Because then it is this sort of thing, we do not have scientific knowledge of it, for we know it [only] through something that is in motion. For matter is the object   20 of opinion and not of scientific knowledge – as Plato says, it is known by a kind of bastard reason [*Tim.* 52B], and as Aristotle says in the *Physics*, it can be known by analogy and through opinion (*doxa*) [191a8]. Thus the above text must have the same meaning as if it read, 'But it is necessary to think about matter too in what is in motion.'

Some [scribes], however, write, 'the matter that is in motion', and interpret the text to mean that matter is not infinite in the way in which actually infinite things are. Hence these latter are [truly]   25 unknowable whereas matter is and is said to be infinite by reason of the fact that it is always in motion and [undergoing] some change, because, having no shape of its own nor any quality (*poiotês*), it [assumes] at one time a form which at another time it exchanges for some other form, and [thus] changes. Being infinite, then, in this way, inasmuch, that is, as it is said to be such because of its continuous motion, matter is intelligible and knowable;[144] for it is not infinite in the same way as those things that are [truly]   165,1 unknowable. [Interpreted thus], Aristotle's statement is equivalent to saying that matter is constantly in motion and flux, and for this reason is said to be infinite, just as the line too must be thought of by means of its [actual] divisions, since it is not infinite with respect to them. – Or [Aristotle says], 'to think of the matter that is in motion', instead of 'as it is in motion and flux and subject to this kind of   5 infinity'; for this reason matter is not the object of scientific knowledge.[145]

After this discussion Aristotle introduces the general statement,

---

[143] 164,17. Causes are infinite if they proceed forever in one direction, so that they never come to a *peras*, terminus. Matter is *a-peiros* in a more radical sense: by its own nature and apart from form, it is without internal boundaries or dimensions of any sort, so that it is totally unlimited and undefined.

[144] 164,26, *noêsai*, which cannot be construed, is omitted in the translation. Were it *noeisthai*, passive, it could be taken with *legomenê*; 'is said to be known', thus complementing the preceding *agnôsta*, but *legomenê* is better understood as continuing the explanation of matter's infinity (cf. 28-9 below). *einai* or *gignesthai* would fit well here, but it is unlikely that *noêsai* would have replaced either of them.

[145] 165,5, *epistêtê*. In the preceding interpretation, matter was said to be *noêtê kai epistêtê*, where the latter term has its general sense of 'knowable'. Here however, where matter is said to be *ouk epistêtê*, the term must have its technical sense of 'known scientifically', as opposed to 'known by way of opinion', (cf. 148,12-13 and 163,20, where *epistêtê* is explicitly contrasted with *doxastê*). *rhusis* (flux) in the present text is reminiscent of Plato, who is mentioned specifically in the earlier text.

'And nothing infinite can exist; and if it could, at least to be infinite
is not infinite' [994b26-7].[146] What he means is the following: 'man'
and 'to be man' are different[147] and [this is true] in all cases in which
the thing in question is composite (*sunthetos*). (For each thing has
10 its being in virtue of its definition (*logos*) and its form. Man [is a
composite] of matter and form, but to be man is something simple,
for it is in virtue of his form that he is man.[148] In the case of

[146] 165,7, *to apeirôi einai*, 'the [what it is] to be infinite'. This use of the possessive
dative with *einai* is Aristotle's usual formula to describe a thing's essence. The
answer to the question, What is it to be such and such? is, as Alexander goes on to
explain, the definition that reveals the essence, and the definition itself is clearly an
object of thought (cf. 24-5 below). Hence Bonitz interprets Aristotle's text, 'the *notion
itself* of infinity, because it is a notion, will not be infinite' (op. cit. ad b25-7), and Ross
so translates the text. The remark does not bear directly on Aristotle's main point,
the impossibility of an infinite series of causes, but he has by implication raised the
question, whether and how infinity can be *known*, and that is Alexander's emphasis
from 165,15 to the end of his commentary on this text.

[147] 165,8. A reference to *Metaph.* 1043b2-4. The complete text is: 'Soul and to be
soul are the same' (quoted by Alexander at 13 below), 'but to be man and man are not
the same, unless even the soul is to be called man.' The statement is occasioned by the
question, whether the name 'animal' signifies 'a soul in a body' or 'a soul', the
actuality of a certain body.
In Alexander's text, the statement that 'Man and to be man are different' is
introduced by *hôsper* (just as), omitted from the translation because the correlative
houtôs (so) does not occur at 14 after the parenthesis. But *hôsper* points to
Alexander's main argument, somewhat obscured by the lengthy parenthesis. This
argument is in the form of an analogy: as an actually existing man is a composite of
body and soul, but his essence, to be man, is simple, so an actual infinity is
unknowable, but what it is for a thing to be infinite is something that can be known.

[148] 165,9-11. It might be objected that in light of this statement, what it is 'to be
man', i.e. man's essence, is simply 'to be soul', a Platonic conclusion that Alexander
could not accept. But since substantial form confers on the composite not only its
being but the fact that it exists as a thing of this kind with certain specifying
characteristics, Alexander does in fact tend to identify essence with the formal
principle that determines it. Cf. the text quoted in n. 132, and these further texts
from his commentary on *Metaph.* 1: 'Each thing has its essence too in virtue of its
form. ... The substance of each thing in the proper sense is the form, in virtue of
which it has its being' (96,18 and 23), 'bones owe the fact that they are bone to their
definition (*logos*), that is to their form and essence (for this is what the definition is)'
(135,18). It can perhaps be argued that the form referred to in such statements is that
of the species, not that of individuals (see n. 56), as the terms 'man', 'bone', etc., name
the essence or definition that is predicated of the individual; thus ps.-Alexander on
the text of Aristotle quoted in n. 147: 'He does not answer the question [whether the
name animal signifies the composite] because it is obvious that names signify forms
but not composites. For since the name is a sign of that which the definition
manifests, but definitions are of forms, it is clear that names are of forms. ... Essence
is not said with reference to the composite, but belongs to the form, i.e. the actuality'
(*in Metaph.* 8, 551,19ff.).
A further problem is that in asserting that the definition of a composite being is
simple, Alexander seems to overlook the doctrine that definition is made up of a
proximate genus and a specific difference. (See Berti, op. cit. 285, for the same
problem in Aristotle's text.) The reason may be that definition, like the essence it
manifests, does not contain quantified matter as does the actually existing composite
being, and thus is simple in comparison with this latter.

incorporeal (*asômatos*) things, the thing and to be that thing are identical, for 'soul' and 'to be soul' are the same, whereas in the case of things that have their being in matter the two are different.) And so what is actually infinite is unknowable, but for a thing to be infinite is neither infinite nor unknowable, for the definition that reveals its nature and its form is not infinite or unknowable. After saying, 'And nothing infinite can exist', which means that it is impossible for the actually infinite to exist, Aristotle adds, 'and if it could, at least to be infinite is not infinite' – that is to say, inasmuch as the infinite is knowable (it can be known through its definition) it is not infinite, for the infinite is not knowable *qua* infinite. He says, 'And nothing infinite can exist', either instead of saying that there is no actual infinite, or because there is nothing whatever to which the definition of infinity applies – because, obviously, nothing [actually] infinite exists. And even were it to be posited that the definition of infinity does apply to something, at least the definition itself through which the infinite is known is not infinite.

Aristotle does not go on to offer a separate proof that the productive causes too are not infinite because that point is obvious. For if the things that come to be are not infinite with respect to their formal cause, but the [process of their coming-to-be] turns back, it is clear that the productive causes are even less likely to be infinite.

994b27 But if the kinds of causes were infinite in number, [then knowledge would also be impossible].

Aristotle had set out to prove that the causes cannot be infinite either [1] as a series or [2] as kinds of cause. He has proved that they are not infinite as a series in either an upward or a downward direction, and now proves that it is also impossible for them to be infinite in their kinds. He makes use of the point previously stated, that things actually infinite are unknowable; but since it is clear that if the causes are infinite in kind they are actually infinite, it follows that they are unknowable. But if the causes and principles are unknowable, obviously the things [derived] from them will be unknowable as well, for we think we know a thing when we have learned its causes. Hence, if the infinity of the causes is of this sort, scientific knowledge will again be destroyed because knowledge of the causes has been destroyed.

The following statement, 'What is infinite by addition cannot be traversed in a finite period of time' [994b30-1], means the following. Every [act of] thinking (*noêsis*) is an apprehension of the object known taking place within a finite period of time; but the infinite by addition (*prosthesis*) is the actually infinite (for the actually infinite is that which has always something outside the point at which [we] apprehend it, and in which there is something outside every part apprehended).[149] It is impossible, then, to traverse this sort of infinity in a finite period of time. What is potentially infinite can indeed be traversed in a finite period of time by cutting it in half; but the infinite that is actually such, i.e. by addition, cannot be so traversed, because there always remains something else [that

15 continues] to be added to the part that is encompassed by thought. If then the intellect thinks of its objects and passes them in review within a finite period of time, but it is impossible to think of infinite things while going through them in a finite period of time because something is constantly being added to the objects [already] comprehended by thought, the intellect could not think of infinite things.

Aristotle himself proved, as he proceeded in this way, that the

20 causes cannot be infinite; but our Aristotle[150] used to give a dialectical proof.[151] Since there are causes of the things that exist,

---

[149] 166,10-13. For this definition of the infinite, see *Phys.* 207a1-9. Alexander gives two ways in which to understand Aristotle's *exô* (outside): as a whole to which something can always be added, and as the parts within that whole, each of which has always something outside it. Infinity 'by division' (*Phys.* 204a7) is that of a completed addition, in contrast to infinity 'by addition' (*Metaph.* 994b30), an incomplete process of division extending indefinitely.

[150] 166,19. I.e. Aristotle of Mytilene, Alexander's teacher. This reference to Aristotle was regarded as a textual corruption by both of Alexander's editors, Bonitz and Hayduck, and another reference to a second Aristotle in his (?) *Mantissa* ('I heard from Aristotle about the intellect that is from without', Bruns 110,4) was similarly rejected by Zeller and others. But in 1967 Paul Moraux argued that the man mentioned in the *Mantissa* text was not Aristocles (Zeller), or Aristotle of Messene, as others had conjectured, but Aristotle of Mytilene ('Aristoteles, der Lehrer Alexanders von Aphrodisias', *Archiv für Geschichte der Philosophie* 49, 1967, 169-82); and in volume two of his monumental *Der Aristotelismus bei den Griechen*, Berlin and New York, 1984, he devoted a chapter to this man (399-425). In neither of the above, however, did Moraux take cognisance of the present text, but in a later article he signalised the importance of this testimony in establishing definitively his thesis ('Ein neues Zeugnis über Aristoteles, der Lehrer Alexanders von Aphrodisias', *Archiv für Geschichte der Philosophie* 67, 1985, 266-69). See further P. Accattino, 'Alessandro di Afrodisia e Aristotele di Mitilene', *Elenchos* 6, 1985, 67-74; and H.B. Gottschalk, 'Aristotelian philosophy in the Roman world', *Aufstieg und Niedergang der römischen Welt* 36.2 (Berlin, 1987) 1160-2. Both these men accept Moraux's conclusion; for Accattino the present text from Alpha Elatton is the decisive factor. P. Thillet, however, after a lengthy review of the sources cited by Moraux in his first *Archiv* article, concluded that it is impossible to accord to Aristotle of Mytilene the role of teacher of Alexander (Alexandre d'Aphrodise *Traité du destin*, Paris 1984, reviewed by R.W. Sharples, *Classical Review* 36, 1986, 33-5, ix-xxi). But in his second *Archiv* article, Moraux notes (269) that Thillet had written to him that he would not have expressed himself as he did had he been aware of the Alpha Elatton text.

[151] 166,20, *epikheirôn edeiknuen*, lit. 'he used to prove the point by means of an *epikheirêsis*', arguing, that is, as the dialectician does in order to refute an opponent rather than to establish the truth (*in Top.* 1 and 2, Wallies 76,10 and 133,29; *in Metaph.* 4, 260,22ff.). An *epikheirêsis* is a form of argument useful for debate and logical exercises (*in Top.* 8, Wallies, 547, 8-14), but like dialectic itself (*in Top.* 1, Wallies, 30, 10-14), it also serves a more serious philosophic purpose. Thus in his

these causes are either more than one or one. But it is impossible
that there should be only one cause of the things that exist and come
to be, a point that has been proved elsewhere; for what comes to be
needs both a substrate and something to produce it. But it has also
been proved that a thing comes to be by virtue of its form; so that
there is not [only] one cause. Therefore the causes are more than
one; but if more than one, either all of them are infinite, or some, or   25
one. That all or some of them should be infinite is impossible, for
there cannot be many infinities. But it is equally impossible to say
that one cause is infinite, the others finite, for since what is infinite
is everywhere, it allows no point of entry to another thing, whether
infinite or finite. But further, even if there were to be only one cause,
this could not be infinite; for then it would not be a cause of anything
because, since the cause is everywhere, that of which it is cause   30
would have no place [to be]. For inasmuch as it is infinite, it will
obviously be infinite in extent as well, whether this infinity is one of
quantity, [so that the one cause] is everywhere, or whether it is one   167,1
of time. – This argument, seems to have a somewhat dialectical
character and to be logical, but not to be equally appropriate to the
matters previously discussed.[152]

[CHAPTER 3]

994b32 Lectures affect the hearer according to his habits.

In this passage Aristotle teaches us what persons are capable of   5
attending lectures (*logoi*) such as these, [saying] that those who
intend to follow [the] lectures must have been educated and
thoroughly trained. For [the effect produced by] lectures is
determined by the habits of the individual [auditors],[153] for we
demand that the [lecturer's] words agree with the things to which
we have become accustomed, and if [he] says anything beyond what
is familiar to us we think it somewhat unintelligible because it is

---

Beta-commentary, Alexander remarks that most of Aristotle's arguments in that
book are *epikheirêseis logikôterai*, overtly logical, i.e. dialectical (*in Metaph.* 3,
206,12), and says that it would in fact be impossible even to debate the *aporiai* that
are the subject of Beta without making use of such arguments (236,26-9), which
enable Aristotle to argue both sides of disputed questions.

[152] 167,1-2. Alexander means that the dialectical argument proposed by his teacher
is adequate to refute the proponent of infinite causes, but that this subject requires a
more positive type of reasoning, presumably *apodeixis*, demonstration, the sort of
argument that, by implication, Aristotle himself has employed in his treatment of the
question. In this context, *logikos* seems only to reinforce the preceding 'dialectical'; cf.
in Top. 1, Wallies, 30,13: *logikôs = dialektikôs*.

[153] 167,7, *kata tên idian tôn ethôn oikeiotêta*, almost impossible to translate
literally; perhaps 'according to the individual appropriation of habits'. Cf. *oikeiotêta*,
168,12 and 170,10 below.

10   foreign to us. This he expresses by the words 'Moreover, what is said
      beyond that [with which we are familiar] seems incongruous'. (The
      word 'moreover' (*eti*) seems superfluous,[154] but if it is to be written it
      would require [the addition of] *allôs* (in another way) to *legesthai* (to
      say); for to say things in another way, one that we are not
      accustomed to hearing – this last he expresses by the words, 'and
      beyond what [is familiar to us]' – makes what is said somewhat
      unintelligible.)
           After this remark, Aristotle goes on to show how great is the force
15   of customs. For lawgivers retain many legendary elements in their
      legislation because it is advantageous that [people] should believe
      the legends are true; [thus] the legislators keep those who are
      subject to the law obedient to it through tales familiar to them from
      childhood. Such, e.g., is the story that some people are indigenous to
      their native land, having sprung up from the earth itself, and that
      others originated from [the dragon's] teeth sown [in the ground]. For
      this reason these people ought to fight for the earth as their mother,
20   or because the gods quarrelled over it, and thus it is worthy of their
      utmost devotion. The statement that '[Legendary and childish tales]
      prevail over our knowledge about these matters because of habit'
      [995a4-6] means that habit prevails over the truth about these
      matters, for knowledge looks to the truth.
           By these considerations Aristotle has shown the force of habits.
      Next he discusses how auditors differ from one another because of
      their habits. Some of them, because they are oriented towards
25   mathematics, demand exact mathematical proofs for everything
      that is said, and refuse to listen to those who speak in another way.
168,1 Others, accustomed to learn through examples, are delighted [to
      hear] lecturers who make use of examples; while still others,
      nurtured in the love of poetry, do not approve of lecturers who fail to
      cite a poet too in support of their statements. There are some, again,
      who examine everything with great accuracy,[155] but others who are
      irritated by precise language (*akribologia*),[156] either because they
5   are incapable of following it (this is what Aristotle means by '[to be
      unable] to make connections') and grow weary in the attempt, or
      because they assume from the start that to speak with absolute
      precision is hair-splitting (*mikrologia*) (this is the meaning of 'on
      account of hair-splitting'). For an exaggerated precision in speech

---

[154] 167,10. The words *eti to* which introduce the text from Aristotle do not appear in
the received text of *Metaphysics*.

[155] 168,4. In view of what follows, this may mean 'subject every statement to exact
analysis'.

[156] 168,4, *akribologia*. This term occurs later in Aristotle's text (995a15), but not in
direct contrast to the pejorative *mikrologia*, as Alexander here uses it. As he later
uses it, the etymological sense of 'precise *language*' is not obvious, so that 'precision'
(Ross, 'minute accuracy') seems an adequate translation.

does create the impression [that one is quibbling], a reputation it derives from business contracts and loans, for to some people too much precision in language and [the tendency] to explore minutiae 10 seems illiberal, just as [hard bargaining] in business matters.

After making these initial remarks to show the force of habits, and why it is that [auditors] react to what is said according to the personal attitude that results from their habits, Aristotle says, 'Hence a person must have been educated to know how each kind of argument is to be taken' [995a12-13]. This statement is equivalent to what is actually said in the *Ethics* too: 'For it is the mark of an 15 educated man to look for just as much precision in each class of things as the nature of the subject permits' [1094a23]. He makes this [same] point in the *Posterior Analytics*, telling us that we must have a general education and know how each of the things being discussed is to be understood (for all things are not alike or capable of being treated with the same degree of precision). And [this requirement applies] especially to those who intend to listen to 20 these [lectures], for [their subject-matter] is not perceptible or concerned with perceptible objects, nor is it something ordinary to which we are accustomed. This is Aristotle's way of pointing out to us that we must first of all be well trained in the principles of analysis and in logic generally, and know the modes of demonstration and the conclusions [that can be drawn] from arguments; for it is ridiculous to be seeking scientific knowledge of something while at the same time asking how scientific knowledge 25 itself is produced and acquired, for not even just one of these inquiries is found to be easy. 169,1

Aristotle now says the same thing that he said in the first book of the *Nicomachean Ethics* when he was saying how those arguments (*logoi*)[157] ought to be received (for he said, '[It is equally foolish] to accept probable reasoning from a mathematician and to demand scientific proofs from a rhetorician' [1094b27]). 'For we must not', he says, 'demand the precision of mathematics in all things' 5 [995a14-15], but [only] in the case of immaterial (*aülos*) things such as the objects of mathematics, [which are derived] from abstraction

[157] 169,2, *tous logous*. Those, that is, appropriate to the subject-matter of ethics. From 167 to 169 of Alexander's text, the plural *hoi logoi* occurs no less than nine times. The term has different meanings, all clearly enough defined, at 167,5 and 7 and 168,10 and 23; but from this point on it is difficult to determine whether Alexander understands it in a precise way on each occasion, or whether, as seems more likely, he uses it loosely. In translation, however, it must be given different meanings according to the context. Here and at 13 and 17 below, it seems to have the sense of 'arguments' that is clear at 168,23; but at 27 and 29 below, perhaps too at 15, it seems to mean either 'discussion' in general, or specifically 'lectures', as at 167,5 and 7; in fact *hoi phusikoi logoi* at 29 is reminiscent of *hê phusikê akroasis*, his usual way of referring to the *Physics*.

(*aphairesis*).[158] Perhaps he is pointing out to us that precision of this sort is needed for the present inquiry too, for the treatise on the first principles deals with immaterial objects, not with things to which we are accustomed. He says, 'For this reason the treatise[159] is not [part of] natural [philosophy]', perhaps because it is precise,[160] for
10   he said this previously. (The text also has the reading *tropos* (method), and the sense of this would be that [such precision] is not characteristic of the natural philosopher.) Or the statement means the following. All natural objects seem to exist with matter, but the objects of mathematics are immaterial; hence the latter also admit of precise treatment, but natural objects do not do so in the same way. Certainly the arguments about mathematical objects, since they deal with immaterial things, are not [the kind used in] natural philosophy; for natural objects do not permit the same degree of
15   precise statement, at least [inasmuch as] they exist with matter. But Aristotle might also be saying this about the arguments that concern us now – that sc. they are not [the kind used in] natural [philosophy]; for it is immaterial objects about which we propose to speak, and they require more accurate arguments than do natural objects. – He adds 'perhaps' to the words, 'For the whole of nature has matter' [995a17], because the body that moves in a circle is also a natural body, but matter is not the substrate for this body.[161]
20   What Aristotle says next, 'Hence we must first inquire what nature is, for thus it will also be clear what things natural philosophy deals with' [995a17-19] [can be understood in two ways]. [1] If it is to be taken simply as it stands (and this seems to be the case), it would indicate that this book, [Alpha Elatton,] does not belong to the treatise [called] *Metaphysics*, but is, as we pointed out at the beginning of [our commentary on] this book, a kind of prolegomenon to theoretical philosophy as a whole [137.12ff]; and since the first part of theoretical philosophy, so far as we are
25   concerned,[162] is natural philosophy, we would find out what sort of

---

[158] 169,6. Cf. *in Metaph.* 1, 52,15 and 3, 201,4-11; and see I. Mueller, 'Aristotle's doctrine of abstraction in the Commentators' (*Aristotle Transformed*, 463-80), 467-70.

[159] 169,9. Alexander read *logos* (treatise) for the *tropos* (method) of the received text of *Metaphysics* (995a17). As the sequence shows, he also knew the latter reading.

[160] 169,9. He says *ētoi* (either), but the correlative *ē* (or) comes only after the long parenthetical clause, so that it is best to make the two interpretations separate sentences.

[161] 169,19-20. Cf. *in Metaph.* 1, 22,2-3: 'the substrate in the divine bodies is not matter.' But according to Aristotle, such bodies do have *hulē topikē*, matter that enables them to change place (*Metaph.* 1042b5). Alexander deals with this topic in his (?) *Quaestiones* 1. 10 and 15.

[162] 169,24. Alexander has in mind the distinction between what is *per se* more knowable and what is more knowable to us, i.e. natural objects. Considered in reference to its subject-matter, natural philosophy is *not* the first part of theoretical philosophy; that priority belongs to philosophy *proprie dicta*, wisdom.

[knowledge] this latter is and what are its objects if we were first to inquire what nature in general is. But one could also understand [2] that he stated the matter thus in order to distinguish the lectures (*logoi*) on natural subjects from the treatise that now occupies us, for one who has first investigated what nature is and has learned with what objects natural philosophy deals knows that these [present] discussions are not [concerned with] natural [objects], but that they are more accurate and deal with immaterial objects. [If the statement is interpreted in this way,] it would not mean that we must here and now investigate what nature is, but that the treatise on natural philosophy must precede the present one [on first philosophy]; for this is the order of the treatises, and one who has been trained in the theoretical investigation of these [natural topics] will thus also be able to understand the [theoretical considerations] that pertain to this treatise.

'Lectures affect the hearer according to his habits.' The meaning of this text is clear from our previous comments,[163] but it can also be understood as follows. Aristotle has said that the knowledge [acquired through] learning [depends] on things known beforehand (for things whose causes are unknowable are themselves unknowable). To convince [us] that knowledge comes from things known beforehand, he adds that [the effect of] lectures depends on the habits [of their auditors], and that thus each auditor wishes to understand what is said [in light of that] to which he has been accustomed, because the auditors interpret what they hear in accordance with the personal disposition and prior knowledge [they have acquired] through their habits.[164]

---

[163] 170,4-5. There is a lacuna in the text at this point; the translation adopts the reading from S: *ex iis quae memoravimus est aperta*. The quotation from *Metaph.* is simply a repetition of 994b32, and it seems strange that Alexander does not mention this fact if he found the text repeated in his MSS. 170,4-11 is in fact so inept a conclusion to the whole commentary that one wonders whether the lines are genuine, or, if so, whether they do not belong at an earlier point. Note too that Aristotle's doctrine of the necessity of prior knowledge for the learning process is not mentioned in Alpha Elatton.

[164] 170,11. Alexander does not quote *Metaph.* 995a19-20, 'whether it belongs to one or more sciences to investigate the causes and principles', a clause found in the received text of *Metaphysics* but bracketed by modern editors. But in his commentary on Beta 995b5-6, he remarks that 'certain people' have written the words at the end of Alpha Elatton, where they do not belong (174,25-7). On this point see Reale, op. cit., 44-5.

Select Bibliography

This Bibliography is restricted to works cited in the footnotes. A comprehensive Alexander-bibliography can be found in R.W. Sharples, 'Alexander of Aphrodisias: Scholasticism and Innovation' (*Aufstieg und Niedergang der römischen Welt*, 36.2), 1226-43; see also his translation of Alexander's *Ethical Questions* (London and Ithaca N.Y. 1990).

1. Primary Sources

Alexandri Aphrodisiensis in Aristotelis Metaphysica Commentaria, ed. Michael Hayduck (*CAG* 1), Berlin 1891.

Alexandri Aphrodisiensis in Topicorum Libros Octo Commentaria, ed. Maximilian Wallies (*CAG* 2.2), Berlin 1891.

Alexandri Aphrodisiensis praeter Commentaria Scripta Minora: De Anima Liber cum Mantissa, ed. Ivo Bruns (Supplementum Aristotelicum 2.1), Berlin 1887.

Alexandri Aphrodisiensis praeter Commentaria Scripta Minora: Quaestiones, De Fato, De Mixtione, ed. Ivo Bruns (Supplementum Aristotelicum 2.2), Berlin 1882.

Alexander of Aphrodisias On Fate, text, translation and commentary by R.W. Sharples, London 1983.

Alexander of Aphrodisias on Aristotle Metaphysics 1, tr. by William E. Dooley, London and Ithaca N.Y. 1989.

The Complete Works of Aristotle. The Revised Oxford Translation, ed. Jonathan Barnes, 2 vols, Princeton 1984.

Aristotelis Metaphysica, recognovit W. Jaeger, Oxford 1957, reprinted 1969.

Aristotle's Metaphysics, a revised text with introduction and commentary by W.D. Ross, 2 vols, Oxford 1924; reprinted 1948.

The Works of Aristotle Translated into English, vol. 8: *Metaphysica*, tr. by W.D. Ross, 2nd ed. Oxford 1928, reprinted 1948.

Aristotelis Fragmenta Selecta, recognovit W.D. Ross, Oxford 1955; reprinted 1970.

Asclepii in Metaphysicorum A-Z Commentaria, ed. Michael Hayduck (*CAG* 6.2), Berlin 1892.

Simplicii in Aristotelis Physicorum libros quattuor posteriores Commentaria, ed. Hermannus Diels (*CAG* 10), Berlin 1895.

2. Secondary Sources

Accattino, P., 'Alessandro di Afrodisia e Aristotele di Mitilene', *Elenchos* 6, 1985, 67-74.

Aristotle Transformed: the ancient commentators and their influence, ed. R. Sorabji, London and Ithaca N.Y. 1990.

Aufstieg und Niedergang der römischen Welt, Part 2. *Principat*, vol. 36.2, *Philosophie und Wissenschaften*, ed. W. Haase and H. Temporini, Berlin 1987.

Berti, E., 'La fonction de Métaph. Alpha Elatton dans la philosophie d'Aristote', *Zweifelhaftes im Corpus Aristotelicum*, 260-94.

Bonitz, H., *Aristotelis Metaphysica Commentarius*, Bonn 1849; reprinted Hildesheim 1960.

Brown, P., 'Infinite causal regression', *Philosophical Review* 75, 1966, 510-25.

Genequand, C., 'L'objet de la métaphysique selon Alexandre d'Aphrodisias', *Museum Helveticum* 36, 1979, 48-57.

Gigon, O., 'Versuch einer Interpretation von Metaphysik Alpha Elatton', *Zweifelhaftes im Corpus Aristotelicum*, 193-220.

Gottschalk, H.B., 'Aristotelian philosophy in the Roman world', *Aufstieg und Niedergang der römischen Welt* 36.2, 1079-174.

Jaeger, W., *Aristotle: fundamentals of the history of his development*, tr. by R. Robinson, 2nd ed., Oxford 1948.

Kenny, A., *The Five Ways: St. Thomas Aquinas' proofs of God's existence*, New York 1969.

Moraux, P., 'Aristoteles, der Lehrer Alexanders von Aphrodisias', *Archiv für Geschichte der Philosophie* 49, 1967, 169-82.

——, *Der Aristotelismus bei den Griechen* II (Peripatoi 6), Berlin 1984.

——, 'Ein neues Zeugnis über Aristoteles, der Lehrer Alexanders von Aphrodisias', *Archiv für Geschichte der Philosophie* 67, 1985, 266-9.

Mueller, I., 'Aristotle's doctrine of abstraction in the commentators', in *Aristotle Transformed*, 463-80.

Owens, J., 'The present status of Alpha Elatton in the Aristotelian *Metaphysics*', *Archiv für Geschichte der Philosophie* 66, 1984, 148-69.

Pines, S., 'An Arabic summary of a lost work of John Philoponus', *Israel Oriental Studies* 2, 1972, 320-52.

Reale, G., *The Concept of First Philosophy and the Unity of the Metaphysics of Aristotle*, ed. and tr. by J.A. Catan, Albany N.Y. 1980.

Sharples, R.W., 'Alexander of Aphrodisias: scholasticism and innovation', *Aufstieg und Niedergang der römischen Welt* 36.2, 1176-1243.

——, 'If what is earlier, then of necessity what is later?' *Bulletin of the Institute of Classical Studies* 26, 1979, 27-44.

——, 'Alexander of Aphrodisias, *Quaestiones on Possibility* I and II', *Bulletin of the Institute of Classical Studies* 29, 1982, 91-108 and 30, 1983, 99-110.

Sorabji, R., *Time, Creation and the Continuum*, London and Ithaca N.Y. 1983.

Szlezák, T., 'Alpha Elatton: Einheit und Einordnung in die Metaphysik', *Zweifelhaftes im Corpus Aristotelicum*, 221-59.

Vuillemin-Diem, G., 'Anmerkungungen zum Pasikles-Bericht und zu Echtheitszweifeln am grösseren und kleineren Alpha in Handschriften und Kommentatoren', *Zweifelhaftes im Corpus Aristotelicum*, 157-92.

Zweifelhaftes im Corpus Aristotelicum: Studien zu einigen Dubia. Akten des 9. Symposium Aristotelicum, eds P. Moraux and J. Wiesner (Peripatoi 14), Berlin 1983.

English–Greek Glossary

The Glossary lists key terms in the translation, and supplies the Greek words which they represent. It is also an aid to locating terms in the Greek-English Index.

(n) = noun; (v) = verb; (a) = adjective

abstraction: *aphairesis*
absurd: *atopos*
accurate: *akribês*
action: *praxis*
  men of: *hoi praktikoi*
activity: *energeia*
actual(ly): *energeiai, kat' energeian*
ad infinitum: *ep', eis apeiron*
affective: *pathêtikos*
alteration: *alloiôsis*
animal: *zôion*
animate: *empsukhos*
argument: *epikheirêsis, logos*
art: *tekhnê*
attributes: *ta huparkhonta*

become: *gignesthai*
  becoming (n): *genesis*
beginning: *arkhê*
being (n): *to einai, to on*
body: *sôma*

cause (n): *aitia, aition*
change (n): *metabolê*
  change(v): *metaballein*
come to be: *gignesthai*
  coming-to-be: *genesis*
complete: *teleios*
  completion, completed state:
    teleiotês
composite: *sunthetos*
continual, continuous: *sunekhês*
contradictory assertion: *antiphasis*
contraries, the: *ta enantia*

define: *horizesthai*

definite: *hôrismenos*
definition: *horismos, horos, logos*
demonstration: *apodeixis*
desire: *orexis*
destroy: *anairein*
dialectical: *dialektikos*
difference, differentia: *diaphora*
difficulty: *aporia, khalepotês*
discussion: *logos, hoi logoi*
disposition: *diathesis*

effect: *to aitiaton*
end (n): *telos*
essence: *to ti ên einai*
  essential: *kath' hauto*
eternal: *aïdios*

false: *pseudês*
finite: *peperasmenos*
flesh: *sarx*
form: *eidos*
  formal cause: *aition eidikon*
formula: *logos*

generation: *genesis*
genus: *genos*
goal: *skopos*
good, the: *to agathon*
growth: *auxêsis*

habitual capacity: *hexis*
hot, heat: *thermos, to thermon*

ignorance: *amathia*
immaterial: *aülos*
immediate: *amesos*

64

imperfect: *atelês*
imperishable: *aphthartos*
impression: *phantasia*
in itself: *kath' hauto*
in the proper sense: *kuriôs*
incorporeal: *asômatos*
individuals: *ta atoma, ta kath'
    hekasta*
indivisible: *atomos*
indolence: *argia*
induction: *epagôgê*
infinite, infinity: *apeiros, apeiria*
intellect: *nous*
    intelligible: *noêtos*
intermediates: *ta metaxu*
investigation: *theôria*

kind (n): *eidos*
    of a different kind: *anomoeidês*
    of the same kind: *homoeidês*
knowledge: *epistêmê, gnôsis*
    scientific knowledge: *epistêmê*
    knowable: *epistêtos, gnôstos*
    unknowable: *agnôstos*

learn, learner: *manthanein, ho
    manthanôn*
lecture(s): *akroasis, logoi*
light (n): *phôs*
limit: *peras*
    limited: *peperasmenos*

man: *anthrôpos*
mathematics: *ta mathêmata*
    objects of mathematics: *ta
    mathêmatika*
matter: *hulê*
    material cause: *aitia hulikê*
motion, movement: *kinêsis*

notion: *ennoia*

object: *pragma*
order: *taxis*

participate: *metekhein*

particulars: *ta kath' hekasta*
perish, perishing: *phtheiresthai,
    phthora*
premise: *protasis*
privation: *sterêsis*
productive cause: *aitia poiêtikê*
progression: *proodos*
proof: *deixis*

quality: *poiotês*

reason (n): *logos, nous*
    rational: *logikos*
relationship: *skhesis*

science, scientific knowledge:
    epistêmê
    scientific discipline: *methodos*
sense perception: *aisthêsis*
    sensible objects: *ta aisthêta*
separated: *kekhôrismenos*
series: *euthuôria*
shape: *skhêma*
    without shape: *askhêmatistos*
simple: *haplous*
size: *megethos*
soul: *psukhê*
species: *eidos*
speculation: *theôria*
structure: *suntaxis*
subject: *to hupokeimenon*
substantial: *kath' hauto*
substrate: *to hupokeimenon*

thing: *pragma*
thought, thinking: *noêsis*
time: *khronos*
treatise: *pragmateia*
true, truth: *alêthês, alêtheia*
turn back: *anakamptein*

universe: *kosmos*

weakness: *astheneia*
whole (n): *to holon*
wisdom: *sophia*

Greek-English Index

This index lists the principal Greek terms that occur in the commentary, together with the meaning or meanings given to them in the translation. Cognate terms are grouped together, so that the listing of terms does not always follow strict alphabetical order. Only the first occurrence of less important terms is given, the citation being followed by *passim*; but all significant occurrences of key philosophical terms are noted. This index is confined to a listing of citations; for the relevant philosophical topics contained in these citations, the Subject Index should be consulted. In cases in which a key term (e.g. *aitiai, aitia*, causes) occurs so frequently that its uses must be distinguished, the reader is referred to the Subject Index for the citations, which are there grouped according to the various contexts in which the term is used. Page and line references are to the Greek text.

adiexitêtos, cannot be traversed: 152,22

agathon, to, the good: 160,8-12

aïdios, eternal: 139,5; 145,10-21 *passim*; 148,2; 149,10
  ta aïdia, eternal things: 147,7.11; 148,5.24; 149,11-12.20
  aïdiotês, eternity: 148,25

aisthêsis, sense perception: 142,20.23; 145,2
  aisthêtikos, capable of sensing: 161,9; 163,1
  ta aisthêta, sensible things: 142,22; 168,20

aitia, aition, cause: 146,7-15; 147,19-27; 148,4-10.30-2; 149,3.27-8; 150,21.25.33-4; 151,5-152,32 *passim*

aitiai, aitia, causes: see Subject Index: Causes
  aitiaton, to, effect: 148,8; 150,34; 153,7

akribes, to, precision: 168,10
  akribeia, accuracy, precision: 168,8.19
  akribologia, precise language, precision: 168,4; 169,7

akroasis, lecture: 167,7
  akroatês, auditor: 167,5.24

alêthês, true: 146,12.15; 147,7-149,13 *passim*

alêtheia, truth: 138,18.21.28; 144,17; 145,4-146,25 *passim*; 148,1-19

alloiôsis, alteration: 153,20; 154,24

amathia, ignorance: 156,20

amesoi protaseis, immediate premises: 163,5
  amesôs, immediately: 162,19.24.27

anakamptein, bend, turn, back: 153,9; 154,22; 155,6-7; 156,30; 159,23; 165,26
  an. eis allêla change back into one another: 155,1; 157,18.24.33; 159,17

analutika, ta: analytics: 168,22

aneleutheros, illiberal: 168,9

anthrôpos, man: 150,5 *passim*

antiphasis, contradictory proposition: 156,14

apeiros, infinite: 149,24 *passim*
  ep', eis apeiron, ad infinitum: 137,12 *passim*
  ta sunekhê apeira, infinite continua: 163,20
  to apeiron, apeiria, infinity: 151,26; 152,16; 163,16;

164,10; 166,9-14
aphairesis, abstraction: 169,6
aphthartos, imperishable: 158,18
apodeixis, demonstration: 146,20;
 163,6; 168,23
aretê, virtue: 145,17
argia, indolence: 142,10
arkhê, beginning: 137,4.11; 149,21;
 152,9-12; 153,5-6
 tês kinêseôs, of motion: 150,2
arkhê, arkhai, principle, principles:
 see Subject Index: Principle
askhêmatistos, without shape:
 164,17
asômatos, incorporeal: 165,12
astron, star: 148,25
atelês, incomplete: 153,25; 155,20;
 156,32; 157,11.14
atomos, indivisible: 163,5
 ta atoma, the indivisible things,
 i.e. attributes: 162,19-163,14
 passim
aülos, immaterial: 169,8-16
auxêsis, growth: 153,19; 154,24

diairein, divide: 163,25.27
diairetos, divisible: 164,6.9
diairesis, division: 164,3
dialektikos, dilectical: 167,2
diaphora, difference: 150,17;
 157,26; differentia: 162.14
diexienai, pass over, traverse:
 164,5-10
doxa, opinion: 139,15 *passim*, reputation: 168,9, theory:
 143,20.22
 doxastos, object of opinion:
 148,12; 164,21
dunamis, power: 142,21; 143,14;
 potentiality: 159,21
 dunamei,potential(ly): 164,10;
 166,12

eidos, form: 153,21.23; 155,20.24;
 159,20; 161,1.12; 162,8;
 164,27; 165,9.11.16
eidos, kind: 149,26; 153,7.10;
 160,30; 165,31-167,3 *passim*
 anomoeidês, of a different kind:
 152,1
 homoeidês, of the same kind:
 151,3; 152,2

eidos, species: 148,25
einai, to, being (*esse*): 138,20; 145,5;
 147,10; 148,11; 156,3-13
 to on, being (*ens*), that which
 exists: 148,1.14.16.18;
 156,2-13
 to mê on, not-being: 147,11;
 156,2-13
 ta onta, the things that are, that
 exist: 141,9 *passim*
 ek tinos, from something: 153,16-
 154,15 *passim*
empsukhos, animate: 161,9; 163,1
enantia, ta, the contraries: 159,23
energeia, activity: 142,22-3; 145,17
 energeiai, kat' energeian, actu-
 al(ly): 151,26 *passim*
ennoia, idea, notion: 141,23; 143,18
epagôgê, induction: 160,9
epikheirein, argue dialectically:
 166,20
epikheirêsis, argument: 167,1
epistasis, consideration: 141,23
epistêmê, scientific knowledge, science: 145,20; 146,11.20; 163,6
 philosophic knowledge: 147,12;
 148,17
 hai epistêmai, the sciences: see
 Subject Index, Science
 epistêtos, object of scientific knowledge: 148,12-13; 163,7;
 164,20; 165,5
eskhatos, last: 151,6 *passim*
ethê, ta, habits: 167,7.22-4
euporia, ready familiarity: 143,21
euthuôria, series: 149,26 *passim*

gignesthai, become, come to be; *genesis*, becoming, coming-to-be:
 see Subject Index: Come to be
gnôsis, knowledge: 138,18 *passim*
 hê kuriôs gn., knowledge in the
 proper sense: 146,12
grammê, line: 163,25; 164,2.5

hêlios, sun: 150,6
hexis, habitual capacity: 139,3;
 144,5
horizein, set a limit: 152,24
 horizesthai, define: 161,12
 horismos, horos, definition: 161,1-
 163,14 *passim*

hôrismenos, definite:
150,16; 160,24
hulê, matter: 149,29-30; 153,11;
157,23; 158,16-17; 159,2-29
passim; 164,16-165,5.10.13;
169,11.19
huparkhein, belong: 162,19-163,10
passim
hupokeimenon, to, subject: 145,10;
162,26; substrate:
154,7.16.21; 158,9-159,27
passim; 166,22

kata sumbebêkos, per accidens:
158,15-16
kath' hauto, essentially, *per se*:
145,23; 158,18
kath' hekasta, ta, particulars:
145,18; 163,6-10
katholou, universally: 145,15
kekhôrismenos, separate, separated: 142,20.22
khalepon, to, khalepotês, difficulty:
140,5 *passim*
khronos, time: 150,20-7; 151,2;
152,15; 154,14; 166,9-17
kosmos, universe: 148,24; 150,18
kuriôs, in the proper sense: 146,12
passim

logos, account: 137,5; 150,7; argument: 151,1.13; 154,13; reason,
160,13; formula, i.e. definition: 161,2-162,16 *passim*;
164,17; 165,10.15.20-4
logikos, rational: 162,15; logical;
167,2
ta logika, logic: 168,22
hoi logoi, arguments: 168,23;
169,2.13-17; discussion,
lectures: 167,5; 169,29;
speech: 168,10

manthanein, act of learning: 156,19
ho manthanôn, the learner:
155,21-156,21 *passim*
mathêmata, ta, mathematics:
167,24
mathêmatika, ta, objects of mathematics: 169,6.13
megethos, grandeur: 140,5; size,
152,15

mesa, ta, the intermediates
(in a series): 150,31 *passim*
Meta ta phusika, Metaphysics (as
title) 169,22
metaballein, change (v.i.): 154,24;
159,19-24
metabolê, change (n): 153,18.21-
2.27; 154,3.16; 157,1.3; 159,24
metaxu, ta, intermediates, intermediate stages: 154,22-155,5
metekhein, participate: 147,10;
148,1; 149,9
methodos, scientific discipline:
145,5

noein, think: 155,23; 163,26-7;
164,2-5; 165,3; 166,15
ho noôn, the thinker: 153,21;
155,22
to nooumenon, object of thought,
thing known: 155,23; 166,7
nous, intellect: 138,14; 142,5-23
passim; 143,15; 150,13;
155,24; 166,15.18; reason:
160,16-19
noêsis, act of thinking: 166,8
noêtos, intelligible: 164,29
nomos, law: 167,16
nomothetês, lawgiver: 167,15

oikeiotês, personal attitude, habits:
167,7; 168,12
orexis, desire: 160,25

pathêtikos, affective: 142,21
peras, limit: 152,17; 160,26-7;
164,18
peperasmenos, finite, limited:
164,3-4; 166,7-16.27-28
phaneros, perspicuous: 142,18-19
phantasia, impression: 141,32;
168,7
philosophein, philosophise: 139,13;
147,6
philosophia, philosophy: 138,8
passim. See Subject Index:
Philosophy
phôs, light (n): 142,14-17
phtheiresthai, phthora, perish,
perishing: 153,2-159,26
passim
phusis, nature: 137,14-18; 138,14;

Subject Index

This index lists topics of interest, including the proper names of persons mentioned by Alexander. The textual references in this index duplicate those given in the Greek-English Index, but here the citations are distributed according to the multiple contexts in which a term occurs. In cases in which a key term (e.g. *aitiai, aitia*, causes) occurs so frequently that its uses must be distinguished, all citations are found in the Subject Index. Page and line references are to the Greek text.

action, *praxis*, its goal not truth: 145,6-21
  actions, *ta prakta*, contingent and variable: 145,14-19
  activity, *energeia*, that proper to the intellect: 142,22-3
Alpha Elatton (Book 2 of *Metaphysics*), authenticity and character of: 137,2-138,23; 139,22-140,2; 143,23-144,3; 169,20-4
alteration, *alloiôsis*, change by way of: 153,2
Aristotle (of Mytilene): 166,20
art, *tekhnê*, truth in: 139,2-3
attributes, immediate, *ta amesôs huparkhonta*: 162,19-163,5

being (*esse*), *to einai*, causes of: 138,19-21; 147,12-14.27-8
  and form: 165,9.11
  and truth: 147,10-148,19 *passim*
  becoming is between being and not-being: 156,2-13
being (*ens*), *to on*, and truth: 148,1.14-19
  what comes to be from something that exists is between what is (*to on*) and what is not (*to mê on*): 156,2-13
body, *sôma kuklophorikon*, moving in a circle, a natural body but without matter: 169,18
  the four primary bodies, how eternal: 148,25; their specific

differences not infinite: 157,25

cause, *aitia, aition*, first: 149,22; last: 160,4
  relation of causes in a series: 151,1-152,32 *passim*
  and effect: 148,8-10
  and knowledge: 146,7-16
  and truth: 145,27-146,17
  the first causes, eternity of: 147,7-148,32 *passim*. See also Principles
  the four causes: final: 150,8; 159,27-160,27 *passim*; formal: 150,10; 160,30-162,16 *passim*; material: 149,29; 158,7-159,27 *passim*; productive: 150,1.3; 160,17; 165,25-7
  infinite regress of the causes: see Infinity
change (v.i.) *metaballein*, (n) *metabolê*, 'from the becoming' and 'from that which is coming to be': 153,15-157,27 *passim*
  reversal of substantial c.: 155,6-7; 157,19-27; 159,17-24
come to be, *gignesthai*, coming-to-be, *genesis*, two types of: 153,15-157,27 *passim*
  hê kuriôs g., coming-to-be in the proper sense: 154,2-4
composite, *sunthetos*, a c. thing different from its essence: 165,8-10

Alexander of Aphrodisias

On Aristotle Metaphysics 3

translated by
Arthur Madigan

To the Memory of my Mother and my Father

Introduction

The commentary on *Metaphysics* 3

The purpose of this brief introduction is to alert the reader to what he or she will find in Alexander's commentary on *Metaphysics* 3, and to give some indications of what may be of interest.[1]

To this end it may be helpful to begin with a summary of the contents of *Metaphysics* 3 itself. The book falls into three unequal parts. The first part of chapter 1 (995a24-995b4) is a statement of purpose, in which Aristotle explains the advantage, even the necessity, of addressing certain aporiae or problems which block the advance of thought. The latter part of chapter 1 (995b4-996a17) lists the aporiae or problems to be addressed and remarks on the difficulty of presenting them correctly. Chapters 2-6 discuss the aporiae in detail. For the most part they follow the order of chapter 1, but with occasional variation in the way the aporiae are framed, the omission of two aporiae, and the addition of one aporia not mentioned in chapter 1. Neither Aristotle nor Alexander numbers the aporiae, but commentators commonly recognise about fifteen of them. Chapter 2: whether the science of wisdom includes all four Aristotelian causes; whether it will include study of the principles of demonstration; whether it will cover all kinds of substances; whether it will study essential attributes or accidents as well as substances; whether there are substances distinct from sensible substances (the occasion for attacks on Platonic Forms and intermediates). Chapter 3: whether the principles of things are their kinds or their constituents; whether the higher or the lower kinds have a better claim to be principles. Chapter 4: whether there exists anything distinct from particulars; whether principles are one merely in form or one in number as well; whether the principles of perishable things and imperishable things are the same (the

---

[1] For a general account of Alexander of Aphrodisias the reader may consult R.W. Sharples, 'Alexander of Aphrodisias, scholasticism and innovation,' in W. Haase ed., *Aufstieg und Niedergang der römischen Welt* II, 36.2, Berlin 1987, 1176-243. For an introduction to Alexander's commentary on the *Metaphysics* the reader may consult R. Sorabji and R.W. Sharples, 'Introduction' in Alexander of Aphrodisias, *On Aristotle Metaphysics 1*, tr. W.E. Dooley, London and Ithaca N.Y. 1989, 1-4.

occasion for a criticism of Empedocles); whether the Pythagorean-Platonic theory of One and Being is true or false. Chapter 5: whether mathematical and in particular geometrical entities are genuine substances. Chapter 6: whether there are good reasons to posit Platonic Forms as distinct from intermediates; whether the principles exist in potentiality or in actuality; whether the principles are universal or particular.

Unlike *Metaphysics* 1, 7 and 12, *Metaphysics* 3 has received relatively little attention. The student of Aristotle who is interested in this book may then be pleased to have at his or her disposal the full and careful commentary of Alexander. Alexander goes through *Metaphysics* 3 line by line, with careful attention to the logical sequence of the arguments, marking variant readings, and noting places where Aristotle's words are susceptible of more than one interpretation. In some places the reader will find that the text of Aristotle explained by Alexander differs from the text as printed by modern editors such as Ross and Jaeger; in some places the reader will find that the text of Aristotle found in Alexander's introductory lemmata differs from that found in the citations embedded in Alexander's commentary.[2] The translator has tried to mark these divergences; and they are not so frequent or so important as to detract from the usefulness of the commentary.

While Alexander's commentary on *Metaphysics* 1 has been of special value as a source of material from Aristotle's *Peri Ideôn*, no such claim can be made for the commentary on *Metaphysics* 3, though there appears to be at least one reference to the *Peri Ideôn* overlooked by Hayduck.[3]

While dialectical reasoning is found throughout the *Metaphysics*, *Metaphysics* 3 stands out as the book of dialectical problems. Alexander is well aware of this fact, often noting the dialectical character of the arguments, the merely probable character of their premises, the use of premises drawn from non-Aristotelian sources. Alexander's commentary on the *Topics* suggests, however, that his notion of dialectic is different from Aristotle's, at least in emphasis. Whereas Aristotle stresses the tentative and probing character of dialectic, Alexander stresses the fact that dialectical argumentation on both sides of a question involves the presence of false premises.[4]

---

[2] On the importance of Alexander's commentary for the constitution of the text of the *Metaphysics*, see W.D. Ross, *Aristotle's Metaphysics*, London 1924, I.clxi-clxiii. I have tried to mark every place where Alexander's lemma or citation differs from the texts of Ross and Jaeger, and every place where lemma and citation differ from one another. In the latter case it is at least possible that the embedded citation preserves the reading of Alexander's MS or MSS of Aristotle, and that the lemma has suffered contamination.

[3] See 201,18-19.

[4] See Alexander *in Top.* 2,15-3,24, especially 3,8-20, and *in Metaph.* 236,26-9. In at

Of course Alexander's way of reading Aristotle is not that of contemporary developmental theorists. Where a developmental theorist might read large parts of *Metaphysics* 3 as indicating honest perplexity on the part of an Aristotle who feels the force of opposed positions and strives to accommodate the truth in them, Alexander reads the book in the light of his knowledge of Aristotle's system, and so distinguishes, at least part of the time, the arguments which are merely dialectical from the arguments which are well founded. At no point does Alexander suggest that Aristotle himself is seriously perplexed. Perhaps surprisingly, however, Alexander does not volunteer information about how or where in the *Metaphysics* Aristotle's aporiae are supposed to be solved.

Here and there one might wish that Alexander would reach out and address a question that begs to be asked; for example, why does Aristotle raise an aporia about the possibility of one science including all four causes, when his own *Physics* is a clear case of such a science? But perhaps the moral is to read Alexander for what he does say rather than looking for what he does not say. Whatever its limitations, Alexander's commentary is still fundamental to the work of any student or commentator who attempts to understand *Metaphysics* 3.

The commentary may also claim a special interest for students of philosophy in late antiquity. It was well known to Proclus' teacher, the Athenian Neoplatonist Syrianus (died *c*. 437), who makes his own commentary on *Metaphysics* 3 the occasion for a polemical defence of Platonism against Aristotelianism. Alexander's commentary was also well known to the sixth-century Alexandrian Neoplatonist Asclepius (or perhaps we should speak of Ammonius, son of Hermeias, his source), whose approach to Aristotle is in general more accommodating than that of Syrianus, and who inserts extended chunks of Alexander into his own commentary on the book.[5] *Metaphysics* 3 and 4 are the only books of the *Metaphysics* for which we have Greek commentaries from all three: Alexander, Syrianus and Asclepius. This affords the possibility of a three-way comparison which reveals something about late Aristotelianism and about the different ways in which Aristotle is handled in the Neoplatonic commentary tradition.[6]

Finally, students whose interests run to Neoplatonism rather

least one place, 218,17, the adverb *dialektikôs*, 'dialectically', appears to be pejorative.

[5] Michael Hayduck, who edited both Alexander and Asclepius for the *CAG*, often draws on these excerpts for readings and for supplements to fill lacunae in the text of Alexander.

[6] For an attempt in this direction see A. Madigan, 'Syrianus and Asclepius on forms and intermediates in Plato and Aristotle', *Journal of the History of Philosophy* 24, 1986, 149-71.

than to Aristotelianism must reckon with Porphyry's statement in chapter 14 of his *Life of Plotinus*, that Alexander's commentaries were among those read in Plotinus' school. If Porphyry is right in saying that Aristotle's *Metaphysics* is concentrated in the writings of Plotinus, perhaps research may show that Alexander's commentary on *Metaphysics* 3 has left its traces in Plotinus as well.

The present translation

This translation is made from the Greek text edited by Michael Hayduck, *Alexandri Aphrodisiensis in Aristotelis Metaphysica Commentaria* (*CAG* 1: Berlin 1891).

Some readers will come to this translation looking for help in understanding Aristotle; these readers, who may have no Greek, will require a clear, accurate, and unencumbered presentation of what Alexander says about Aristotle. Other readers will be interested in Alexander himself; they will want to know which English words correspond to which Greek words, and where the translator departs from Hayduck's text, and why; and they may well wish to distinguish between what Alexander actually says and what the translator thinks Alexander means. I have tried to keep in mind the requirements of these two sorts of readers.

Departures from Hayduck's text are listed consecutively under Textual Emendations, and are explained in the notes at the points where they occur.

Square brackets [ ] in the translation enclose words not found as such in the Greek text but necessary or at least helpful to an understanding of the text. While not attempting to put brackets around the numerous parallelisms in the text, I have otherwise used the device fairly freely.

Angle brackets < > enclose conjectural supplements to Hayduck's Greek text. In his text of Alexander Hayduck frequently notes the presence of lacunae. In his critical apparatus he often proposes to fill in these lacunae with material drawn from the excerpts from Alexander that are embedded in the corresponding commentary of Asclepius. I have generally followed Hayduck's advice in this matter. A few proposed supplements are my own.

The Aristotelian lemmata that mark the beginning of each section of the commentary, and the citations embedded within the commentary, present a combination of problems. At times the lemmata and citations witness to a text of Aristotle different from that found in the principal MSS of the *Metaphysics*. These instances are important for textual criticism, but may cause difficulty for students working with the modern editions of Ross and Jaeger, or with translations based on modern editions. Hence I have tried to mark every place where Alexander's lemmata or citations differ from the texts of Ross or Jaeger. At times the text of Aristotle given in a lemma differs from the text found in a citation embedded in Alexander's commentary itself; this suggests the possibility that the citation preserves the reading of Alexander's MS or MSS and that the lemma has suffered contamination. I have tried to mark these cases. At times a lemma or citation seems to be missing words which it needs to make sense. I have tried to indicate in footnotes when a lemma or citation is incomplete in the Greek, and have placed the necessary supplement in square brackets in the translation.

Apart from the divisions required by the lemmata, the paragraphing is my work, as are the occasional numbering devices, [i], [ii] etc.

Material from the *altera recensio* (*alt. rec.*) or parallel version of Alexander's commentary on *Metaphysics* 3 appears in the *apparatus criticus* at the foot of the first three pages of Hayduck's text. This parallel material is translated in footnotes as it occurs.

Those seeking information on Hayduck's text are urged to consult his preface, as well as the remarks of William E. Dooley SJ in his Translator's Preface to Alexander of Aphrodisias, *On Aristotle Metaphysics 1*, and the further references he provides.

Acknowledgments

The translator's debts are many and various. The beginnings of this work were funded by a Summer Research Grant from Boston College administered by Dean Donald J. White. A year's Junior Fellowship at the Center for Hellenic Studies, directed by Professor Zeph Stewart, taught me much about how to interpret Alexander's Greek. Two visits to the Seminar für Klassische Philologie at the Freie Universität, Berlin enabled me to make further progress; for this I thank Dieter Harlfinger and Christian Brockmann. Among those who have read the translation in whole or in part are my confrere William Dooley SJ, Brad Inwood, Robert Sharples, Frederic Schroeder and Robert Todd. Mistakes and infelicities which remain in the translation are mine, not theirs. Margaret Holland has helped in the correction of the proofs. My greatest debt is to Richard Sorabji, for his patience, encouragement and sound counsel.

Textual Emendations

Except as noted below, I translate the text of Alexander as printed by Hayduck, omitting words which he brackets and accepting the supplements which he incorporates into his text. Where I have adopted an emendation or supplement proposed or mentioned by Hayduck in his apparatus, or drawn from some other source, that fact is noted below and the source is credited in parentheses. These emendations are also recorded in footnotes at the point of their occurrence in the text.

175,8-9	Reading *to kai peri tôn arkhôn· akolouthon gar tôi proeirêmenôi* for *to †akolouthon gar tôi proeirêmenôi tôi kai peri tôn arkhôn* (S, Bonitz).
177,23	Deleting *tinos* (Ascl.)
177,28	Supplying, after *arkhai ê, tauta eis ha diaireitai hekaston enuparkhonta en tois meresin (hekaston gar enuparkhei en tois heautou meresin) hôs hê ousia* (Ascl., Hayduck).
179,8	Supplying, after *peperasmenai, kat' arithmon de ou, ê kai kat' arithmon eisi peperasmenai* (Ascl., Hayduck).
181,12	Reading *monon* for *monôn*.
183,17	Reading *hekastên tôn epistêmôn* for *hekaston tôn epistêtôn*.
183,26	Reading *tên deiknuousan* for *to mê einai deiknuousan* (Bonitz).
186,13	Supplying, after *einai, hoti to men proüparkhei (toiouton gar to poiêtikon aition) to de husteron epiginetai* (Ascl., Hayduck).
187,14	Reading *kai peri tôn* for *kai tôn* (*Metaph.* 996b26, Hayduck).
188,27	Supplying, after *axiômata, einai hapanta hen ti genos kai mian tina phusin hupokeimenên* (Ascl., Hayduck).
189,18	Deleting *ek*.
189,28	Supplying, after *apodeixeis, ha dei prôta einai*.
191,30	Supplying, after *doxôn, tês autês* (Sharples).
192,29	Reading *kai allês kai allês to* for *kai allês ê peri to* (Hayduck).

193,28	Supplying, after *autês*, *eite allês eiê an legôn eite tês autês* (Ascl., Hayduck).
194,9	Reading *kai peri ta* for *kai ta* (*Metaph.* 997a26, Hayduck).
195,7	Full stop after *geômetrêi*.
195,24	Reading *ouden elatton* for *ouketi*.
196,25-26	Reading *ousias horistas kai autas kath' hautas* for *ousias horistikas autas kath' hautas*.
197,2	Reading *hêi* (adverb) *ousia* for *hê ousia*.
200,11	Supplying, after *euthu*, *hoias legei ho geômetrês* (*Metaph.* 998a1).
201,6	*panta kata* for *panta ta kata*.
201,18-19	Supplying *peri ideôn* after *deuterôi*.
202,13-14	Supplying *hois* before *khrômetha* (Bonitz).
203,6	Supplying, after *arkhai*, *alla mên palin autôn tôn horismôn ta genê arkhai* (Ascl., Hayduck).
204,22	Reading *arkhai* for *stoikheia*.
205,2	Reading *ousiai* for *ousia*.
206,1-2	Reading *oute ara* for *oute gar* (Ascl., Hayduck).
208,17-18	*to tôi eidei adiaireton tou kata to poson (sc. adiairetou) tou de kata to poson diairoumenou to tôi posôi adiaireton* for *to tôi eidei adiaireton †tou kata to poson diairoumenou to de tôi posôi adiaireton*.
209,17	Supplying, after *katêgoreitai*, *polu hêtton epi tôn allôn genôn* (S, Hayduck).
209,17	*êtoi de touto ê* for *touto de êtoi*.
209,18	*mê ousês tinos diaphoras* for *mesês tinos diaphoras* (Hayduck).
212,2	Supplying, after *einai*, *oud' an dunaito ti para ta kath' hekasta einai* (S, Bonitz).
212,5	Reading *toiauta* for *toiouton* (Bonitz).
215,31	Interrogation mark after *ou gar hen hapanta hôn hê ousia mia*.
216,4	Reading *ta proüparkhonta êdê kai hopôsoun onta eidê* for *ta proüparkhonta †eidê ê hopôsoun ta eidê* (Hayduck).
216,9-10	Reading *kai menein en autêi eis touto metaballousêi* for *kai menein en hautêi eis touto metaballousan*.
217,17	Reading *ei ekhei kata ti koinônian allêlois, ho mê esti kat' arithmon hen* for *†ekhonta an koinônian allêlois, ha mê esti ta kat' arithmon hen* (Hayduck).
218,4-5	Begin parenthesis at *ei hen* rather than at *ou pleiô*.
218,27	Reading *pithanon einai to ta men* for *pithanon einai tou ta men* (Brandis).
219,31	Reading *ou gar monon geneseôs* for *ou gar geneseôs* (S).

221,8   Reading *sunthesis tis ôn* for *auto sunthesis tis* (Hayduck).

221,9   Reading *oukh hôs eulogon ara* for *oukh hôs eulogon gar*.

221,11-12   Deleting *ton theon* (A²S).

222,13   Supplying, after *ekeina*, *ex hôn gegone to phtheiromenon* (LF, S).

222,24   Reading *aphairousi* for *aporousi* (Hayduck).

224,22   Reading *ousiai* for *ousia* (S, Bonitz).

226,6-7   Reading *ta de para to hen para to on ên, ta de para to on ouk esti* for *to de para to hen †ouk ên, ta de para to on ouk ên* (Ascl., Hayduck).

227,1   *ekeino* for *ekeinôn* (Bonitz, Hayduck).

228,6   *aporêsai* (infinitive) for *aporêsei*.

229,3   *pathê te kai kinêseis* for *pathêtikas kinêseis*.

230,28   Supplying, after *sômatôn*, *toutesti kata tauta tas tôn sômatôn diaireseis* (Ascl., Hayduck).

230,30-1   Reading *kata men gar to platos* for *kata mentoi to platos*.

232,20   Supplying, after *ouk esti*, *ousia* (S, Ascl., Hayduck).

233,30-1   Reading *houtô de oude arkhai ousiôn kuriôs tines kai hôrismenai* for *houtô de †oude arkhôn ousôn ousiai kuriôs tais kai hôrismenais*.

235,26   Reading *dunatai gar mê einai* for *dunatai gar einai*.

Alexander of Aphrodisias

On Aristotle Metaphysics 3

Translation

The Commentary of Alexander of Aphrodisias on [Book 3] (Beta) of the *Metaphysics* of Aristotle

995a24 It is necessary, with regard to the science that is the object of inquiry, for us to proceed first ...

The science (*epistêmê*)[1] that is the object of the inquiry and that is 5 proposed here is both wisdom (*sophia*) and the theological science which Aristotle entitles metaphysics because it comes after physics in the order relative to us. He also calls it primary wisdom, because it is able to consider the things which are primary and of highest dignity.[2] For this same reason it is also theological, for Aristotle's discussion in these [books] is concerned first and foremost with the cause (*aition*), the form (*eidos*), which is on his view an utterly 10 immaterial substance (*ousia*), which he also calls the primary god and mind (*nous*). He says that it is necessary, for the discovery of the science itself and of the objects of inquiry belonging to it, to proceed first of all to enumerate those points about which one must first face an aporia (*aporein*), and then to face the aporia about these points.[3]

---

[1] Important terms are transliterated at their first occurrence (or sometimes, if a contrast is at stake, at the first occurrence of the contrast) but thereafter only if the translation differs notably from that first given. Substantives are generally given in the nominative, verbs in the infinitive, unless there is some reason to give the form actually occurring in the text.

[2] In the *alt. rec.* found in MSS LF the commentary begins as follows: Having said in Alpha Meizon of the present treatise what the goal of it is, that it is concerned with being as being, as has been clearly dealt with in that book, and having said what science it is that considers this, that it is primary philosophy, which he also entitles theological science and metaphysics, as well as primary philosophy, because it is [science] of the primary things.

[3] An *aporia* is an obstacle. Alexander uses *aporia* in at least four senses: a physical impediment to movement in a certain direction (the original sense); a state of perplexity (the *aporia* in us); a problematic object or issue, such as to give rise to perplexity (the *aporia* in the thing); a philosophical discussion which seeks to clarify a problematic issue, and to relieve perplexity, by arguing on both sides of the issue. The ideal translation would communicate the last three senses of the term, while preserving the original sense of a physical impediment. Aristotle complicates the translator's task by mixing the metaphor of an obstacle in a person's path with the metaphor of a knot preventing a person from moving. More importantly, he employs a whole family of cognates: the adjective *aporos*, and the verbs *aporein* (in passive as

172,1   And so he does.[4] One can also understand the phrase 'points about
which one must first face an aporia' [995a25] in an even more
universal sense; for it is by way of these points that the discovery of
the sciences occurs.[5] If this is true for every science, so too for the
science proposed here.

Aristotle next indicates the points about which one must, in each
science, face an aporia, in the words 'These are the points on which
5   certain [thinkers] have held different views' [995a25-6].[6] This could
mean either that they held views which were not suitable or as they
ought to have been but rather erroneous, or [simply] that different
thinkers have held different views (for the points which present
aporiae most of all are those on which diverse opinions have been
laid down previously by those who have concerned themselves with
them). Or it could mean those points which, though knowledge of
them is indispensable, have been overlooked by previous thinkers;
he speaks as though he will work through aporiae (diaporein)[7]
concerning these as well.

Having said that one must face the aporiae, Aristotle then
10   establishes and proves universally that for all who are going to
concern themselves with some matter, it is useful for the discovery

---

well as active voice) *diaporein, euporein, proaporein, prosaporein.* Depending on
context the verb *aporein* may mean to state or face an obstacle, or to have resolved it.
To preserve the connection among the different senses of *aporia* and *aporein*, and
among the cognates, I use aporia as an English word, admitting its absence (in the
required sense) from the *Oxford English Dictionary*, but finding support in its
appearance in *Webster's Third International*. For a fuller discussion, see J. Owens,
The Doctrine of Being in the Aristotelian 'Metaphysics', 2nd ed. Toronto, 1963, 211-19.

[4] In place of 'He says that it is necessary ... And so he does.' the *alt. rec.* reads: but
[it is] metaphysics [*meta ta phusika*, after the physics] because it comes after that
[treatise] in the order relative to us. Having proceeded [in Alpha Meizon] to the views
about causes and principles held by those who philosophised before him, and having
tested these and swept them away, and having dealt in Alpha Elatton with these very
matters and having proved that causes do not go on to infinity either in a direct line
or in kind, he says here, beginning his discussion 'It is necessary, with regard to the
science that is the object of inquiry, for us to proceed to the points concerning which
one must first face an aporia' [999a24-5; but note the absence of the first *prôton*,
'first']. The science that is now the object of his inquiry is, as has been said, primary
philosophy. He says, 'the points about which one must first face an aporia' [995a25] in
the sense that he will first speak about the matters about which one must face an
aporia, then, having faced an aporia [*aporêsas*, perhaps a mistake for infinitive
aporêsai, 'to face an aporia'] about them .... And so he does.

[5] The *alt. rec.* reads: One can also understand the phrase on the supposition that he
is saying in universal terms that it is necessary, for every science that is an object of
inquiry, to proceed to the 'points about which one must first face an aporia' [995a25];
for it is by way of these that the discovery of the sciences occurs.

[6] At this point the *alt. rec.* inserts: For he says that the points about which certain
[thinkers] have held different views are such.

[7] The verb *diaporein* involves more than merely raising or mentioning an aporia,
but less than actually solving it; it involves consideration of arguments on both sides
of an issue, enough to make it clear that there is a genuine difficulty.

of the objects of the inquiry to begin by working through the aporiae about them. For the advance (*euporia*) [of thought], the discovery and establishment of these objects of inquiry, depends on the discovery of the points of aporia. It would be more consistent with this if, instead of 'but it is' (*esti de*) [995a27], he had written 'for it is' (*esti gar*); for the subsequent advance is the solution of the matters of aporia already mentioned. This is equivalent to saying 'for the solution of the previous points of aporia is the cause of the subsequent advance'. Or [one might put it] this way: 'for the resulting subsequent advance results from the solution of the primary points of aporia.' For Aristotle this is the starting point (*arkhê*) of the proposed treatise (*pragmateia*); for here he begins to speak of matters which have a necessary bearing on the issues proposed. (The matters discussed in Alpha would be preliminary to this treatise and contribute to putting it on the right footing.) This is why some have thought that the present book is the first book of the treatise *Metaphysics*.[8]

995a29 It is impossible for people to untie a knot that they do not know.

If the discovery and establishment of the objects of the inquiry depends on the solution of the points of aporia, and it is not possible for people to untie a knot unless they first know it, i.e. how it has been tied (how could one untie an unknown knot in a knowledgeable way?), and if the aporia of thought (*dianoia*) is the knot in the matters under inquiry (for it is this aporia that shows the knot in the object (*pragma*)), it is necessary first of all to face the aporia concerning the matters under inquiry, the matters that are to be proven – given that discovery comes from solving the points of aporia, and only those who know how the aporia has developed can solve the points of aporia.

'But the aporia of thought makes this clear concerning the object' [995a30-1]. This is equivalent to saying, 'but the aporia of thought makes clear the knot which is in the object'. Having called the aporia a knot, Aristotle then indicates in what respect it is like a knot. A knot prevents forward movement and progress towards the [goal] proposed, and this is what an aporia does as well: thought is prevented from going forward because of the aporia concerning the object.

15

20

25

30

173,1

---

[8] See W. Jaeger, *Aristotle, fundamentals of the history of his development*, 2nd ed. Oxford 1948, 177-8. As Jaeger sees it, Aristotle's use of the first person plural, suggesting that he considered himself a Platonist, led some to doubt the authenticity of *Metaph*. 1. Jaeger cites Alexander 196,19, Syrianus *in Metaph*. 23,9 and a report in Albert the Great that some credited Theophrastus with adding *Metaph*. 1 to the *Metaphysics*.

5   **995a32 For it is impossible to move forward either way.**

Neither the man tied up with a knot nor the man facing an aporia can go forward towards the [goal] proposed. Hence, because one has to know the knot if one is to untie it, Aristotle says that it is necessary to begin by facing the aporiae, and because those who inquire about something without working through the aporiae are

10 walking like blind men. For those who speak about objects of inquiry without having examined the points of aporia concerning those objects have no goal (*skopos*) towards which to direct what they say,[9] no goal towards which to bear. For it is [facing] the points of aporia in advance that guides those who face the aporiae to conduct their inquiries in an orderly way. For those who inquire about things without facing the aporiae are inquiring without knowing what they have to inquire about.

15 Aristotle adds to this that those who inquire about something without facing the aporiae can never know[10] whether the inquiry has advanced and come to a [successful] end (*telos*). He gives the reason: to those who inquire in this manner the end of the inquiry is unknown. This is why he says that they resemble and are like people who do not know the place towards which they have to walk,

20 people who do not know the end;[11] to these people the end, the goal, is not known even if it has been found.[12] For it is the solution of the possible aporiae concerning certain matters which is the end, and the discovery of the thing itself.

Aristotle adds to the preceding another reason why it is necessary to begin by facing the aporiae: just as in [legal] judgments those who have heard both sides pleading against each other, and not just one

25 side or the other, make better judgments, so too in the case of the [present] objects of inquiry: one's judgment about them is sounder if one begins by confronting and solving all the possible aporiae, and all that can be said to confirm and establish them.

---

[9] For the remainder of this sentence the *alt. rec.* substitutes: for it is with a view to the goal that one should direct and harmonise what one says and do what leads logically to it.

[10] In the *alt. rec.* the verb 'know' (*gnôrizein*) is in a different position in the sentence.

[11] In Hayduck's text this is *hois agnoeitai to telos*; in the *alt. rec.* it is *mê eidosi to telos*, with basically the same meaning. The *alt. rec.* continues: to these people the end, the goal, has never been found or become known.

[12] Reading *oud' ei pote* with Bonitz and Hayduck; MSS of Alexander give *oudepote*, 'never'. Hayduck says that Bonitz adopted *oud' ei pote* on the basis of Aristotle, cf. 995a36. Of MSS of *Metaph.* E gives *oud' ei pote*, which Ross prints; JA[b] (and Ascl.) give *oudepote*; Jaeger emends to *oude pot<eron>*.

These remarks about the need first of all to work through the
aporiae would also show the usefulness of dialectic for philosophy   174,1
and for the discovery of truth. For it is characteristic of dialectic to
work through aporiae and to argue on both sides [of a case]. So what
was said in the *Topics* (1.2), that dialectic is useful for philosophical
inquiries, is true.[13]

995b4 The first aporia concerns matters about which we   5
worked through aporiae in our prefatory remarks.[14]

Aristotle is not saying that the aporia he presents here has
[actually] been faced in his prefatory remarks. It is, as he says, the
first aporia that ought to be faced: whether it belongs to one science
to consider the causes (*aitiai*) of all things, *or* to more than one
science, in the sense that different sciences are able to consider   10
different principles and causes. He does not seem to have raised *this*
aporia in the previous books [of the *Metaphysics*] (he seems to have
mentioned it in the first book of *On the Soul* [*de Anima* 1.1]). Hence
the statement 'the first aporia', i.e. the aporia which he also presents
as first, 'is concerned with matters *about which* we faced aporiae in
our prefatory remarks'.[15] For in those books he did face aporiae
about causes; he is saying, then, that the first aporia which he   15
mentions is [also] about causes. He worked though aporiae about
causes in Alpha Meizon, inquiring how many kinds of causes there
are, presenting the views of others about causes, and addressing
them; and he confirmed that there were four kinds of causes. In
Alpha Elatton he inquired whether causality goes on to infinity,
either in a direct series or in kind, or whether it comes to a halt and
is limited. But the aporia about these [causes], i.e. the aporia now   20
spoken of, would be first.[16] In any case, either this is what he means,
or he means that 'the first aporia is concerned with *these* matters
[i.e. with causes] about which we worked through aporiae in our
prefatory remarks', in the sense that not all the aporiae are

---

[13] Alexander's positive judgment on the usefulness of dialectic for philosophy
should be taken together with his concluding remarks at 236,26-9: 'The aporiae
presented in Beta contain arguments [drawn] from accepted opinions (*endoxa*) and
[conducted] on the level of plausibility (*kata to pithanon*). And indeed, it is
impossible for people to argue for opposed positions, except by using [merely]
verbal arguments; nor, for that matter, could the aporiae be solved, if this were not
the case.'

[14] This will be aporia 1 in the full-length discussion of chapters 2-6.

[15] In *Metaph*. 1 Aristotle faced aporiae about causes, but he has not faced the
present aporia about causes.

[16] i.e. primary.

concerned with these [causes] about which we faced aporiae in those
books, when we inquired whether they exist and how many they are,
[but that] the first aporia, which we are now about to face, *is*
25 concerned with these things, for it too is concerned with causes.[17]
Some, however, on account of the statement Aristotle has just made,
insert this aporia at the end of Alpha Elatton, placing it there without
reason.[18] The statement 'whether it belongs to one science or to many
to consider' would be equivalent in meaning to 'whether one science is
able to consider all four causes which we have posited, or whether
there is one science of one cause, another of another cause', as
30 Aristotle will argue[19] later on when he faces the aporia. And it would
be reasonable for him to say 'about which we worked through aporiae
in our prefatory remarks', for in Alpha Meizon he inquired whether
there are four kinds of causes, and he is now about to inquire about
those four kinds, whether the knowledge (*gnôsis*) of them belongs to
one science.

175,1		**995b6 And whether it belongs to the science to survey only the**
			primary principles of substance.[20]

The second aporia which Aristotle says we must face is whether it
belongs to the wise man, the primary philosopher, and to the
5 primary science, to survey only the primary principles of substance,
or whether it is proper for it to survey the principles of
demonstration as well – the common principles (*koinai arkhai*) from
which demonstrations are derived, which are called axioms
(*axiômata*) – for these are the principles of every science. Aristotle
makes it clear that this is what he means by adding the word 'only'
(*monon*).

It will appear that the phrase 'concerning the principles as well' is
lacking in the text, for it follows naturally on what has already been

---

[17] There are two possible senses in which this aporia is 'first': (i) it is primary
relative to the other aporiae about causality, i.e. the question of which science is to
study the causes is prior to questions about the number and finitude of the causes; (ii)
the aporia about causes is primary relative to other aporiae which are not about
causes.
[18] These unidentified parties find, or rather create, a previous reference to the first
aporia by inserting a mention of it, in language very close to that of 995b5-6, at the
very end of Alpha Elatton. Ross and Jaeger bracket the phrase, citing Alexander; see
their apparatus on 995a19-20 and Ross's commentary on 995a19 and 995b5.
[19] *epikheirêsei*. The verb *epikheirein* and the corresponding noun *epikheirêsis*
(Alexander favours this word, while Aristotle favours *epikheirêma*) are associated
with dialectical as opposed to scientific argument. See H. Bonitz, *Index Aristotelicus*,
s. vv. *epikheirein, epikheirêma*.
[20] Aporia 2 in the full-length discussion.

said.[21] It is an axiom that a pair of contradictories (*antiphasis*)[22] 10
cannot both be true at the same time or both false at the same time;
so too, that things equal to the same thing are equal to each other;
and that if equals are subtracted from equals the remainders are
equal; and that every effort is either for a good or for an apparent
good; and the like. And the [axiom] of non-contradiction[23] is the
most common of all axioms, for it is true in all cases.

995b10 If it is concerned with substance, whether there is one 15
science concerning all substances, or more than one.[24]

The third aporia of those proposed is whether, if it belongs to the
proposed science to consider substance (*ousia*)[25] and its causes,
and if there is more than one kind of substance, some being
intelligible and others sensible, so that their principles are different
– whether, then, it belongs to the proposed science to consider all the 20
principles which are principles of substances, so that one science
would be able to know all the principles which are principles of
substances, *or* whether there are several different [sciences] of
principles, principles which are the principles of different kinds of
substances. But if there are several [sciences], Aristotle says the
aporia deserves to be faced, whether these several sciences are akin
to one another, so that it would be reasonable to call them all types 25
of wisdom,[26] or whether they are not all types of wisdom, but rather
some will be types of wisdom while others will receive some other
classification (*genos*).

Having said this, Aristotle says we must also inquire about this
very point, whether these sensible substances are the only
substances, *or* there exist some other substances distinct from
(*para*) these as well;[27] for this point is neither obvious nor free of
dispute. This aporia would differ from the first: in the first, Aristotle 30

---

[21] Hayduck prints *leipein de têi lexei doxei to †akolouthon gar tôi proeirêmenôi tôi kai peri tôn arkhôn*, noting corruption. Bonitz proposes, in line with the Latin translation S, to delete the second *tôi* and to transpose *kai peri tôn arkhôn*, thus: *leipein de têi lexei doxei to kai peri tôn arkhôn· akolouthon gar tôi proeirêmenôi.* I translate Bonitz' proposal. The formula *akolouthon ... tôi proeirêmenôi* is also found at 176,11-12. Alexander is working with a MS or MSS lacking the words *kai peri tôn arkhôn* at 995b8. Neither Ross nor Jaeger reports such a MS or MSS.
[22] Literally the singular, 'a contradiction'.
[23] Literally 'of contradiction'.
[24] Aporia 3 in the full-length discussion.
[25] The lemma reads *esti peri tên ousian*, 'is concerned with substance', while Alexander's paraphrase is *peri tês ousias ... theôrein*, 'to consider concerning substance'. I detect no significant difference between Alexander's use of *peri* with the accusative and his use of *peri* with the genitive.
[26] Literally 'wisdoms'.
[27] Aporia 5 in the full-length discussion.

spoke about causes without qualification (*haplôs*), not about the causes of substance; in the present aporia [he is asking] whether there is one science of the causes of *substance*, or more than one; and if there be more than one, whether they are all akin and types of wisdom, or whether some are types of wisdom, while the others are some other kind (*eidos*) of science.[28]

176,1

Next Aristotle adds that the aporia deserves to be faced about whether all substances are substances in one sense (*monakhôs*), that is, according to one formula (*logos*), *or* whether there are several sorts of substances and several formulae. He makes it clear how he means this by adding the words 'for example, those who
5 posit the Forms (*eidê*), and the mathematicals (*mathêmatika*) intermediate (*metaxu*) between the Forms and the sensibles (*aisthêta*)' [995b16-18]. Those who posited the Ideas (*ideai*) said that the mathematicals were substances, and that as substances and Things Themselves (*auta onta*) they were not the same in kind as the Ideas or the sensible substances; on the contrary, they said that this grade (*phusin*) of substances was intermediate between the other two; thus there would be three types of substance, as Aristotle
10 said about Plato in Alpha Meizon [1.6]. And this inquiry would involve something more than the one before it; for in it Aristotle does not inquire whether there are several sorts (*eidê*) of substances (this point has already been posited), but whether these are the same as certain [thinkers] have said they are.

Aristotle would have said the phrase 'whether in one sense' [995b15-16] as following naturally on what precedes it. Having first asked whether one should say that only sensible substances exist, or others distinct from these as well, he added the phrase 'whether in one sense', [as applying to the substances] distinct from the sensible
15 substances. For those who made [substances] intermediate between the Forms and the sensibles were clearly making more than one kind of substance distinct from the sensible substances.

995b18 And whether the consideration is about substances alone, or whether it is also about the essential accidents of substances.[29]

By accidents (*sumbebêkota*) he means the things that belong
20 (*huparkhein*) essentially (*kath' hauto*), so that the meaning is, 'whether the wise man will deal with substances alone, *or* whether he will also deal with the things that belong essentially [to substances]'.

---

[28] While Alexander knows the distinction between *genos*, 'genus' and *eidos*, 'species', he sometimes (cf. 175,26 with 176,1) uses the two terms without any distinction in meaning.
[29] Aporia 4 in the full-length discussion.

The things that belong essentially, in the proper sense (*kuriôs*), are the things that are included in definitions; and about these things [the wise man] must speak, for there is no other way of getting science of things apart from knowing the things that belong to them in this way. By essential accidents Aristotle means things that are insepara- ble and proper (*idia*) and almost of the essence of a thing, in terms of   25 which descriptive accounts (*hoi di' hupographês logoi*) are commonly framed about certain things. For example, it would be an essential accident of a triangle to have three angles equal to two right angles, and to have two sides greater than the third, any way they are taken; but it is *not* from these features that the triangle gets its definition. It would be an essential accident of number that it is odd or even, and of each being (*on*)[30] that it is one insofar as it is a 'this something' (*tode*   30 *ti*); and whatever accidents belong in this manner [would be essential accidents].

995b20 In addition, concerning the same and different and like and unlike and contrary and contrariety and concerning prior and posterior.[31]

Aristotle also inquires, concerning these notions which dialectic uses (dialectic being an activity that argues from accepted opinions   35 (*endoxa*) and proves [from accepted opinions] the things that are proposed), whether it belongs to the wise man to deal with what   177,1 these are, with a view to truth and science.[32] For if it belongs to the dialectician to deal with these things on the level of accepted opinion (*endoxôs*), to whom does it belong to deal with them on the level of truth (*alêthôs*)? Aristotle proposes to inquire about these things as well, since he himself makes use of them in his own demonstrations in this treatise. For example, he uses sameness (*to t' auto*), precisely that (*hoper*) which is spoken of in the case of substances; at least he   5 inquires whether all substances are the same as one another, or not the same but rather different. But it is also necessary for him, in demonstrations, to make further use of all the other things which he listed; for they are the common tools of those who demonstrate.

As Aristotle goes on he will show in what respect the inquiry into and the consideration of these things is also appropriate to the primary philosopher. For this treatise[33] is not [merely] verbal   10

---

[30] I regularly translate *on* as 'being', *onta* as 'beings', *mê on* as 'non-being', and the Platonic principle *to on* as 'Being'.

[31] This aporia does not figure in the full-length discussion.

[32] i.e. scientifically, in contrast to the less than fully scientific procedure of dialectic.

[33] Metaphysics or first philosophy, specifically that part of it concerned with sameness, otherness, and similar items.

(*logikos*),³⁴ as some have thought due to the fact that many such things are objects of inquiry in it; for Aristotle does not deal with these things for their own sake, nor does he make this his goal; on the contrary, he deals with them because it belongs to primary philosophy, which considers being as being (*to on hêi on*), to carry out a consideration of those things which commonly belong to being. These are also of this kind, as he will prove.

15   **995b25** Further [we must examine] the essential accidents of these things: not only what each of these things is [but also whether one thing is contrary to one thing].

Aristotle has explained which essential accidents he means by saying 'not only what [each of these things] is' (*ti esti*) [995b26]. For the things that belong essentially (*ta kath' hauta huparkhonta*) are included in what [a thing] is (*en tôi ti esti*).³⁵ He says that they are

20   essential accidents,³⁶ such as: every contrariety has as an essential accident the intermediate and the extreme; or the case he mentions: [the problem] whether one thing has one contrary or not, which seems to be a dialectical consideration.³⁷ One must, he says,

---

³⁴ The adjective *logikos* and the adverb *logikôs* indicate that an argument or discussion is based on a *logos* or *logoi*, on what is said about a thing, as opposed to what the thing is in itself. The word is associated with dialectical argument. To proceed *logikôs* is contrasted with proceeding *analutikôs*, *An. Post.* 1.22, 84a7-11, with proceeding *phusikôs*, *Phys.* 3.5, 204b4-10, and with proceeding *epistêmonikôs*, Alexander *in Metaph.* 344,18-20. For more information see H. Bonitz, *Index Aristotelicus*, s.v. *logikos*. For fuller discussion see M. Kappes, *Aristoteles-Lexikon*, 1894, 35-6; W.D. Ross, *Aristotle's Metaphysics*, Oxford 1924, I.168. William Dooley SJ and Kevin Flannery SJ have helped me here, which is not to say that they agree with the translation 'verbal'.

³⁵ There are two kinds or two levels of essential accidents or properties: (i) essential accidents or properties of substances; (ii) essential accidents or properties *of* essential accidents or properties of substances. Alexander takes Aristotle's 'not only what [each of these things] is' as equivalent to 'not only essential accidents of level (i), essential accidents of substances, included in the *ti esti* of substance, but also essential accidents of level (ii), essential accidents *of* essential accidents'. At 177,18-19 'are included' translates *emperiekhetai*, supported by ALF, the Latin translation S, Asclepius 145,2-3, and printed by Hayduck. Bonitz proposed *ouk emperiekhetai* or *ou periekhetai*, 'are not included'. Perhaps Bonitz took *en tôi ti esti* as 'in the category of substance', and wanted to keep Alexander from saying that mere properties or accidents fell into the category of substance. Alexander, however, supposes that substance's essential properties do fall within the *ti esti* of substances; to consider 'not only the *ti esti*' of substances means to consider not only essential properties (i) but also essential properties (ii), viz. the essential properties *of* essential properties (i).

³⁶ That is, essential accidents *of* essential accidents.

³⁷ Contrariety is an example of an essential accident; if it is true that every contrary has exactly one contrary, that would be an essential accident *of* an essential accident.

examine whether it also belongs to the wise man to scrutinise the truth about this matter.[38]

995b27 And whether the principles and elements are the kinds, or the constituents into which each thing is divided.[39]   25

The issue about which Aristotle now says we must inquire is whether the kinds (*genê*)[40] are the principles of these things whose kinds they are (for the kinds appear to be primary in nature, and things that are primary are principles), *or* <these things into which each thing is divided, constituent (*enuparkhonta*) in its parts (for each thing consists of its own parts)>[41] – as substance seems to be divided into matter and form, or into the four elements, or into whatever such thing one may suppose; for each thing is divided into those things which are its primary components, while the primary   30 components of each thing seem to be its principles, for example, the letters (*stoikheia*)[42] [seem to be the principles] of sound.

But if the kinds are principles as well, Aristotle says in turn that it deserves inquiry whether the highest kinds [are principles], *or* those closest to the individuals (*atoma*);[43] these are the indivisible   178,1 species (*eidê atoma*), but speaking loosely (*koinoteron*) he calls them too 'kinds' (*genê*), using the word 'kind' in place of the word 'common' (*koinon*).[44]

995b31 Most of all we should inquire into and investigate the issue, whether there is any cause in its own right distinct from matter.[45]

What Aristotle means is this. Some of the natural philosophers of   5 old supposed that matter alone was a cause in its own right (*kath' hauto*), and spoke of the modifications (*pathê*) of matter as accidental causes, not causes in their own right. For, according to them, Air, or Water, or the Intermediate, or something else that they supposed to be the principle and element [of things], was a

---

[38] Deleting *tinos*, in line with the parallel passage in Asclepius 145,6.

[39] Aporia 6 in the full-length discussion.

[40] Here *genê* are 'kinds' as opposed to *enuparkhonta*, 'constituents' and including *eidê*, 'species'. Later on *genê* will be 'genera' as opposed to *eidê*, 'species'.

[41] I follow Hayduck in recognising a lacuna and filling it from Asclepius 145,20-1.

[42] The word also has the more general sense of 'elements'.

[43] Aporia 7 in the full-length discussion.

[44] Here Alexander adverts to the distinction between *genos* and *eidos*. Aristotle's calling indivisible species 'kinds' is loose usage, but understandable if he is using 'kind' as co-extensive with 'common', which would include indivisible species. The adverb *koinoteron* means 'loosely', as opposed to strictly or precisely, but *koinon* means the word 'common' in the sense of general or universal.

[45] Aporia 8 in the full-length discussion.

cause in its own right since, on their view, each of these[46] was the
10   only thing existing in its own right, while rarity (*manotês*) and
density (*puknotês*), mixture (*sunkrisis*) and separation (*diakrisis*),
existed in an accidental way. These thinkers, then, said that matter,
i.e. the subject, was a cause in its own right, but posited some other
cause as well – but in an accidental way, for these things were
accidents of matter.

Aristotle is not saying, at this point, that we must inquire
whether there is some accidental cause distinct from matter, but
rather whether [it is a cause] in its own right, as he showed in the
15   *Physics*.[47] For the other causes would appear to be causes no less
than matter but rather even more so. But even if there is some cause
in its own right distinct from matter, Aristotle says that we must
examine another point: whether this cause is separated from
matter and exists Itself in virtue of Itself,[48] *or* whether it is in
matter, like the enmattered form (*enulon eidos*), and as the Stoics
thought god and the productive cause were in matter. And if there is
20   some separate (*khôriston*) and immaterial (*aülon*) cause, [we must
inquire] whether this is one in number or more than one, matters
which Aristotle discusses in *Metaphysics* Lambda [*Metaph.* 12.7-8].

995b34 And whether there is something besides the composite.
By composite I mean when something is predicated of matter.

By composite (*sunolon*) Aristotle may mean that which is common
25   (*to koinon*),[49] meaning that which is [said] of particulars and of
things in matter. And if this is what he means by composite, then he
would mean, whether there is, distinct from that which is common,
i.e. the composite which is predicated of the enmattered thing, some
other separated Form, *or* whether there is no Form or Idea distinct
from that which is common, *or* whether there is for some things but
not for others – as seems to be the view of those who say that there
are no Ideas of things not found in nature, or of artifacts.

Or he may mean by composite the complex entity (*to*
30   *sunamphoteron*). Having called it a composite, he makes clear the

---

[46] *toutôn hekasta*. The translation 'each group of these' would more accurately
reflect the plural; but that would seem to exclude the monists.

[47] Hayduck takes this to refer to *Phys.* 1.7-9, and the argument in *Phys.* 1.7 that the
contraries (as well as the subject) are principles seems relevant. But that discussion
does not use the terminology of cause *kath' hauto* and cause *kata sumbebêkos*.
Perhaps Alexander is thinking of *Phys.* 2.3, which begins with an explanation of the
four Aristotelian causes and explains different modes of causality, including
accidental causality (*Phys.* 2.3, 195a32-195b12).

[48] *auto kath' hauto*. The formula suggests the kind of existence characteristic of a
Platonic Form, hence the capitalisation.

[49] This term is often equivalent to 'universal', but I have tried to reserve 'universal'
as a translation of *to katholou*.

sense in which it is a composite, by adding 'when something is predicated of matter', that is, when matter is taken together with some form.

Or he may mean by the composite that which is enmattered (*to enulon*).[50] [On this interpretation] he would be inquiring whether there is some separated form besides the enmattered form (for this is what is predicated of the matter, and the composite is the matter along with the form that is in the matter), *or* whether there is no such thing, *or* whether some forms are separated from matter, and some not. This is what he would mean by the words 'or of some but not of others' [995b36]. And if there are any immaterial forms at all, then [he would be inquiring] how many these are; as I have said, he will discuss these matters in his consideration of the counteracting spheres [*Metaph*. 12.7-8].[51] In the preceding aporia he would be inquiring whether there is some cause in its own right besides matter, and if there is, whether it is separated from matter or itself together with matter; in the subsequent[52] aporia he would be inquiring simply whether there is some immaterial form.

179,1

5

996a1 Further, whether the principles are definite in number (*arithmôi*) or in kind (*eidei*).[53]

We must inquire, Aristotle says, concerning the principles and causes as well: if they are limited, whether they are limited in kind (*kata to eidos*) alone <but not in number (*kat' arithmon*), or whether they are limited in number as well>,[54] so that the productive cause would be numerically one and matter would be one in number, and likewise in the case of the other causes, *or* whether the cause, even if not one in number according to each kind of cause, is still limited.[55]

10

Aristotle declines to consider the supposition that the principles are indefinite in kind, as a view that is absurd and has been shown [to be absurd] in the preceding book [*Metaph*. 2.2, 994a1-2].[56] It was also shown in the preceding book that for each kind of cause the causes are limited [*Metaph*. 2.2].

He says that we must inquire in like manner about the formal

---

[50] Or 'material'; but I have tried to reserve 'material' for *hulikos*.
[51] cf. 178,21 above.
[52] *deuteras*, literally 'second', i.e. second to or subsequent to the preceding.
[53] Aporia 9 in the full-length discussion.
[54] Recognising a lacuna with Hayduck and supplying from Asclepius 147,13-14.
[55] The three possibilities are: causes limited in kind but unlimited in number within each kind; causes limited in kind with exactly one cause within each kind; causes limited in kind with a definite finite plurality of causes within each kind.
[56] *Metaph*. 2.2, 994a1-2 asserts this point, but the proof of it lies in the survey of Aristotle's predecessors in *Metaph*. 1: no one has found any type of cause beyond the four causes of the *Physics*; cf. *Metaph*. 1.10, 993a11-13.

15   (*eidika*) causes (these are the ones contained in the formula of a
thing; for it is terms of them that the formula (*logos*) of each thing,·
its definition (*horismos*), is framed), and about the material (*hulika*)
causes, for these are the subjects (*hupokeimena*). If the productive
(*poiêtikon*) cause and the final (*telikon*) cause are also themselves
kinds [of causes], as he said in the *Physics* [*Phys.* 2.7], he would have
mentioned all the causes.

20   By 'causes in formulae' (*en tois logois*) [996a1-2], Aristotle may
have meant the principles of demonstrations. These are the axioms,
and in fact he has already mentioned them [995b6-10]. By [causes]
'in the subject' [996a2], he may have meant the principles of
substances, for substances are subjects.

To this aporia Aristotle adds that a further aporia deserves to be
faced: whether the principles of perishable (*phtharta*) things and of
imperishable (*aphtharta*) things are the same principles *or* different
principles; and if they are different, whether they are all
imperishable, *or* whether those of the perishable are perishable and
those of the imperishable imperishable.[57]

25   **996a4 Further, the most difficult issue of all, posing the
greatest aporia: <whether>[58] One and Being are nothing
other [than the substances of beings] as the Pythagoreans and
Plato <claimed>.[59,60]**

The aporia which Aristotle says presents the greatest difficulty[61] is
the following: whether One (*to hen*)[62] and Being (*to on*) Themselves
30   are substances and principles of beings (this he expressed in the
words 'but rather substances of beings' [996a7]), the view of the
Pythagoreans and of Plato, who speaks of a Being Itself and a One
Itself (Aristotle has also mentioned this view in his discussion
(*logos*) of the infinite in the third book of the *Physics* [*Phys.* 3.4] and
in *Metaphysics* Alpha Meizon [*Metaph.* 1.5-6]), *or* whether certain
180,1   other natures function as subjects (*hupokeisthai*), and these things,
One[63] and Being, are accidents of those natures, as the natural
philosophers said, supposing that Water or Air or Friendship or
Mind or some such thing was the principle of beings; for they said
that these things, One and Being, were accidents of those things.

---

[57] Aporia 10 in the full-length discussion.
[58] Supplying <*poteron*> with Hayduck, in line with the MSS of *Metaph.* Ross and
Jaeger report no dissent.
[59] Hayduck supplies <*elegen*>, the reading of MSS of *Metaph.* A^bE^1, printed by
Ross; Jaeger prints *elegon*, in line with E^2JG.
[60] Aporia 11 in the full-length discussion.
[61] Literally, 'the aporia which he says presents the greatest aporia'.
[62] Or 'Unity'.
[63] Or 'Unity'.

Further, whether the principles have a reality of their own (*oikeia hupostasis*), in their own right, as particular beings have, *or* they do 5
not, but are like kinds and universals and common terms, whose existence (*einai*) consists in their being predicated of particulars.[64]
This aporia would differ from the one faced a short while ago [177,26-31], 'and whether the principles and elements are the kinds, or the constituents into which each thing is divided' [995b27-9]; in that aporia the object of inquiry was whether the constituents into which particulars are divided are their principles, rather than the 10
common terms which are predicated of them; in the present aporia the inquiry about the principles is framed in general terms (*koinôs*) and universally: whether [the principles] exist in the way common terms, which do not have a reality proper to themselves (*kat' idian hupostasis*), exist, or in the way particulars exist.

And if [principles exist] in this latter way, [we must inquire] whether the principles subsist in a potential way (*dunamei*), as matter seems to exist, *or* in the way of actuality (*kat' energeian*), the view of those for whom Fire or one of the bodies is the element.[65] 15

996a11 Further, whether in the way of motion or in some other way;[66] and indeed these points <would>[67] present great difficulty.[68]

What Aristotle inquires about is this: whether the principles are principles by moving, i.e. producing, the things whose principles 20
they are, *or* in some other way. For one principle, namely the productive cause, seems to be able to move (*kinêtikê*) [things], while another, namely the material (*hulikê*) cause, does not.

But something like the following may also be meant: whether it is by being in motion[69] that these principles are causes of the things that derive from them, *or* by themselves being unmoved[70] – as the proponents of the Ideas said about them, and as the primary cause in fact is.

Or, from what was said previously [*Metaph.* 2.2, 994b5-6], the words may be understood this way: whether the principles are in

---

[64] Aporia 15 in the full-length discussion.

[65] Aporia 14 in the full-length discussion.

[66] Ross understands this question in close connection with the aporia about the potential or actual status of the principles; he translates 'and further, whether they are potential or actual in any other sense than with reference to movement'. Alexander, however, takes it as a new question.

[67] Hayduck supplies <*an*> in line with MSS of *Metaph.*

[68] This may be classed as part of aporia 14, but it is not addressed in the full-length discussion.

[69] Or simply 'while being in motion'.

[70] Or simply 'while themselves being unmoved'.

motion (*kineisthai*) and change (*metaballein*) into one another, *or* are changeless.

25   In addition to these points, Aristotle says it is worthwhile to face aporiae about the mathematicals (*mathêmatika*) as well. Mathematicals include numbers, lengths, shapes (he would mean plane figures: triangle, square, circle, and the like), as well as points. Concerning these [we must inquire] whether these too are substances, as some think, *or* not; and if they are substances, whether they are separated from sensibles and exist in their own right,[71] *or* whether the mathe-
30   maticals have their existence by being in sensibles.[72]

Having begun by speaking of the points about which he says we must begin with aporiae,[73] Aristotle now says that in these matters not only is it difficult to discover how the truth stands (the discovery of the truth about the matters previously mentioned is the sum and substance of the proposed science), it is even difficult to work through the aporiae.

CHAPTER 2

[Aporia 1]
[The case against one science of all the causes]

Aristotle returns to the first aporia which he proposed to face, and
35   that was: whether it belongs to one science to speak about all the principles and all the causes, *or* to more than one, a different science for each kind of cause.

181,1   First he argues (*epikheirei*)[74] for the view that it does *not* belong to one science to speak about all the causes. To this end he first employs an argument which is in effect (*dunamei*) as follows: things which differ in kind (*kat' eidos*) but belong to the same science are contraries (*enantia*) to one another; but the causes are not
5   contraries to one another; hence causes, which differ in kind, do not belong to the same science.

---

[71] *autai kath' hautas*. Alternatively, in view of the Platonic overtones, 'Themselves by Themselves'.

[72] Aporia 12 in the full-length discussion.

[73] Reading *proaporêsai* with Bonitz and Hayduck; ALF read *prosaporêsai*, 'face an additional aporia'.

[74] Alexander tends to use *epikheirein* for the dialectical arguments of *Metaph*. 3. When Alexander says that an argument is dialectical, this does not mean simply that its premises are assumed rather than known, it suggests that the argument has a false premise. Note that the *endoxa* used by dialectic may include premises which are false; this must be the case when, as in *Metaph*. 3, pairs of arguments argue for contradictory conclusions. Cf. 236,26-9, and Alexander *in Top*. 2,20-3,24.

The argument (*logos*) is in the second figure;[75] so far as its form (*tropos*) is concerned, it is valid (*hugiês*) and conclusive; but it has assumed a first premise (*protasis*) that is not true. For it is not true that 'things which differ in kind but belong to the same science are contraries to one another'. But 'contraries belong to the same science' is true (*hugiês*),[76] which is why its contrapositive (*antistrephon*), 'things which do not belong to the same science are 10 not contraries', is not the same as the premise given above, 'things which [differ in kind but] belong to the same science are contraries to one another'. For on that view[77] it is thought that things which differ in kind belong to the same science only[78] if they are contraries; this is what Aristotle means by asking 'for how could it belong to one science to know the principles, if they were not contraries?' [996a20-1]. Whereas the assumption here[79] is that 15 contraries belong to the same science, but not that *only* contraries belong to the same science. For nothing prevents certain things which are not contraries from belonging to the same science; for example, the objects of geometry are not contrary to one another. On the contrary: natural philosophy and practical philosophy differ in kind, but are not contraries, and they are ranged under one science.[80]

Further, someone will say that the principles *can* be reduced to 20 opposites (*antikeimena*), viz. the productive (*poiêtikon*) and the receptive (*pathêtikon*), given that matter is receptive, and that the three causes besides matter are reduced to the formal cause and this is productive; for everything that produces does so according to its form (*eidos*) and the perfection (*teleiotês*) which it possesses.

996a21 Further, for many beings, not all [the causes] pertain.

This argument (*epikheirêsis*) too is constructed in favour of the view 25 that there is no one science able to know all the causes. Aristotle bases the argument on the objects of science (*epistêta*). If it should

[75] This is, a syllogism in which the middle term figures as predicate of both the premises.

[76] It is common to distinguish the logical validity of a syllogism, i.e. the conclusion's following from the premises, from the overall soundness of the syllogism, i.e. logical validity plus true premises. One would like to reserve *hugiês*, 'sound', for the latter; but at 181,6 Alexander uses it for logical validity, while at 181,8 he uses it for the truth of a proposition.

[77] i.e. according to the false first premise.

[78] Hayduck prints *monôn tôn diapherontôn kat' eidos ei enantia eien tên autên epistêmên einai*, 'only of things which differ in kind is there the same science if they are contraries'. I read *monon* in place of *monôn*, and take it with *ei enantia eien*; cf. the contrasted position in 181,15-16: *tôn enantiôn ... ou mên kai monôn*.

[79] i.e. on the true alternative to the false first premise.

[80] Alexander appears to make the striking suggestion that natural philosophy and

appear that not all the objects of science involve all the causes,[81] and
if the sciences are able to know their proper objects, it is clear that
<each science>[82] would know those causes which pertain to its own
30   proper objects. Thus one science would be able to know some causes,
while another science would be able to know others: each [would
know the causes] which pertain to its proper objects.

That not all the causes pertain to all the objects of science, he
shows by reference to the unmoved entities (*ta akinêta*). By
'unmoved entities' Aristotle would mean the ungenerated (*agenêta*)
and imperishable (*aphtharta*), and by the 'principle of motion'
[996a22] he means the productive cause. He includes the
mathematicals too among the unmoved, for the source of the
35   principle of motion, that is, the productive cause, is not a cause in
their case either; for how could a productive, i.e. a moving
(*kinêtikon*) cause pertain to things that are ungenerated and
unmoved?

But neither does the nature of the good, i.e. the end,
that-for-the-sake-of-which (*to hou heneka*) pertain to these things.[83]
For that which is a cause *qua* good is that for the sake of which (*to
hou kharin*) other things are, and which is itself not for the sake of
182,1   anything, and such a thing is an end. But the end, and the doing of
things preliminary to the end for the sake of something, pertain to
actions, and to the sciences of production and of action. But where
there is production and action, there is motion. Hence neither could
5   this cause, that is, the final cause, which is the good simply and by
its own nature – this is what he means by the phrase 'in its own
right and in virtue of its own nature' [996a24]; he also calls it the
'Good Itself' [996a28-9] – pertain to the unmoved.

Wishing to prove that the final cause does not pertain to all things
either, as the productive cause does not (for neither cause pertains
to the unmoved), Aristotle did not say directly that the final cause
(*hê kata to telos aitia*)[84] does not pertain to them, but rather that the
10   nature of the good (*hê tou agathou phusis*), which happens to be an
end (*telos*), does not pertain to them. Hence, having begun with the
good, he goes on to prove that not even the final cause pertains to
things unmoved, by showing that the good is in all cases the end.[85]

---

practical philosophy are subdivisions of one more inclusive science. He could have
illustrated his point just as well by saying that the objects of natural philosophy differ
in kind without all being contraries, and that the objects of practical philosophy differ
in kind without all being contraries. Perhaps that is what he meant to say.

[81] i.e. if some objects of science do not involve all four causes.

[82] Following Hayduck, who inserts *hekastê* on the basis of the Latin translation S.

[83] viz. to the unmoved.

[84] Literally, 'the cause in the mode of end'.

[85] i.e. instead of arguing simply and directly that there are objects to which the
cause in the mode of end does not pertain, he argues that there are objects to which

But since there are some goods which are also productive, he makes clear which goods are final, in the words 'if indeed everything which is good *in its own right and in virtue of its own nature* is an end' [996a23-4]. Assuming the good in its own right to be a final cause, and showing that the final cause is the end of some action,[86] and that all actions involve motion (the activities according to the virtues, which have that which is noble as a goal, involve motion, but each of the arts as well strives for some good and attains it through activity and motion), he thus proves that the cause in the mode of good, the final cause, does not pertain to things unmoved.

Aristotle means the phrase 'nor is there any Good Itself' [996a28-9] as equivalent to 'it is not good as an end *for anything*'. The Good Itself is good in its own right and by its own nature, and that which is good in this way Aristotle calls an end.[87]

To prove that this[88] is the case, Aristotle cites the mathematicals. Neither the productive cause nor the final cause pertains to them. Nor is there in geometry any demonstration of anything that uses the argument 'because it is better that way'.[89] For example, [there is no demonstration] that the angles of a triangle are equal to two right angles because it is better that way (in the way that that-for-the-sake-of-which figures in the case of things that come to be by nature and in the case of things that are moved according to art), nor does anyone who does geometry attend to the final cause at all. Since this is the case, different sciences would be able to know different causes; it was in order to reach (*lambanein*) this [conclusion] that Aristotle mentioned these considerations.

Having said that the final cause, viz. the good, does not pertain to the mathematicals, Aristotle cites in confirmation the tale told by the sophists, and mentions Aristippus [996a32] who, like some other sophists, spoke of the mathematical sciences as deficient relative to

15

20

25

30

---

the nature of the good does not pertain, that the nature of the good includes the notion of end, and so, that there are objects to which the notion of end does not pertain. The point would be clearer if Alexander had said that the notion of end included the nature of the good.

[86] Literally, 'that the cause in the mode of end is the end of some action'.

[87] At *Metaph.* 996a28-9 *oude einai* depends on *ouk an endekhoito*, and it would be natural to understand the phrase 'nor could it be possible for there to be any Good Itself' as denying the existence of the Platonic Good Itself. But that would make the phrase a parenthetical remark. Alexander, trying to fit the phrase into the argument, paraphrases *oude einai* as *oudeni esti*: the Good Itself is not a final cause *for anything*. He then points out that the Good Itself is not a final cause for mathematical or geometrical objects; thus mathematics and geometry make no use of final causes. On the way he rules out a misunderstanding: he is not denying that the Good Itself is good in itself, only that it serves as a good or final cause for anything else.

[88] i.e. the point stated at 181,31, that not all the causes pertain to every object of science.

[89] The kind of argument desired by Socrates at *Phaedo* 98-9.

35 the most complete and perfect arts, on the ground that each of these
arts has an end and a good proposed to it, and in what takes place
under their influence they attend to the argument 'because it is
better that way', while the mathematical sciences have no such
cause, nor do they take any account of goods and evils.

There seems to be, in turn, a fallacy (*paragôgê*) in this line of
183,1 argument.[90] For, even if not all the causes pertain to certain of the
objects of science (*epistêta*), it will not follow that it does not belong
to one science to know about all [causes]. People could use the same
line of argument to prove that, since all the causes pertain to certain
objects of science, it belongs to one science to know them.[91] For
[even] if not all the sciences know all the causes – if, on the contrary,
5 there are some sciences to which [only] certain of the causes pertain
– it will not follow from this that *no* science will know them all.
Aristotle himself will make this evident a little further on, when he
inquires [about sciences], to which all the causes pertain (because
their subject matter involves the four causes), which is the cause
knowledge of which is the principal factor in bringing about science
of the proposed subject matter.[92]

Further, not every good is by its own nature something to be
achieved by action. On the contrary, there is the good to be achieved
10 by action; and there is the good that is an object of contemplation,
not to be achieved by action, which pertains even to the
mathematicals; for the truth about those realities is a good and an
end for them. Now the end of wisdom is this sort of a good; for the
knowledge of that which is supreme (*kuriôtaton*) and the best of
beings, that which in the highest degree is (*malista on*), is the
greatest good and the end of wisdom.

[The case for distinct sciences for distinct causes]

996b1 But if there are several sciences ...

15 Aristotle proceeds to the opposite side of the argument. He states
the aporia: if there are several sciences able to know the causes and
the principles, and not just one – as seems to have been shown in the
preceding treatment of the aporia, by the fact that each of the
sciences[93] does not make use of all the causes – which of the causes

---

[90] i.e. the whole argument since 181,25, not the parenthetical remark about
Aristippus.

[91] viz. all the causes.

[92] cf. 183,15ff.; 184,7ff.

[93] Reading *hekastên tôn epistêmôn*, 'each of the sciences', in place of *hekaston tôn
epistêtôn*, 'each of the objects of science', which Hayduck prints as the reading of the
MSS. One might speak of objects of science as *having* or not having all the causes, but
it is rough to speak of them as *using* (*khrêsthai*) or not using the causes. The basic

must the science that is the object of the inquiry (this is, as he indicates, wisdom) be able to know? Or, of those who have all the causes, 'which one' should be said 'to be in the highest degree the possessor of science about the thing that is the object of the inquiry?' 20 [996b3-4]. 'For it is possible for all the types (*tropoi*) of causes to belong to the same thing' [996b5-6]. By knowledge of which cause, by knowing which of these causes, will one possess science of the object that is the subject matter? If one science is able to know one cause and another science able to know another cause, [then] in the case of objects to which the four causes pertain, which of the four 25 causes will confer on the one who knows it scientific knowledge of the objects?

By [this] reference to the simultaneous presence of these causes, Aristotle also refutes the aporia that tries to prove, on the ground that all causes are not to be found in all sciences, that different sciences are able to know different causes, not one science all causes.[94] [He refutes it], citing the fact that, if all the causes pertain to certain objects, it is clear that the corresponding sciences will be sciences of all the causes. This is the case with the science he cites, that is, house-building: in this case he says that the form is the 30 formula [cf. 996b8], because the definition of each thing is in terms of its form. 'That-for-the-sake-of-which' he calls 'the product' [996b7], in the sense that that-for-the-sake-of-which, in house-building, is that for the sake of which the product comes to be (it comes to be for the sake of shelter); or in the sense that the product which comes to be is, in house-building, that-for-the-sake-of-which, viz. the form (Aristotle supposes that the final cause and the formal 184,1 cause are the same, as can be discovered in the case of some things that come to be by nature); or in the sense that the product is not the form but rather the complex entity (*sunamphoteron*),[95] which could not be the same as the cause according to the formula.

The meaning[96] may also be something like the following: for things to which the four causes pertain, which is the cause 5 knowledge of which is principally responsible for producing scientific knowledge, in a man who knows all the causes of the

---

aporia is whether it belongs to one science to know all the causes. Objects which seem to involve, or not to involve, all four causes are introduced in order to solve this basic aporia.

[94] Hayduck indicates corruption. I am following S as a guide to the sense, taking the initial phrase *dia de toutôn ontôn hama* as referring to the co-presence, in certain cases, of all four causes (*eo argumento quod eaedem nonnumquam simul consistant*), and taking *deiknuousan* as conative (*nititur ostendere*); and I accept Bonitz' proposal of *tên* for *to mê einai* at 183,26.

[95] i.e. composed of both form and matter.

[96] i.e. the meaning of *Metaph.* 996b3-4, 'which one should be said to be in the highest degree the possessor of science about the thing that is the object of the inquiry?'

object? For the knowledge of such a cause would belong properly to wisdom.

Having shown the absurdity of supposing that the causes of the same object are known by several sciences, one knowing one cause,
10   another knowing another, with the [question] 'or of those who possess the causes, which one [should be said] to be in the highest degree the possessor of science about the thing that is the object of the inquiry?' [996b3-5],[97] Aristotle leaves this topic, and addresses the [question] 'which of these should be said to be the science that is the object of the inquiry?' [996b3].

996b8 Now from the points previously determined, there is no clear account (*oudamôs ekhei logon*)[98] of which of the sciences one ought to call wisdom.

Having asked 'which of these [sciences should be said to be] the one
15   that is the object of the inquiry?' [996b3], Aristotle shows that it is possible to say that all of them are. He uses the points about wisdom that he enunciated in Alpha [*Metaph.* 1.2]. For in the previous book [Alpha] Meizon he listed what are the common preconceptions (*koinai prolêpseis*) about the wise man, and among them were, that wisdom must be most suited to rule and most architectonic, also most precise and in the highest degree knowledgeable, also capable of knowing difficult things, also knowing all things insofar as
20   they admit of being known, also capable of teaching. On the basis of these views he says it is equally possible for those who proceed according to each cause to prove that the science that is able to know that cause is wisdom. For insofar as wisdom is a science most suited to lead and most architectonic, and inasmuch as it is the mistress of the other sciences, it would be the knowledge of the end; for the end is the good, and the other things are for the sake of it; for it is with a
25   view to the end that people ordain what must be done. So the knowledge most suited to rule, the most complete and the best, would be the knowledge of the best of the causes; and such is that for the sake of which other things are. From this point of view, then, wisdom will appear to be the science that is able to know the end.

---

[97] Alexander takes 996b3-5 as a rhetorical question which demolishes the supposition of several different sciences knowing the different causes of a single object.
[98] Alexander and A^b read *oudamôs ekhei logon*, followed by a full stop. Ross and Jaeger print *ekhei logon*, and take with the following *hekastên prosagoreuein*. Ross translates 'there is reason for applying the name to each of them'.

996b13 But insofar as it [wisdom] has been determined (*diôristai*)[99] to be [science] of the primary causes and of that which is in the highest degree an object of science, the science of essence (*ousia*)[100] would be such.

Inasmuch, he says, as wisdom has in turn been said to be able to 30 know the primary causes and things in the highest degree objects of science, it will appear in turn, from this point of view, that the knowledge of the form and of the corresponding cause is wisdom. Having spoken first about the final cause in matters of action, he speaks in second place about the final cause in objects of contemplation. He shows that the form is in the highest degree knowable (*gnôston*), on the ground that in all cases we say that there 35 is scientific knowledge when someone knows the form of something and the corresponding cause: 'For, while people have science of the 185,1 same object in many ways, we say that the one who knows what the object is by way of its being (*tôi einai*)[101] knows it to a higher degree [than one who knows it] by way of its non-being (*tôi mê einai*)' [996b14-16].[102] To prove that the one who knows the formal cause of the object of science knows the object in the highest degree, he first assumes that we know a proposed object to a higher degree when we 5 know it from those things that belong to it, than we do when we know it from things that do not belong to it. This latter is what 'by way of its non-being' [996b16] means: some bits of instruction, formulae of certain items, come from negations (*apophaseis*); this would be knowledge [derived] from non-being. For example, one who defines a point as that which has no parts knows it by way of non-being, and renders an account of its formula [derived] from what does not belong to it. The very one who says that an accident is 10 that which belongs to an object, not as a definition (*horos*) or as a genus or as a property, is defining from non-being. The one who says that an accident is what is such as to belong or[103] not to belong to the same thing knows it in terms of its being, for he [defines] it from that which belongs to it.

Of those who know something in terms of its being, we say that the one who knows what the object is (*ti esti to pragma*) has knowledge in the highest degree, [more] than the one who knows the

[99] Ross and Jaeger print the aorist *diôristhê* and indicate no divergence among MSS of *Metaph.*

[100] Or perhaps 'substance'. But here 'science of *ousia*' means 'science of the formal cause'.

[101] i.e. by what it is.

[102] i.e. by what it is not.

[103] Literally, 'and' (*kai*); but an accident is not something that can belong and at the same time not belong to a certain thing; it is something that can belong at one time and not belong at another time, or in brief, something that can belong or not belong.

15   thing's accidents; for [we say] he is the one who knows the object in
terms of its essence (*ousia*), not the one who knows it in terms of some
accident. Each thing is that which it is according to its form, so that
the one who knows the form knows the thing in the highest degree. If,
then, the knowledge of the form, of this cause, is in the highest degree
science of the object, and if science in the highest degree is wisdom,
20   then in turn according to this argument the science of the formal
cause would be wisdom.

996b18 But further, in the other cases too [we think that there
is] knowledge of each thing ...

The logical order of the text is: 'But further, in the other cases too
which admit of demonstrations, we think that there is knowledge of
each thing when we know what the thing is.'[104] The expression 'in
the other cases too' is equivalent to 'in all things which admit of
25   demonstrations'. That knowledge of the form is knowledge in the
highest degree of the object, he proves through the fact that in
demonstrations too we think we have demonstration of the thing
proposed when we know its formula, its definition. For when we
know the definition of the thing proposed, and when we prove
through the definition that that which is to be proven to belong to
the object does belong to it, we then believe that we have
30   demonstration of it in the strictest sense. (For example, we know
what an eclipse of the moon is, at the point when we understand
that it is an interposition of the earth, which is the definition of an
eclipse. Likewise we know what the squaring of a rectangle is, at the
point when we understand that it is the discovery of a mean; for the
square based on the mean line is equal [in area] to the rectangle; the
line is a mean because it is longer than the shorter side of the
35   rectangle, but shorter than the longer side; and the square based on
186,1   it is equal to the given rectangle.) For the definition together with
the cause is a demonstration, though different in the position

---

104 'The logical order of the text is' renders *to katallêlon esti tes lexeôs*. MSS of
Metaph. 996b18-20 read *eti de kai en tois allois to eidenai hekaston kai hôn apodeixeis
eisi tote oiometha huparkhein hotan eidômen ti estin.* (Ross prints *kai hôn apodeixeis
eisi*, and translates 'even of the things of which demonstration is possible', but Jaeger
brackets the phrase. The issue is whether Aristotle can speak of demonstration, as
opposed to definition, as conferring knowledge of what a thing is.) Alexander is
commending a different word order (and giving a slightly different text: omitting *kai*
before *hôn*, and including *to* before *ti estin*): *eti de kai en tois allois to eidenai hekaston
tote oiometha huparkhein hôn apodeixeis eisin hotan eidômen to ti estin.* This I
translate. I have not found a way of expressing the contrast between the different
word orders in intelligible English.

(*thesis*) [of the terms], as Aristotle has shown in the *Posterior Analytics* [*An. Post.* 2.10, 94a2].[105]

996b22 But concerning instances of becoming,[106] and actions ...

Having shown that there can be wisdom by way of the knowledge of the formal cause, Aristotle now shows that wisdom can also be by   5
way of the knowledge of the productive cause. For in the case of all things which come into being (*gignesthai*) and all actions which are performed (*prattesthai*), and in general all things that change (*metaballein*), the cause of knowledge of these things is knowledge of the productive cause, viz. the source of the principle of motion. For we know the cause of the Trojan War at the point when we know that it was on account of the abduction of Helen, viz. the principle and cause of the war. We know the cause of the fight at the point   10
when we know the insult which was the beginning of the fight.

Having spoken of the productive cause, Aristotle goes on to say 'this is different from (*heteron*), and opposite to, the end' [996b24], meaning that these causes are opposed and opposed in this respect, <that the one precedes (*proüparkhein*) (such is the productive cause) while the other supervenes (*epiginesthai*) later on>.[107] He goes on to say 'therefore it would seem to belong to another science (*allês epistêmês*) to consider each of these causes' [996b24-6], a   15
statement which hardly seems consistent with the [topic] proposed.[108] The [topic] which Aristotle proposed to himself was to inquire, on the supposition that knowledge of all the causes did not belong to the same science, knowledge of *which* of the causes ought to be called wisdom. He then showed, in line with the preconceptions about wisdom, that there is a sense in which one can call the knowledge of the final cause wisdom, and the knowledge of the formal cause wisdom, and the knowledge of the productive cause   20
wisdom. Once he had shown these things, the logical conclusion

---

[105] In *An. Post.* 2.10, 93b38-94a14 Aristotle first distinguishes a kind of definition which is not a demonstration at all from a kind of definition which is a sort of demonstration because it gives the cause of the thing defined, but differs from demonstration in the position of the terms (*thesis*). Ultimately (94a11-14) he distinguishes three types of definition: undemonstrated statement of what a thing is; a reasoning that leads to what a thing is but differs in grammatical(?) form (*ptôsis*) from a demonstration; the conclusion of a demonstration of what something is.

[106] Aristotle's Greek is *geneseis*, literally 'becomings' or 'comings-to-be'.

[107] I follow Hayduck in filling the lacuna from Asclepius 157,14-15; but I see no need for Bonitz' suggested addition *tauta d' eipôn*.

[108] Not inconsistent in the sense of contradicting something in the argument, but inconsistent in the sense of not pursuing the original goal of the discussion (to find out which of the distinct causal sciences was wisdom) but rather simply repeating the original assumption (that there are distinct sciences for the different causes).

(*akolouthon*) was to go on [to say] that the types of wisdom would be several in number. So one must understand Aristotle's statement as equivalent in meaning to 'so it would belong to different types of wisdom[109] to consider each of these causes', and wisdom could not be one, given that it does not belong to one science to consider [all] the

25   causes, and that the science which considers each of the three is a [type of] wisdom.[110]

Aristotle may have added the statement 'so that it would seem to belong to a different science to consider each of these causes' [996b24-6], not as a logical conclusion (*akolouthon*) from what he had just said, but rather to connect the claim that one science is able to know one cause, another science another cause, with the first of his previous statements.[111]

Or, having previously said about the productive cause that it is

30   different from and opposite to the end, he was making the further point about these [two causes] that, because they are contraries, the knowledge of each of them will belong not to the same science but to a different science.[112]

Or a better text might be 'so that it would *not* seem to belong to a different science to consider each of these causes'. For this is the

187,1 reason why it was *not* granted that the same[113] science is able to know all the causes: that they [the causes] were *not* contraries.[114] Now that Aristotle has found a contrariety between causes, between the final cause and the productive cause – and on the basis of the other things he has said to show that it is not reasonable for there to be several sciences concerned with the knowledge of the causes[115] –

he may be making the further point that in line with what has been

5   said the knowledge of these causes would *not* belong to different

---

[109] First explanation: Alexander explains Aristotle's *allês epistêmês*, 'a different science' as equivalent to *allês ... sophias kai allês*, 'different types of wisdom'.

[110] i.e. each of the three sciences is a type of wisdom. Three: no mention has been made of a science of the material cause; cf. 187,8-13.

[111] Second explanation: the statement violates the logical order of the argument in the antithesis in order to make a connection with 'the first of his previous statements' (*tois prôtois proeirêmenois*); these would presumably be the arguments against one science of all the causes, 996a20-996b1.

[112] i.e. to different sciences. This third explanation comes to an absurd conclusion – absurd because Aristotle's regular doctrine is that knowledge of contraries belongs to the same science. I leave the absurd conclusion as it stands, because Alexander next proposes an emendation to remove precisely this absurdity.

[113] Accepting Hayduck's correction of *hautê* (accent on penult), 'this', to *hautê* (= *hê autê*, accent on final syllable), 'the same'.

[114] The fourth explanation affirms the principle that contraries belong to the same science (cf. *Metaph.* 996a20-1 and 181,2-23, especially 8-9). It also supposes that Aristotle has shown the productive cause and the final cause are contraries. If they are contraries, they must belong to the same science. The drastic but seemingly necessary remedy is to emend the text by adding the negative *ouk* at 996b24. According to Ross and Jaeger MS E of the *Metaphysics* reports the reading *ouk allês*.

[115] i.e. the arguments for the thesis.

sciences. This would also prove at the same time that discussion of all the causes is proper to wisdom.

We should note that in what he has just said Aristotle has again mentioned Alpha Meizon [*Metaph.* 1.2], for it was there that he presented the common preconceptions about the wise man.[116]

While he has mentioned the three causes, and has shown from what point of view the science that is able to know each of them can be the wisdom that is the object of the inquiry, Aristotle has not 10 mentioned the material cause, for he supposes that knowledge of those [three] causes is [knowledge] in a stricter sense and is science to a higher degree than [the science of] the material cause; for they are [causes] in a stricter sense and causes to a higher degree; for matter, in the things that come to be from it, seems to have the status (*logos*) of a [mere] necessary condition.[117]

[Aporia 2]

996b26 But <concerning>[118] the principles of demonstration, it
is a matter of dispute whether it belongs to one science or to 15
more than one [to consider them].[119]

This was the second of the points that he enumerated among aporiae to be faced. It concerns the axioms, which are the principles of demonstrations, and which he calls 'common opinions' (*koinai doxai*) because all those who demonstrate make use of them. When he mentioned the aporia, he called them principles 'from which all prove [things]' [995b8].[120] He inquires, then, whether it belongs to 20 the same science to know about these principles as it does to know about the principles of substance (*ousia*) and of being, *or* to another science – so that there would be more than one science about the principles, one about these principles and another about the principles of substance. And if the knowledge of the principles of substance and the knowledge of the principles of demonstration belong to different sciences, which science (concerning itself with 25 which causes, with which principles) ought one to call wisdom?

---

[116] cf. 196,20-3, where Alexander is concerned to confirm the authenticity of *Metaphysics* 1.

[117] As opposed to the status of a genuine cause.

[118] Alexander has *kai tôn* with no preposition; I translate *kai peri tôn*, following MSS of *Metaphysics* and Hayduck's suggestion.

[119] The bracketed material has to be supplied in thought in the *Metaphysics* as well. No emendation of Alexander or of Aristotle is proposed.

[120] I follow Brandis and Hayduck in bracketing *ex hôn peri toutôn*.

[The case against one science of the principles of substance
and the principles of demonstration]

Aristotle, then, faces the aporia on this point; and in support of the
view that it does *not* belong to the same science to deal with both the
former principles and the latter principles, he uses the following
first argument. If all the demonstrative sciences use the axioms in
like manner, in line with their proper objects of demonstration, and
if they do not all speak about them, then none of the sciences which
30   use the axioms in like manner will speak about them. But the
antecedent (*to prôton*) [is true]: all the sciences use the axioms, just
as the science which is concerned with the principles of substance
does; and they do not all speak about them, for neither geometry nor
music speaks about the axioms, even though they use them. Hence
the consequent (*to deuteron*) [is true].

Or as follows. If all sciences are concerned with axioms in like
manner as the science concerned with substance is, then either all
188,1   sciences will speak about them, or not even that science will speak
about them. But all are concerned with the axioms in like manner as
that science is (for all of them use the axioms for the demonstration
of their own proper objects, just as it does); and they do not all speak
about them; so neither could the science concerned with substance
speak about them. But if this is so, then the same science is not
5   concerned with substance and with the axioms. For, as speaking
about the axioms is not the proper function of the other sciences that
use them in like manner as this science[121] does, neither could it be
the proper function of this science [to speak about the axioms].

996b35 If, then, it belongs in like manner to any science
whatever [to know about the axioms], it cannot belong to all
the sciences ...[122]

Why can it not belong to all sciences? Because a science is able to
10   demonstrate the essential properties of its subject, and sciences
with different subjects have different things to prove. For it is not
possible for the same properties to belong essentially to different
subjects; this is why it is not possible for the axioms to belong
essentially to the subjects of all the different sciences either. But if
this is not the case,[123] then neither could all the sciences

---

121 viz. the science of substance.

122 The negative *mê* at 996b35 indicates that Aristotle regards 'it cannot belong to
all the sciences' as part of the protasis, as Ross takes it. Alexander's question in 188,9,
and the reply which follows, suggest that he regards it as the apodosis. Alexander
does not always observe the classical distinction between *ou* and *mê*.

123 i.e. if the axioms cannot belong essentially to the subjects of all the different
sciences.

demonstrate them.[124]

Having argued for the view that it does not belong to one science[125] to speak about the principles of substance and about the 15 axioms which are the principles of demonstration, Aristotle next argues that there is not even a science of the axioms, saying, 'And at the same time, in what manner will the knowledge (*hê gnôsis*)[126] of them exist? For even now we know what each of them happens to be' [997a2-4]. What he means is the following. We have scientific knowledge of something either by way of definition or by way of demonstration. If, then, there is science of the axioms, it would be a 20 demonstrative science, concerned with some one of their properties.[127] But on the one hand, what each of them is, is immediately evident (*gnôrimon*) to all. For example, it is evident, apart from science, what 'in every case, either the affirmation or the negation [is true]' means, or what 'things equal to the same thing are equal to each other' means. For all the sciences use these as things that are evident, and have no need of a science to teach them. Hence there 25 will be no definite (*aphôrismenê*) science of what each of these is.[128] If, on the other hand, there is demonstration about these things, and some demonstrative science, <all> the axioms will have to <be some one genus, some one nature as subject>,[129] and they will have to have both attributes (*pathê*), that is, the things demonstrated to belong to them (Aristotle calls the essential properties, that are the objects of demonstration, 'attributes'), and certain axioms, by way of 30 which their essential properties are demonstrated (by axioms Aristotle means indemonstrable and immediate premises (*protaseis*)).[130]

[124] viz. the axioms. If the axioms cannot belong essentially to the subjects of different sciences, then the axioms are not matter for demonstration by those sciences. In the context of the present argument Alexander neglects the fundamental indemonstrability of the axioms. He adverts to this point at 189,6-8, à propos of 997a7-8.

[125] This refers back to *Metaph.* 996b33-4, explained by Alexander in 187,25-188,6, rather than to the immediately preceding argument against the axioms' being the subject matter of all the sciences.

[126] In Alexander's citation *he gnôsis* is the subject of the sentence. Ross and Jaeger follow the MSS of *Metaph.*, which have *epistêmê*, 'science', instead of *gnôsis*, and no article; that makes *epistêmê* the predicate: 'in what manner will there be science?'

[127] This sentence, 188,19-21, would fit better at 188,26, after the first horn of the dilemma.

[128] The first horn of the dilemma: if the science of principles of demonstration is supposed to be definitional, it is pointless, and there really is no such science. The sentence 188,19-21 would fit better here.

[129] Hayduck recognises a lacuna and fills it from Asclepius 161,3-4, citing Alexander 189,13-14 in support. MSS of Asclepius give *ta pote*, 'the (axioms) at that time'. In his edition of Asclepius Hayduck emends this to *ta prôta*, 'the primary (axioms)'. In his apparatus to Alexander Hayduck proposes either *ta prôta* or *hapanta*, 'all (the axioms)'. I translate *hapanta*.

[130] The second horn of the dilemma: if the science of principles of demonstration is

Aristotle makes the statement 'for it is impossible for there to be demonstration about all things' [997a7-8] as a logical consequence of the statement that 'there will have to be some genus as subject, including both attributes and axioms' [997a6-7]. For 'it is impossible

189,1 for there to be demonstration about all things' follows from this. For demonstrations are concerned with essential properties of the subject of a science, with what Aristotle calls attributes, not with all things, nor with any chance things; but neither is it possible for there to be demonstration of all the things assumed for the proof of anything.[131]

The next statement, 'it is necessary that demonstration be from
5 some things and about some thing and of some things' [997a8-9] is connected with the statement 'there will have to be some genus as subject, including both attributes and axioms' [997a6-7]. (The statement 'for it is impossible for there to be demonstration about all things' [997a7-8] is parenthetical and said on account of the axioms.)[132] The phrase 'from some things' (*ek tinôn*) indicates the axioms through which the proof is achieved; 'about some thing' (*peri ti*) indicates the genus which is subject, to which something is
10 proven to belong or not to belong; 'of some things' (*tinôn*) indicates the things demonstrated to belong or not to belong to the subject, or what he calls attributes.

The statement 'So it results that there is some one genus of all the things that are proven' [997a9-10] would be equivalent to 'it *will* result', *if* there is demonstration about the axioms, and *if* the axioms are some one genus and some one nature as subject, 'that all
15 things demonstrated by way of the axioms will be of one nature', because all sciences and demonstrations prove the things proposed [to them] by way of the axioms, and the axioms are of one and the same nature, and, being of the same nature as one another, are able to prove [things of] some one nature – given that demonstrations are of[133] essential properties, and that it is necessary that things of one
20 and the same nature as one another belong essentially to one nature. Aristotle uses the expression 'one genus' (*genos*) [997a9] in place of 'one nature' (*phusis*).

Or the meaning is this. If there is a science and a demonstration of the axioms, there will have to be some genus as subject for them. For every demonstration, and every demonstrative science, is concerned

supposed to be demonstrative, a demonstrative science of principles of demonstration is absurd. The explanation of the absurdity runs to 190,17.
[131] *tinôn*, literally 'of certain things'.
[132] i.e. to make the important but hitherto neglected point that there is no demonstration of the axioms.
[133] Deleting *ek* at 189,18, in line with Alexander's explanation at 189,8-11. If *ek* were retained the translation would be 'proceed from essential properties', whereas demonstration proceeds from axioms to essential properties.

with some definite (*hôrismenon*) genus, and every object of demonstration belongs to a definite genus. Hence the axioms too, if they are objects of demonstration and there is a demonstrative science of them, have some definite genus as 25 subject, to which they are proven to belong. For every demonstration proves that the things which it demonstrates (which Aristotle calls attributes) belong to some genus, i.e. to one nature as subject, [and it does so] by way of certain axioms, by way of which demonstrations [are achieved], <and these must be primary>, that is, immediate and indemonstrable premises.[134] For [i] if things proven must be proven by way of axioms, but axioms too are subject to proof, then 30 [proof] would go on to infinity, and thus nothing could be demonstrable; [and] [ii] for not all things are demonstrable[135] – a proposition that Aristotle could also have used to demonstrate that there is no demonstration of the axioms.

That the items mentioned must be present in every demonstration, Aristotle has made clear by adding 'it is necessary that demonstration be from some things', by way of which the proof is achieved, 'and about some thing', which is the subject of the 35 demonstration, 'and of some things', that is, the things demonstrated themselves [997a8-9]. But if the axioms have some one genus as subject, then one and the same genus will be the subject of all things that are demonstrated and of all the sciences. For the one who uses something to achieve a demonstration, something which 190,1 belongs essentially to some genus, i.e. to one nature, is not using it with reference to any other [genus] than that to which it belongs essentially. For one does not prove any chance thing through any chance thing; nor does the man who uses [theorems] proven in

---

[134] Hayduck marks the explanatory phrase *toutestin amesous protaseis kai anapodeiktous* as corrupt, presumably because of the unexplained accusatives. I supply *ha dei prôta einai* just before the explanatory phrase in an attempt to explain the accusatives. For axioms as *prôta* cf. 190,26-7. For axioms as undemonstrated and immediate cf. 188,30-1.

[135] This sentence has caused trouble. Asclepius 161,12-13 inverts the order, and the logical relationship: 'for it is not possible for all things to be demonstrable, since thus nothing will be demonstrable.' The Latin translation S (and perhaps, behind it, S's MS of Alexander), retains the order of our MSS of Alexander, but introduces a supplement, and changes 'demonstrable' to 'indemonstrable': 'and so none of them will be demonstrable (which, however, ought to have been the case), because not all things are *in*demonstrable.' I take it that both Asclepius and S think that Alexander is offering one reason or one argument for the claim made in 189,26-9, that demonstration requires immediate and undemonstrable premises; they recognise that the last part of it ('for not all things are demonstrable') does not really support what precedes it ('nothing could be demonstrable'); and they adopt expedients to get around the difficulty. The difficulty is removed, or at least lessened, if we take 'for not all things are demonstrable' as a second and independent argument. I number accordingly. It is the second reason which Alexander says Aristotle could also (*kai*) have used to show that that there is no demonstration of axioms.

5   geometry use them on anything other than geometrical subjects,
     because it is to these that they belong essentially; nor does the man
     engaged in music who uses any [theorem of music] use it on
     anything other than the subjects of musical [theorems].[136] For it is
     by way of essential properties that demonstrations of essential
     properties are achieved. Those, then, who use the axioms would be
     using them on that genus to which the axioms belong essentially, for
10   they belong to some one [genus], given that there is a demonstrative
     science of them. But all the sciences use the axioms which they use
     on the things which they demonstrate. Hence all the sciences will
     have the same genus as subject, because all the sciences use the
     axioms, and the axioms belong to some one genus, and it is not
     possible, in a demonstration, to use things which belong essentially
     to a genus on any genus other than that genus to which they belong
15   essentially. But if all the sciences have the same genus as subject,
     and all prove by way of the same things (for they prove by way of the
     axioms), then all sciences would be the same.[137]

     [The case for one science of the principles of substance and
                the principles of demonstration]

     997a11 But if the [science] of substance and the [science] of
     these things are different ...

     Having argued for the position that it does *not* belong to the same
20   [science] to speak about the principles of substance as it does to
     speak about the principles of demonstration, but to a different
     science, and having added a further argument, on different grounds
     (*exôthen*), that the axioms are not even demonstrable, Aristotle next
     faces an aporia that is continuous with the preceding. For he
     inquires, which of them is wisdom, which is [wisdom] in the most
     proper sense and prior: the science concerned with the principles of
     substance, or the science concerned with the principles of
     demonstration?
     And that it is reasonable[138] to say that the science concerned with
25   the axioms is such, he argues as follows. The science concerned with
     primary things is primary; the axioms are primary; he has proven

---

[136] Reading with Hayduck *oute ho en tois mousikois tini*. Bonitz conjectures *oute ho
tois en mousikois* (or *mousikêi) tisi*, 'nor does the man who uses any of the [theorems]
in music apply....' I take this as a guide to the sense, but suspect that Alexander
wrote the rather elliptical sentence that Hayduck prints.

[137] i.e. the same as one another. The Greek for 'the same' is plural, *hai autai*.

[138] The Greek is *hoti dê eulogon einai legein epikheirei*. I understand a finite verb
esti after *hoti*, and take the infinitive *einai* as depending on the following *legein*; but
perhaps *einai* (also found in the parallel, Asclepius 162,17) is simply a mistake for
esti.

this by saying that they are 'universal' (the universals have been proven to be primary by nature, relative to the things below them, and such are the axioms: common to all things and universal, since all things proven are proven by way of them) 'and the principles of all things' [997a12-13]. Principles are primary relative to that whose principles they are, so that in this way too they are universal. The fallacy [here] is that the axioms are assumed to be primary and 30 universal without qualification (*haplôs*). For items common to certain things are not by that very fact their universals, nor are universals primary without qualification and in the proper sense; hence neither is the science concerned with the universals primary without qualification or of higher dignity. Further, principles are not proven by way of axioms; for principles are not demonstrable.

997a14 If it is not the task of the philosopher [to consider the   191,1
axioms] ...

Regarding the aporia which he raised, about to whom it belongs [to consider the axioms] – for either it belongs to all the sciences which use them, or to none – Aristotle now proves that it is reasonable for the philosopher to treat of (*pragmateuesthai*) the axioms, which are the principles of demonstration, the primary means of proving the   5 truth in all matters under inquiry. He makes this evident by proving that it is absurd to say that anyone else treats of truth and falsity. The phrase 'about them' [997a14] would refer to the premises, among which the axioms are included. For to whom else, besides the philosopher, would it belong to deal with truth and falsity in premises? Thus it is proven that even if it is not the task of the *primary* philosopher to deal with demonstration and its principles,   10 it is still the task of the philosopher. These considerations would also establish, in a way, that the treatise on demonstration is a part of philosophy.

[Aporia 3]
[The case against a single science of all substances]

997a15 And in general, whether there is one science of all
substances, or several sciences ...

Since of substances some are intelligible and unmoved, while   15 others are in motion and sensible, Aristotle inquires whether it belongs to one science to consider all substances, *or* to several different sciences; and if it does not belong to one science, which kind of substance is it, science of which should be considered the science now proposed, that is, wisdom.

For he says that to suppose that there is one science of all
20 substances is not reasonable, and he adds why. If [one supposes] one
science [of all substances], the science which demonstrates all the
essential accidents of substances would also be one; for every
demonstrative science is able to demonstrate the essential
properties of that genus with which it is concerned; hence, if there is
also some one science concerned with substance, substance too
would be some one genus (for if there is one science of one genus,
25 then that which is the object of one science is one genus); but if
substance too is one genus, and if it belongs to one science to
demonstrate the essential accidents of one genus, then the science
that demonstrates the essential properties of all substances would
also be one. For it is proper (*idion*) to a demonstrative science to
consider, concerning some subject, the essential accidents [of that
subject], by way of the axioms and common opinions.

Aristotle says, 'so concerning the same genus' (*to auto genos*)
30 [997a21] in place of 'so concerning one genus' (*hen genos*), [i.e.] that
to consider the essential accidents [of that genus], by way of the
common opinions, belongs to <the same science>, that is
(*toutesti*),[139] to one science.[140]

Aristotle appears to introduce the absurdity from [the notion of]
192,1 accident. For, assuming that it belongs to a science to demonstrate
the accidents of the genus that is its subject, [then] since all other
things are accidents of substance, it turns out, according to those
who say that the science concerned with substance is one,[141] that it
belongs to one science to speak concerning all beings; for all beings
besides substance are accidents of substance. This is the reason why
5 Aristotle goes so far as to say: 'For there would be in fact one
demonstrative science concerned with all the accidents' [997a18-19],
though he does not add the next step.[142]

---

[139] Bonitz would delete *toutesti*, presumably on the ground that there is nothing
preceding it which requires explanation. Hayduck suggests adding *protaseôn*,
'premises', as an explanation of 'opinions'. I follow a suggestion of Robert Sharples (in
private correspondence) and read <*tês autês*> *toutesti mias*; Alexander is explaining
Aristotle's words *tês autês*, 'the same science', 997a22.

[140] Brandis takes the sentence to be incomplete as it stands: 'that is, it belongs to
one science to consider ... .' He proposes to conclude it as does Asclepius 163,18-21:
'the essential accidents of magnitudes and it belongs in turn to another science to
consider numbers, so that there would be different sciences of substances, since
[there are different sciences] of the essential properties of substances.' I see no need
for the supplement.

[141] Presumably Alexander is thinking of Platonists.

[142] The 'next step' (*to hexês ... autôi*) would be a further point that Aristotle could
have made but did not make in so many words, namely, that there would be one
demonstrative science concerned with all beings, substances as well as accidents. For
similar notes on what Aristotle does *not* say, cf. 193,14.32. Hayduck finds corruption
running from the negative *ouketi* in 192,5 down to *einai* in 192,7. He cites S: *quod*
vero statim adiecit (Subiectum enim circa quod, unius est scientiae – –) id mihi

'For it belongs to one science [to consider] that about which [the science is], and it belongs to one science [to consider] the things from which [the science proceeds], whether this belongs to the same science or to a different science' [997a22-4]. This seems to me to mean the following. Having said [997a18-21] that, if substance is one subject genus, the science which demonstrates all the essential properties of substance will also be one, Aristotle goes on to speak in universal terms: 'For it belongs to one science [to consider] that 10 about which [the science is], and it belongs to one science [to consider] the things from which [the science proceeds], whether this belongs to the same science or to a different science; hence too the accidents [belong to one science], whether they [the sciences] consider them or one of them does' [997a22-5]. The meaning would be as follows. It belongs to the same science [both] to consider just what the subject is and to consider its essential properties; for it is from these and in these that the subject has its being. But that science whose role it is to know the essential properties of some 15 thing also has the role of demonstrating that thing's essential accidents.

Aristotle may have said 'and it belongs to one science [to consider] the things *from which*' [997a23] in place of 'and [it belongs to one science to consider] the things from which come the demonstrations concerning that subject'. For it is through the essential properties of a thing that demonstrations are achieved, and one who concerns himself with that thing must know these properties. Hence the one whose role it is to know the subject nature will also have the role of knowing the essential properties of this nature, for it is by way of 20 these that knowledge of the substance (*ousia*)[143] of the thing proposed is achieved, [that is] by way of the things by way of which demonstrations of the properties of that substance[144] are achieved.[145] The science which has the role of knowing these things

---

huiusmodi esse videtur. S does not translate, and presumably did not read, the negative *ouketi.* S takes *to hexês ... autôi* as introducing the ensuing citation of 997a22-4. I take *to hexês ... autôi* as the last words of its sentence, and take the citation as beginning the next sentence. I am in debt to Robert Sharples for help on this passage.

[143] Substance in the sense of essence; cf. 193,27. I have retained 'substance' as the translation to avoid confusion with *ti ên einai*, 'essence', and *kath' hauto*, 'essential'.

[144] i.e. essence.

[145] Alexander here distinguishes, in line with *An. Post.* 1.10, 76b11-16, two levels of things that belong essentially to a subject genus: a first level (*axiômata* or basic truths about the genus) serves as the basis for demonstration of a second level (*pathê* or attributes, further essential features of the genus). At 192,22-3.29 Alexander speaks of the second level as *kath' hauta sumbebêkota*, 'essential accidents', which might suggest a useful terminological contrast with *kath' hauta huparkhonta*, 'essential properties'. But the contrast is hardly fixed, because items of the second level are spoken of as *huparkhonta* at 192,21.25. At 192,35-193,1 Alexander speaks of *huparkhonta kai sumbebêkota*; but whether *kai* indicates interchangeability or

also has the role of proving the essential accidents of this genus, that is, the things that are proven by demonstration to belong to the genus. For one whose role it is to know the subject genus and the
25   things by way of which the properties of the genus are proven, also has the role of demonstrating its properties. The one whose role it is to demonstrate things, also has the role of knowing them.

So, if the science that treats of the subject genus, of its substance,[146] is *one*, by reason of the genus' being *one* thing, some one nature, it will also be the role of one science to demonstrate all the essential accidents of this genus. But if it belongs to several
30   sciences, different sciences,[147] to treat of the genus taken [for consideration], of its substance,[148] by reason of the genus' *not* having some one nature (for if certain things are classified under a higher genus, it is not by that very fact the case that it belongs to one science to consider them; on the contrary, the subject of each science, that of which it treats, has to be the same in form and of one nature), it will, then, belong to several sciences, to the same sciences, to demonstrate the properties of that genus. For however
35   many sciences are concerned with the subject, the sciences
193,1 concerned with the subject's essential properties and accidents are equally numerous.

The words 'Therefore too the accidents [belong to one science], whether they[149] [the sciences] consider them or one of them does' [997a24-5] would be equivalent in meaning to: 'The same sciences, to which consideration of the subject genus and consideration of the things through which the properties of the genus are demonstrated
5   belong will also have knowledge of the essential accidents that are demonstrated to belong to the genus.' So, if those sciences are several, in such a way as to be separate from one another, then the sciences which demonstrate these [essential accidents] will be several as well. But if they are one science, composed of several sciences as parts, this will also be the case with the science that proves the essential properties of this genus; for it will be one, even though gathered together out of several sciences as parts. Aristotle
10   adds this remark, because, while the treatise concerning substance seems to be the whole of philosophy, it is not the case that every [branch of] philosophy is concerned with every [kind of] substance;

---

rather distinction is unclear. At 193,4 the *huparkhonta* and the *sumbebēkota* are identical; and that is how I take them at 193,24-5. In *Metaph.* 997a18-25, the text that Alexander is explaining, Aristotle uses the term *sumbebēkota*, not the term *huparkhonta*.

[146] i.e. essence.

[147] Adopting Hayduck's suggestion, made in the light of 191,17: *kai allēs kai allēs to*.

[148] i.e. essence.

[149] Hayduck prints *autai*, 'they'. Ross and Jaeger print *hautai*, 'these'.

on the contrary, in one part it is concerned with sensible and natural substance, in another part with intelligible substance.

Believing that he has reduced to an absurdity the thesis that there will be one demonstrative science of the essential properties of substance, Aristotle stops without going any further;[150] for it will be evident that it is irrational for the same science to consider both the accidents of sensible substance and those of intelligible substance.

[Further considerations][151]

Someone might raise the question: how, then, could substance *not* be one genus, if Aristotle now means, by 'concerning one genus' (*peri hen genos*), not [concerning merely] the common term (*to koinon*), as he did earlier,[152] but rather 'concerning one form' (*peri hen eidos*), some one nature that is the same in form, as well? For this is the sense in which a science is concerned with one genus: not that one science is concerned with all the things that derive from the same highest and most common genus, but that it is concerned with things that share the same form and formula.[153]

One can also understand the words 'For it belongs to one science [to consider] that about which [the science is] and it belongs to one science [to consider] the things from which [the science proceeds]' [997a22-3] in the following way. If a genus has one science that inquires what each of the things ranged under the genus is and [seeks] its definition, that genus also has one science that knows and proves the properties of the genus, the things from which it derives its being.[154] For it is by way of the essential properties of each thing, its essential accidents, that demonstrations are achieved.[155] But it belongs to one science to know the essential properties of some one genus. For if the science that defines [a genus] is one, the science that demonstrates it is also one. The 'which' (*ho*) [997a23] signifies

---

[150] i.e. he stops short of stating the absurdity explicitly.

[151] These do not amount to a case for a single science of all substances.

[152] 'Of one genus' is Alexander's interpretation of 997a21, 'of the same genus'; cf. above 191,29ff.

[153] The objection is as follows. If substance has only the weak generic unity of a common name, then the notion of a science of all substances is absurd. But if substance has specific unity or unity of form, what is so absurd about a science of all substances? They might then form the kind of genus that can be the subject of a science. Alexander leaves the objection unanswered. Presumably he would have said that substance does not in fact possess the specific unity or unity of form requisite for the subject of a science.

[154] In the earlier explanation, the things *ex hôn*, 'from which', were taken as sources of *demonstration* about a genus. In the present explanation they are taken as sources or principles of the *being* of the genus.

[155] Taking *kai* in 193,24 as explicative; cf. note on 192,22.

substance (*ousia*), that is, essence (*ti ên einai*).[156] By the phrase
'whether it belongs to the same science <or to another' [997a23-4] he
would mean: whether it belongs to the same science>[157] both to
define a thing and to demonstrate the essential properties of this
30   same thing – that is, whether the same science defines *and* demonstrates, or whether they are different, and not both parts of one
science – it will follow, then, that one science demonstrates the
essential accidents of the same genus.[158] For this is what is missing in
the phrase 'therefore the accidents as well' [997a24]; it needs to be
supplemented 'it belongs to one science to consider and to prove'. For
a science whose role it is to know the things 'from which' [997a23] also
has the role of proving the accidents of the subject, whether each of
35   these sciences is different from the other in its consideration of the
essential properties of the subject – the science of definition taking
them as given, the science of demonstration demonstrating them – or
194,1 whether there is also some one science composed of both, of defining
and of demonstrating. For, as the science which defines and proves
the essence of one thing is one science, so too the science that
demonstrates [its accidents] is one science.

Some manuscripts read, instead of *eith' hautai* ('whether these')
[997a24], *eith' hai autai* ('whether the same').[159] On this reading, the
5   meaning would be, whether the science that defines and the science
that demonstrates concerning the same genus are the same sciences,
or whether they are not the same, but are parts of one science, in
such a way that the science of the subject genus results from the
combination of the two of them.[160]

[Aporia 4]
[The case against a single science of substance and its essential
accidents]

997a25 Further, whether the consideration is <concerning>
substances alone, or their accidents as well.[161]

---

[156] The most common meaning of *ousia* is 'substance'. Here, however, Alexander
explains *ousia* as essence. Alexander's explanation has led me to gloss *ousia*
'essence' in the commentary on aporia 3; cf. nn. 143, 144.

[157] Following Hayduck's suggestion to supply *eite allês eiê an legôn eite tês autês*
from Asclepius 164,6-7.

[158] That is, one science will demonstrate all essential properties of one genus,
whether or not that science is the same as the science which defines the genus.

[159] Ross and Jaeger print *eith' hautai* but note divergence in the MSS and other
sources of the text of the *Metaphysics*.

[160] The apodosis is unstated but obvious: 'it will belong to one science to consider
the accidents.'

[161] Following Hayduck's suggestion to read *kai <peri> ta sumbebêkota*, in line
with MSS of *Metaph.* and Alexander's citation at 195,4.

This aporia too has been mentioned by Aristotle in his presentation 10
of the aporiae. The aporia he raises in these words will be seen to
follow logically on the preceding statement: 'For it belongs to one
science [to consider] that about which [the science is], and it belongs
to one science [to consider] the things from which [the science
proceeds], whether this belongs to the same science or to a different
science' [997a22-4]. For, having said by those words that, just as it
belongs to one science to define the subject genus, so also it belongs
to one science to demonstrate the essential accidents of that genus,
and having raised the aporia, whether both belong to the same 15
science, *or* whether it belongs to one to define and to another to
demonstrate, he now raises the [present] aporia in its own right, and
inquires whether the science that is proposed to us (that is, wisdom)
considers substances alone, examining what the being (*to einai*) of
substance is and *defining* what the nature of substance is, *or*
whether the same science considers the essential accidents of 20
substance as well, so as to be, at the same time, a *demonstrative*
science as well. For if it belongs to the same science to consider
substance and to consider its essential accidents as well, this science
would be demonstrative; for it belongs to a demonstrative science to
demonstrate the essential properties of substance.

Aristotle adds, as an absurdity, 'the science of substance would
also be demonstrative' [997a30-1],[162] assuming that it follows from
the [notion of a] demonstrative science that it demonstrates those 25
things concerning which it discusses and which it considers. 'But',
Aristotle says 'there does not seem to be demonstration of what [a
thing] is' (*tou ti estin*) [997a31-2], rightly assuming that there is no
demonstration of definition or of what [a thing] is, for he has proven
this in the *Posterior Analytics* [*An. Post.* 2.3-4].

But if the same science considers substance, i.e. what substance
is, *and* the essential properties of substance, it does not at all follow
that that science *demonstrates* what substance is. For, if the science 30
which considers substance is also demonstrative, it does not follow
that it demonstrates *substance*; for it will assume what substance is
by way of definition, while it will demonstrate its essential
properties, for these are subject to demonstration. For, if the same
science is concerned with both objects, it does not follow that it is
concerned with both in like manner. For the two activities, defining
and demonstrating, do not become identical to one another just

---

[162] i.e. the science of substance would be demonstrative *of substance*. The absurdity
would be for the science of substance to demonstrate substance, its own subject
matter. The troublesome assumption, from which the absurdity would follow, is that
a demonstrative science demonstrates its own subject matter. The distinction
between being the subject of a demonstrative science and being an object of
demonstration in such a science is explained at 194,28-195,2.

35   because both are the work of one person.[163] But Aristotle, assuming
195,1   that the science of substance will be demonstrative, infers that
        substance will be [the object] of demonstration, supposing that it is
        proper to a demonstrative science to consider the object proposed to
        it by way of demonstration.

        Wishing to indicate to us in what sense he meant the words,
        'whether the consideration is concerning substances alone, or their
5   accidents' [997a25-6], Aristotle cites the objects of geometry: solids,
        planes, and lines – *if*, that is, he speaks of these as substances[164] –
        since they have certain essential properties, about which a geometer
        practises demonstration. He means,[165] whether it belongs to the
        same person to consider what each of these things is, i.e. to define
        what a solid is or what a plane is, what a line is, *and* to consider the
        essential properties of each of these. For example, while the
10   *definition* of a line is, length without breadth, it is an *essential
        property* of a line to be either straight or curved (depending on how it
        happens); likewise [it is an essential property] that if a straight line
        made to intersect a straight line makes the resultant angles equal to
        one another, then each of the equal angles is a right angle, and the
        line made to intersect is perpendicular to that which it intersects;
        and the like. By introducing this example he all but solves the
15   aporia which he presents. Geometers, at any rate, speak about both
        kinds of things, but they do not demonstrate their definitions; on the
        contrary, they assume without demonstration that a plane is that
        which has length and breadth alone, and make use of this, while
        they do demonstrate the fact that certain things are essential
        properties of rectilinear plane figures, and certain things essential
        properties of curvilinear plane figures; but this involves no
        demonstration of essence.
20   Now geometers do not have substances as their subjects which
        they define, but natural philosophy[166] has substances as its subjects
        and none the less both defines these substances and demonstrates
        what their essential properties are. For it does *not* demonstrate
        what the world is or what the sun is, or what any other natural
        substance is. But none the less[167] it speaks and demonstrates

---

163 Or perhaps 'about one object', that is, substance; but this would blur the
distinction just drawn between what substance is (defined) and substance's essential
properties (demonstrated).
164 Alexander's point is that Aristotle is not committed to taking geometrical
objects as genuine substances; cf. Aristotle's noncommittal *ei* at 997a27, and
195,19-20.
165 Hayduck, perhaps in view of S's *namque*, says that *legei ei* at 195,7 appears to
be corrupt. I place a period, not a comma, after *tôi geômetrêi* and take *legei ei* as
beginning a new sentence explaining 997a25-6.
166 Or 'physics'.
167 Supposing *ouden elatton* (cf. 195,21) or equivalent in place of MSS *ouketi*
printed by Hayduck. The sentence clearly opposes items not demonstrated to items

concerning the forms of motion or of place, or the other essential   25
properties of natural things. Likewise, then, if there is some
accident belonging to the primary substances, the one who considers
their substance (*ousia*)[168] will also speak about and demonstrate
those accidents.

[The case for a single science of substance and its essential accidents]

Having added that there will be demonstration of definition and of
essence (*ti ên einai*), as an absurdity following on 'if it belongs to the
same' [997a30] science to preside over both,[169] Aristotle in turn tells
what absurdity follows if it is *not* the case that it belongs to one   30
science to consider both. It is difficult to discover what science there
will be – distinct from that which considers substance – which will
consider and demonstrate the essential properties of substance –
while remaining different from the first science. He makes a sound
point: that it is not easy to discover one science treating of the
essence (*ti esti*) of its subject, and another science treating of the
subject's essential properties – not easy in the case of any other   35
genus, or in the case of substance. For it is impossible for someone
who does not know the substance (*ousia*)[170] of something to prove its
essential properties.

[Aporia 5]

Aristotle now presents a further aporia, one which he set down at   196,1
the outset (it was the fourth of those he set down): whether one must
think that only sensible substances exist, *or* whether there are also
some other substances, distinct from (*para*) sensibles, [existing] in
their own right. To the issue about there being some substances
distinct from sensible substances, he adds another issue, which he
also mentioned in his initial presentation of the aporiae: whether   5
these [non-sensible] substances exist in one manner only, *or*
whether there are several kinds of such substances, in such a way
that certain substances would be Ideas and patterns, while others,
such as the mathematical substances, would be in between the
Ideas (*ideai*) and sensible substances. For this was the place
assigned to the mathematicals by Plato's disciples, who said that
they were substances in their own right, outside of and separated
from both sensible substances and the Ideas. It is in reference to this   10

---

demonstrated.
[168] Or 'essence'.
[169] i.e. both substance and properties or accidents.
[170] Or 'essence'.

[issue] that Aristotle says the following words, inquiring whether there are 'several kinds of substances' [997b1]. And that it will appear that there are *not* several kinds of substances, he will prove by refuting the things that are said [in their support].

> **997b3** So, then, that we say that the Forms are causes and substances in their own right, has been said in our initial discussions.

15   Having come to pose the aporia, whether sensible substances are the only substances, *or* whether there are others distinct from these, and whether there are several kinds of substances distinct from sensible substances (as was the view of the ancients who were disciples of Plato and who posited both the Ideas and the mathematical substances), Aristotle inquires about these, whether there can exist any such substances. In preparation for his argument against these substances, he begins by reminding us of
20   the kinds of things they[171] said they were, and refers us back to what he said in the first book. (From this it is clear, as it is already clear on several counts, that that book is Aristotle's work and belongs to this treatise;[172] for the manner in which he spoke about these substances there is similar to the manner in which he mentions them here: in both texts he has constructed his arguments as though the theory of Ideas were his own.)[173]
      The words 'So, then, that (*hôs*)' [997b3] are equivalent to 'So, then,
25   in what sense (*pôs*)'. Aristotle said in the first book that the Platonists said that the Ideas were substances, objects of definition, and existing in their own right,[174] separated from sensibles, and that sensible substances had their being by virtue of a relation to patterns; and they placed[175] the Ideas under the formal cause, cause according to essence.

---

[171] The Platonists.

[172] viz. the *Metaphysics*.

[173] Alexander alludes to Aristotle's use of the first person plural, 'we', here and in *Metaph.* 1.9. Cf. n. 8 above.

[174] Reading *ousias horistas kai autas kath' hautas* in place of Hayduck's *ousias horistikas autas kath' hautas*. Hayduck reports that a marginal note in A suggests that *noêtas*, 'intelligible', would be better than *horistikas*, and that S has *per se intelligibiles*. Alexander refers to *Metaph.* 1.6, 987b1-10, where the point is that Plato regarded Ideas, not sensibles, as objects of definition. In his commentary on that passage Alexander uses the neuter plural *horista* at 50,13 and 51,22. I suspect that *horistikas*, 'definitory' or perhaps 'sources of definitions', resulted from a fusion of *horistas* with a following *kai*.

[175] If the plural *hupêgon* is retained, the reference is to the Platonists. But Hayduck suggests that the singular *hupêgen*, 'he assigned', may be right. Hayduck's point, I take it, is that the reference may be to Aristotle. Hayduck may be thinking of *Metaph.* 1.7, 998b4-5 where Aristotle classifies the Forms under the heading of formal causes. Alexander explains that passage at 62,18-20.

[An argument against the Forms]

997b5 While they[176] have many difficulties,[177] it is the height of absurdity to assert that there are certain natures distinct   30
from those in the heaven ...

What the many difficulties are, Aristotle has said in the first book [*Metaph*. 1.6 and 9]. He says, 'distinct from those in the heaven' (*ouranos*) [997b6-7] in place of 'distinct from those that are sensible, i.e. in the world' (*kosmos*) (by 'heaven' he means 'world'), in the sense of their being in a place and existing by nature; for these things could be said in a proper sense to be in heaven.[178]

He says that while there are many absurdities that follow from   197,1
the doctrine (*dogma*) of the Ideas – he means the aporia about what kind of reality (*hupostasis*) they have, whether as[179] substance or not, and what the manner of participation (*methexis*) is, and all the other aporiae that he raised against this theory in the first book – the height of absurdity is the one which he now presents as follow-   ing for them. They say that there are certain natures, distinct from   5
the sensible and naturally existing substances of this world;[180] they then call them Ideas, and they posit that these natures are the same as the sensibles which are in the heaven, and differ from the sensibles only by virtue of being eternal.

Aristotle confirms that this follows from their doctrine, on the basis of what they themselves say. For they say there exists a Man Itself[181] and a Horse Itself and Health Itself, but they say nothing   10
else about them. Now if there also exist Those[182] Men and Horses, differing from sensibles only in virtue of the 'Itself', their other features will be the same as [those of] sensibles (at any rate, those who say that there are definitions of Those realities say that the definitions apply to sensible things as well), and they will differ only by virtue of being eternal; this is what the addition, the 'Itself', seems to indicate. So Those realities, too, will be sensible. For just as   15

---

[176] viz. the Platonist exponents of Forms, or perhaps the Forms themselves.

[177] Following MSS of Alexander and MS A^b of *Metaph.*, which give *pollas d' ekhontôn duskolias;* other MSS of *Metaph.* read *pollakhêi d' ekhontôn duskolian*, 'while they have difficulty in many ways', which is what Ross and Jaeger print.

[178] Not 'up in heaven' but rather 'inside the heaven'.

[179] Reading the adverb *hêi* in place of the article *hê*.

[180] The phrase 'of this world' is my interpretation of *tautas*, 'these'. This is a natural extension of the function of the demonstrative *houtos*, to refer to what is near as opposed to what is far away. For similar uses of *houtos* see 198,27; 199,33-4.

[181] I have capitalised nouns that name Ideas or Forms, as well as the intensive pronoun *auto*, 'Itself', often prefixed or suffixed to nouns naming Ideas or Forms.

[182] The capitalised 'Those' is my interpretation of *ekeina*, 'those'. This is a natural extension of the function of the demonstrative *ekeinos*, to refer to what is far away as opposed to what is near, to designate things outside the sensible world. For similar uses of *ekeinos* see 197,12.14, and perhaps 198,27.

those who said that there were gods and who made them human in form were making them eternal human beings, predicating eternity of them through the word 'god', so those who made the Forms the same as the sensibles, [only] with the benefit of the addition, 'Itself', were making the Ideas eternal sensibles. For it is impossible for something which is a man or a horse, admitting the formulae of

20   these things, not to be sensible and capable of sensation. But if this is the case, the position that only sensible substances exist would not be negated by the positing of the Ideas.

In Alpha Meizon [*Metaph.* 1.9, 990a34-990b4], in his first attack on the Ideas, Aristotle's first point was that [their proponents], wishing to obtain some scientific knowledge of beings, proceeded to

25   seek their causes, but thought that they would obtain scientific knowledge of them by making substances equal in number to those already in existence. He now explains the sense of that statement, by way of [the claim] that those who posited the Ideas were assuming nothing else than eternal substances equal in number to, and the same as, the substances which were the objects of their inquiry – given that they only differ from sensibles by the addition of the word 'Itself' which would signify their eternity.

[The case against the Intermediates]

997b12 Further, if anyone posits things intermediate, distinct
30   **from the Forms and the sensibles, he will get many aporiae.**

Having raised an aporia against the Ideas, Aristotle moves to the things which are said to be intermediate between the Ideas Themselves and the sensibles, that is, the mathematicals, which the Platonists said were substances, existing in their own right; and he says that many aporiae follow from this theory. By way of these

35   aporiae he proves that the nature of the substances distinct from the sensibles is difficult to grasp. And he presents the aporiae.

198,1   [i] As it is in the case of a line – their view is that there exists, distinct from the sensible line and from the Idea, a mathematical line, of which geometry treats – so too it will be in the case of the other things, that is, the mathematicals: all mathematical scientists will have certain intermediate natures to consider. So, since

5   astronomy is one of the mathematical sciences, and is concerned with the heaven and the sun and moon and other stars, each of these things, about which the mathematician or astronomer speaks, will be intermediate between the sensibles (heaven, sun, moon, other stars) and the Ideas. But how could there be some mathematical sun

10   that was not in motion? Or a world? Or any other of the stars? For the essence (*ousia*) and nature of these things is bound up with such

and such a kind of motion. But [the Platonists] say that the mathematicals are immovable.

[ii] But even more irrational than saying that a world and a sun are immovable is saying that they are in motion, but are not sensible but rather mathematical. For it is impossible for something to be in motion unless it is enmattered (*enulon*) and by its own nature sensible. (This absurdity would also follow for those who say 15 that there is some Idea of heaven, Heaven Itself, and of the sun, Sun Itself; for how is it possible to conceive of (*epinoein*) any of these as immovable?)

[iii] The same argument as in the case of astronomy also applies in the case of optics and the objects of which optics treats, and in the case of mathematical harmonics (not that harmonics which fits notes together – for this seems, on their view, to be concerned with sensibles – but rather the harmonics that proves in what ratio 20 (*logos*) of numbers each concord consists: this is the mathematical harmonics which will clearly be concerned with the mathematicals). For all these sciences, being mathematical, will have certain mathematical substances as their subject matter, substances intermediate between sensibles and Ideas. But how is it possible for there to be certain visible things, the objects of optics, if they are not sensible? Or for there to be audible things, the objects of harmonics, if they are not sensible? For the essence of optics (*to optikêi einai*) is 25 to speak about things that are visible, and the essence of harmonics is to speak about things that are audible.

[iv] From this it will follow that one will say that there are, distinct from the senses of this world, certain other intermediate senses as well, through which the apprehension (*antilêpsis*) of those intermediates takes place. But if there are senses, it is clear that there will also be animals possessing those senses, intermediate between the Animals Themselves (the Ideas) and the perishable animals; for it is impossible for there to be senses without animals.   30

997b25 One might raise a further aporia: concerning what kinds of beings must we seek for these sciences?

[v] The aporia Aristotle raises is as follows. Since [the Platonists] said that the mathematical sciences were concerned with things intermediate between sensibles and Ideas, he inquires, distinct from *which* of the sensibles are there these intermediates with which the 35 mathematical sciences are concerned?[183] As they say that geometry 199,1

---

[183] i.e. which kinds of sensibles have intermediates corresponding to them, and which do not? The suggestion is that this question cannot be answered satisfactorily, and that a theory which gives rise to a question which cannot be answered satisfactorily is itself unsatisfactory.

(*geômetria*) is something distinct from surveying (*geôdaisia*), and differs from surveying in no other respect than the fact that surveying is concerned with sensibles and their measures (it was discovered in Egypt due to the need of dividing the land, because the boundary markers which had earlier been set down were disturbed
5   by the flood of the Nile), while geometry is not concerned with sensibles, and they say that there is another science concerned with the Ideas of these things – as,[184] then, in the case of surveying and geometry, so too there ought to be, in the case of medicine, a certain kind of medicine that concerns itself with the health of sensible animals, comparable to surveying, and another kind of medicine, distinct from intelligible Medicine Itself: the kind of medicine intermediate between that Medicine which treats of Health Itself
10 and that which treats of health in sensible things, a kind of medicine comparable to geometry.

But if this is so, there will be a kind of health distinct from Health Itself and the health in sensible things: intelligible health, for intelligible animals. For, if there is a Triangle Itself and a Line Itself, and if there are sensible [triangles and lines] too, with which surveying is concerned, and if there are certain things intermediate between these, things with which geometry is concerned, so
15 likewise, if there is Health Itself, and health in sensible things, with which medicine is concerned, there will also be a kind of health and a kind of medicine intermediate between these; for the reasoning (*logos*) is the same. But if there is to be an intermediate health and an intermediate medicine, there will also be certain other healthful things, through which the intermediate medical man will effect health; and clearly there will be certain animals in which that health will be found.

20 (It does *not* follow, for those who think of the mathematicals by way of abstraction (*aphairesis*) from sensibles, and do not give them a reality (*hupostasis*) of their own, that they also think of some kind of health by way of abstraction, a health comparable to the mathematicals. For it is not possible, by thought (*epinoia*), to separate essence (*ousia*)[185] from the natural body.)[186]

But as in the case of medicine, so too the issue will be raised in the case of the other arts. For why will this be true in the case of geometry and not also in the case of any science whatsoever? There

---

184 Taking *hôs* at 199,6 as resuming the *hôs* of 198,35.

185 Here, the essence that is required for health.

186 Aristotle's objection is that given the Platonic conception of geometry as a science of intermediates, there ought by parity of reasoning to be many other intermediate sciences and intermediate objects. Alexander's point is that Aristotle's conception of geometry as obtaining its objects by abstraction is sufficiently different from the Platonic conception that it is not vulnerable to this objection.

must be some explanation (*aitia*) of why this is said to be the case.[187]   25
   Having presented this aporia, Aristotle next [997b32] says that
the [Platonists'] view – that surveying is concerned with sensibles
while geometry is concerned with certain other things – is unsound;
for surveying is not concerned with sensibles either. He confirms
this with the argument that, if surveying were concerned with
sensibles, then, when they perished, it would perish along with
them. For it is necessary, if something is about an object, and that
object is done away with, for that which is about the object to be   30
done away with as well. For example, if it is about an individual
thing (*tode ti*),[188] then, when this thing has perished, it is necessary
for that which is about it to have perished as well – given that its
own being (*autôi to einai*) consists in its being about that object. But
in fact no art and no science perishes along with these objects,[189]
and neither does surveying. So it is clear that surveying is
concerned not with these things or about these things[190] that are
sensible and perishable, but rather with the universal, which is   35
eternal. For every science and art is constituted (*sunistasthai*) as
[being] about the universal, which is not sensible. For if someone
uses the sciences or the arts to deal with sensibles, it does not follow
that they are *about* sensibles; on the contrary, they are about the
universals and things of that kind; they treat of sensibles, not
insofar as these are sensible and individual (*tade*), but insofar as
they are things of a kind (*toiade*) and share in what is common.
Hence, if surveying is not about sensible magnitudes either,   200,1
geometry could not differ from surveying by virtue of being about
intelligibles; for surveying is also about such things. By the same
reasoning, medicine is not about sensible health either; for [if it
were], then, when the things which it is about perished, it would
perish along with them.
   Next Aristotle proves that astronomy does not speak about   5
sensibles either, for example, about this heaven and these stars.[191]
[He argues this separately] because these are imperishable; and one
can no longer prove that the science that is said to be about them, in
this case astronomy, is not about them, on the ground that when
they perish they do not do away with it as well.[192] On the contrary,

---

[187] viz. of why the Platonists take geometry to be a science of intermediates, but do
not extend this to other sciences and to the arts.
[188] Word for word, 'this something'.
[189] i.e. the sensible objects of this world. See n. 180 above.
[190] The Greek is *oude peri toutôn oude peri tauta*. If Alexander sees an important
difference between *peri* with the genitive and *peri* with the accusative in 199,33-4, he
does not explain it.
[191] i.e. the sensible heaven and stars which we observe.
[192] Alexander's point is that the argument that worked in the case of surveying
('science *x* cannot be about object *y*, because, when *y* perishes, it does not do away with

the essence (*ousia*) of these things[193] is proven in another way and on
10   other grounds. It is not possible to assume sensible lines such as those
which the astronomer uses in his proofs; for no sensible thing is so
perfectly straight <'such as the geometer says that they are'
[998a1]>[194] (instead of 'the astronomer' Aristotle says 'the geometer'). On the contrary, the astronomer uses, for his astronomical
proofs, lines which are such as the geometer says lines are. Likewise
no sensible thing is curved or spherical in the way the geometer
15   defines these. For example, the sensible circle touches the sensible
ruler and the sensible plane not just at a point (*kata stigmên*), while
mathematicians and astronomers speak of the circle and the sphere
in this way, i.e. as touching the plane at a point (*kata sêmeion*).

(So Protagoras thought that by appealing to sensibles he was
refuting the geometers, showing them to be in error, proving that
20   none of these things is such as they say it is; he himself did not realise
that their discussion is not concerned with sensible things – nor is it
in the case of any other artisan.)

Nor are the motions of [bodies] in the heaven, nor even the motions
of the heaven itself, some of which occur in a circular manner and
others in the form of spirals, such as the astronomer assumes them to
be. For the astronomer assumes lines, the spiral and the circle, which
25   are lengths without breadth, and posits that motions occur in accord
with these; but among sensible things there is no length without
breadth. Further, they assume that the stars are certain points, and
have the status (*logos*) of points in the heaven; but a point is
something which has no parts, and none of the stars is such a thing.

But if no craft is about the sensibles, the difference between the
30   crafts and the mathematical sciences could not be that the former are
about sensible substances while the latter are about certain intelligible substances. Instead of proving this Aristotle goes on to say:

---

x') does not work for astronomy. It does not work because the condition is never
realised – because the objects of astronomy cannot perish. I take the initial *kai gar* as
elliptical and supply the bracketed material in the light of this overall interpretation.
Hayduck proposes *kai gar ei* or *kan gar*, making the clause the protasis of a condition.
Assuming the apodosis begins at *kai mêketi*, the sentence would run 'For if these are
imperishable, then one can no longer prove ....'

[193] i.e. the truth about these things.

[194] Supplying *hoias legei ho geometrês* from *Metaph.* 998a1. This supplement is
required if the following explanation is to have anything to explain. The passage from
neuter singular *euthu*, 'straight' to feminine plural *hoias*, 'such as', is rough, but
understandable in a sentence incorporating a citation of Aristotle's own words.

[The case against intermediates present in sensibles]

> **998a7** There are some who say that these things which are said to be intermediate between Forms and sensibles do exist, only not separately from the sensibles.

Having replied to those who say that the mathematicals are 35 substances in their own right, separated from the Ideas and from the sensibles, Aristotle now proceeds against those who say that the mathematicals exist according to a certain proper nature, only not themselves outside of the sensibles, but rather present in them.

This view would differ from the view which says that the 201,1 mathematicals are assumed and thought of by way of abstraction (Aristotle's own view), inasmuch as those thinkers, while assigning the mathematicals a certain proper nature, different from and distinct from the sensibles, say that they are present *in* the sensibles, not as belonging to them,[195] but as being present *in* them while being different *from* them. Whereas those who assume them 5 [the mathematicals] by way of abstraction, who separate some [attributes] of the sensibles by reason (*logos*), leave them [the sensibles], including the [attributes] separated, all in every respect sensible,[196] since those separated [attributes] are not capable, on their own, of making up a complete sensible nature, not even if they are thought of as having some extension (*diastasis*). For the extension that is thought of in the case of the mathematicals, together with the affective attributes (*pathêtika*)[197] separated by reason, *is* the sensible nature. For the sensible nature is naturally in 10 existence (*hupostasis*) in both of these.

Aristotle says that this view[198] is much more absurd than the view which says that they [the mathematicals] are separated. While he declines for the moment to list the majority of the absurdities that follow on this opinion, he does mention [i] that by the same reasoning the Ideas too could be posited as present in the sensibles. For if they [the mathematicals], being intelligible substances in 15 their own right, are present in sensibles, then why in the world

---

[195] i.e. not as being among their attributes. Or perhaps 'not as being among them', i.e. not being themselves sensible. Alexander's point is the distinction between the objects of Aristotelian mathematics, which are tied by their nature to sensible things, and mathematical intermediates, which reside in sensible things but are of a quite different nature from sensible things and their sensible attributes. The Aristotelian mathematician thinks about sensibles in a certain way, but is still thinking about sensibles.

[196] Hayduck follows LF and prints *panta ta kata ta hola aisthêta*. He notes that A omits *ta* after *kata*. I delete *ta* after *panta*: *panta kata ta hola aisthêta*. I take *panta ta* as a dittography; but might it be a corruption of *pantote* 'in all cases'?

[197] i.e. qualities capable of giving rise to sensation.

[198] viz. that mathematicals are present in sensibles.

should not the Ideas, which are also certain intelligible substances, be present in the sensibles? Some account (*logos*) is required of why the mathematicals should be present in sensibles while the Ideas are not.

That many [absurdities] follow from this view,[199] Aristotle has shown in the second book <of *On Ideas*>;[200] he has also mentioned
20   it in the first book, Alpha Meizon, in his discussion of the view of Eudoxus [*Metaph*. 1.9, 991a13-19]; and he will speak of it in *Metaphysics* Nu as well [*Metaph*. 14.3, 1090a20-1090b5].

[ii] Further, there will be two solids in the same place: the mathematical solid (for there is also a mathematical solid, with which stereometry is concerned) and the sensible solid, if the former is to be present in the latter. For there will be, in this manner, a body going right through a body,[201] if each of the two exists according to its proper nature and the one is present in the other.
25   [iii] Further, the mathematicals will not be immovable either, given that they are present in the sensibles. For when these [the sensibles] are in motion, it is necessary that the things present in them be in motion as well: in motion not as accidents, but as things which are themselves present in a place; for if they are magnitudes and have extension, they will be in motion in like manner as those bodies which are moved by force (*bia*) and under some [external] influence, and not according to the internal inclination (*rhopê*) that is in them.

[iv] In general, for what reason must one say that they exist but
30   that they exist in sensibles? For they do not appear to furnish anything necessary for the sensibles, given that they do not exist in their own right.[202]

---

[199] Whose view is it? Aristotle does not say, and up to this point Alexander gives no indication. The reference to *Metaph*. 1.9 and (if I am right in seeing it here) the reference to *On Ideas* 2 suggest Eudoxus; but *Metaph*. 1.9, 991a13-19 is concerned not with intermediates in sensibles but with Forms in sensibles; cf. Ross, *Aristotle's Metaphysics* I.232-3. *Metaph*. 14.3 speaks of the Pythagoreans as holding that mathematicals are present in sensibles. *Metaph*. 13.1, 1076a32-5 mentions the view that mathematicals are present in sensibles, but with no indication of its origin.

[200] As Alexander's text stands, it seems to refer to the second book of the *Metaphysics*. But Hayduck, somewhat exceptionally, gives no specific reference to a relevant passage, and I cannot find any. At 98,21-2 Alexander, commenting on *Metaph*. 1.9, 991a18-19, speaks of a listing of absurdities in the second book of *On Ideas*. Hence I supply <*peri ideôn*>. But as noted above *Metaph*. 1.9, 991a13-19 is concerned not with intermediates but with Forms.

[201] In Greek: *sôma dia sômatos*. Alexander characterises the absurdity in the vocabulary of the Stoic total mixture.

[202] At 201,15, explaining argument [i], Alexander spoke of mathematicals present in sensibles as *ousiai kath' hautas*. Here, explaining argument [iv] he speaks of them as *mê kath' hauta*. At 201,34, explaining argument [v], he speaks of them as *ou kath' hautous*. The characterisation of mathematicals as existing in their own right and/or not existing in their own right is not in the text of Aristotle. It is the work of Alexander, who fits Aristotle's arguments into a dilemmatic structure: if

[v] But in addition to the absurdities already mentioned, all those which followed for those who made the mathematicals separate will follow for these [thinkers] as well. For on their view too there will be another heaven distinct from the sensible heaven, and in like manner a sun and each of the stars, only they will not exist in their own right, but will be present *in* these very sensibles: sun in sun, 35 moon in moon, heaven in heaven; and in addition to that absurdity they [the mathematicals present in sensibles] have incurred this as well, that of having two bodies in the same place.

CHAPTER 3

[Aporia 6]

Concerning all these matters already mentioned, then, Aristotle 202,1 says that the aporia is not a matter of chance, what position to take in order to hit on the truth. Likewise concerning the matters he now proposes.

998a20 And concerning the principles, which must one take as elements (*stoikheia*) or [rather]²⁰³ principles (*arkhai*): the 5 kinds (*genê*),²⁰⁴ or rather those constituents (*enuparkhonta*) of which each thing primarily²⁰⁵ exists?

[The case for constituents as principles]

Concerning this aporia too Aristotle has already spoken in his initial presentation of the aporiae. It is, whether one must posit that the kinds, the common factors (*koina*),²⁰⁶ are the principles and primary

---

mathematicals exist in their own right, absurdities follow; if mathematicals do not exist in their own right, absurdities also follow.

²⁰³ The *kai* is corrective. In Aristotle, and in Alexander's exposition, there is no doubt that constituents are elements; the issue is whether these constituents or elements are the principles of things; cf. below 202,8-9 and 25-6.

²⁰⁴ The Greek *genos* is here translated 'kind' rather than 'genus' because, as used in the initial formulation of this aporia, it includes all kinds, *infimae species* as well as higher genera. To maintain consistency I have retained 'kind' throughout aporia 6, even though *genos* is opposed to difference at 203,3-11 and to species at 203,14-23. In aporia 7 Alexander's usage shifts as the distinction between *infimae species* and higher genera becomes important.

²⁰⁵ Reading the adverb *prôton*, the reading of A²LF, printed by Hayduck. The MSS of *Metaph.* are divided between *prôton* and the neuter plural *prôtôn*; both Ross and Jaeger print *prôtôn*; Ross translates 'primary constituents'. Alexander's paraphrase *ex hôn ... prôtôn* at 202,9 indicates that he understood the expression as neuter plural. I am assuming that Alexander's MS of *Metaph.* read the adverb *prôton* and that he interpreted it as though it were neuter plural; but it is possible that his MS read the neuter plural *prôtôn*, and that the lemma was later influenced by a MS or MSS reading *prôton*.

²⁰⁶ The *koinon* is a universal, understood as common to a plurality of things. I have

among beings, *or* the elements, the primary things out of which
10　beings have come into existence, the ultimate things into which they
are dissolved. Wishing to indicate these things, he shows [them] in
the case of sounds. Sounds are composed of elements,[207] not of sound
in general,[208] which would be the kind of sounds. But in the case of
geometrical propositions (*diagrammata*)[209] as well, it is not the
common factor that is the [basic] element, but rather the
constituents in demonstrations, <which>[210] we use for the
15　demonstration of every theorem, as we speak of the *Elements* of
Euclid. For the reason why such things are called elements, is that
the things through which these are demonstrated are useful to us
for the proofs of all theorems, being present as constituents in all
things. And among these things the primary are the elements of the
secondary, for we use the demonstrations of the primary in order to
prove the secondary.[211]
20　　　Aristotle mentions those of the natural philosophers who assumed
several primary bodies, or one, and shows that they too thought that
the things which they said were the principles of beings were
present as constituents in other things and that those things were
derived from them. Empedocles, for example, who assumed the four
bodies as elements of beings, did not call them principles as being
kinds but rather as being constituents of the things whose coming
into being derives from them. Likewise each of the other natural
25　philosophers who assumed that the principle was of the nature of a
body.
　　　In addition, Aristotle shows from the case of artifacts as well that
[that which is] as constituent and element is the principle, not the
kind. For example, those who wish to see, about a bed or any such
thing, what its nature is, obtain this knowledge from the parts out of
which the thing has come into existence; for it is by knowledge of the
30　principles that that which is derived from the principles comes to be

---

adopted the translation 'common factor' in preference to 'the common' or 'common
thing'.
　[207] At this point LF offer a longer text, regarded by Hayduck as possibly correct: '...
and have as principles the things out of which they are composed ....'
　[208] The Greek is *tês koinês phônês*, literally, 'common sound'.
　[209] cf. Ross, *Aristotle's Metaphysics* I.234 on 998a25 concerning *diagrammata* as
propositions rather than as figures.
　[210] viz. the constituents. I accept Bonitz' suggestion to add <*hois*> to provide a
dative for the verb *khrômetha*.
　[211] One might have expected Alexander to explain as follows: a treatise that proves
the basic theorems of geometry is termed *Elements* because we use these basic
theorems to prove more advanced theorems. What he says is more complicated: the
basic theorems in geometry are termed *Elements* because the things we use to prove
the basic theorems are also the things we use to prove the more advanced theorems.
The steps in the proofs of the basic theorems are thought of as reappearing in the
proofs of the more advanced theorems.

known, and each of these things becomes known when it becomes evident what things it is composed of and what the manner of its composition is; hence these are the principles of these things.

[The case for kinds as principles]

Having argued and shown by induction (*epagôgê*) that the constituents are principles, not the common factors or the kinds, Aristotle next argues in turn that it will seem reasonable to say that the kinds are principles.

998b4 But insofar[212] as we know each thing by way of   203,1
definitions, and the kinds are the principles of definitions ...

The argument is in effect as follows. The things from which we know each thing are the principles of those things (for it is posited that it is from knowledge of the causes and elements of certain things, their   5
principles, that knowledge of the things themselves derives). But it is from definitions that we know each being. Hence the definitions are principles. <But the kinds in turn are principles of the definitions themselves>,[213] for the grasp (*lêpsis*) of the kind is the principle of the definitions.

Differences (*diaphorai*) can also be spoken of as kinds, as Aristotle has said in the *Topics* [*Top.* 1.4, 101b18] so that the meaning would be: the kinds (kinds in the sense of kind[214] and differences) are the principles of definitions, for it is of these that definitions are   10
composed). Therefore the kinds are principles; for definitions are [principles] of things defined, and kinds are [principles] of definitions.

998b6 And if to get science of species (*eidê*) is to get science[215]
of beings ...

The argument is as follows. Science and knowledge of beings come   15
about in terms of their species (for there is no science of particulars), and indeed their definitions are in terms of their species. But if knowledge of beings depends on knowledge of species, the species would be principles of the particulars – the species in terms of which

---

[212] Hayduck prints *hêi* and indicates no dissent in the MSS of Alexander. In their texts of *Metaph.* Ross and Jaeger print *ei*, 'if', but they report *hêi* as the reading of EJ, and Ross notes it as supported by the Latin translation of William of Moerbeke.
[213] Following Hayduck's suggestion to supply <*alla mên palin autôn tôn horismôn ta genê arkhai*> from Asclepius 175,26-7.
[214] i.e. genus.
[215] Ross and Jaeger print the article *tên*, 'the science'.

each group of things have their being as individuals.[216] But the kinds
are principles of the species, for the species result from the division of
the kinds, and the definitions of the species are [stated] in terms of
20   the kinds. Hence the kinds are the principles of all beings.

Or: the knowledge of each thing is in terms of the species (for the
essence (*einai*) of each thing is in terms of these) – not the species
insofar as it is distinguished as being derived from its genus, but the
species insofar as it is distinguished from and opposed to matter; the
one who has grasped species in this latter sense proceeds to species as
derived from genus.

998b9 Even of those who say that the One[217] or Being or the
25   Great and Small are elements of beings, some appear to use
them as kinds.

That it may seem reasonable for the kinds to be the principles of
beings, Aristotle now confirms this view, arguing from those
thinkers who have used the same principles.[218] For those who
assumed the One and Being and the Great and Small as principles
30   of beings assumed these things to be the principles of all beings *as
kinds*. This would be the view of Plato: he assumed the One, which
he said was Being in the proper sense, and the indefinite Dyad,
204,1 which he named Great and Small, as principles. It was as kinds that
he supposed them to be [principles] of beings, because he saw both
One and Inequality predicated of each being.[219] For insofar as each
being is an individual thing (*tode ti*), and is of a kind (*toiouton*)
according to its species, One and Being are predicated of it; but
5   insofar as Plato saw the subject to be in continuous flux (*rhusis*) and
change (*metabolê*), in this respect the Great and Small are
predicated of it. Hence these kinds too are common, and as the
highest kinds they are, on his view, principles.

[Incompatibility of the two views]

998b11 But it is not possible to speak of the principles in both
ways.[220]

---

[216] Or 'their being as these somethings'.

[217] Or Unity.

[218] i.e. the same principles for all things; cf. *Metaph*. 1.6, 987b18-20. At *Metaph*.
1.9, 992b18-993a7 Aristotle criticises the project of searching for the elements
(*stoikheia*) of all things.

[219] Alexander's point is that Plato argued from facts about predicates to claims
about principles, from φ is predicated of *x* to φ is principle of *x*.

[220] Ross and Jaeger print *oude amphoterôs ge hoion te*. The *ge* is not found in
Alexander. I take it that Ross' underlining ('in *both* ways') is meant to render *ge*.

Having argued both for the view that it would be more reasonable for the elements to be principles rather than the kind, and in turn for the view that it is even more reasonable for the kind to be a principle rather than the elements, Aristotle now argues that it is not possible to say that both groups, kinds and elements, are principles of beings. The argument is as follows. He assumes, as proven in the *Posterior Analytics*,[221] that the definition that manifests the essence of each thing is one; for it belongs to each being to be the one thing which it is, and this is what the definition in the proper sense expresses. But the definition is also that which derives from the principles. With these points laid down, Aristotle assumes that both the kinds and the elements are principles of beings, and says that if the definition of each thing derives from its principles, then there will be one definition in terms of the kinds (by 'kinds', as we said [203,7-11], he means differences too), and another definition in terms of the elements. Therefore, if the definition derives from the principles, and there is one definition from the former[222] and another from the latter,[223] there will be more than one definition of the same thing. But there is not more than one definition. For the definition of each thing is one. So both groups are not principles.[224]

10

15

20

[Aporia 7]

998b14 Further, and in addition, if the kinds are principles in the highest degree,[225] which group[226] must we think are the principles, the primary kinds [or the ultimate predicates of indivisibles]?

This aporia too belongs to those already mentioned. It is as follows. Supposing it granted and agreed that the kinds are principles, it is worthy of inquiry, Aristotle says, whether we ought to posit as principles the highest and most common kinds, *or* the ultimate

25

---

[221] Hayduck says that this is found not in the *Posterior Analytics* but at *Top.* 6.4, 141a35.

[222] viz. the kinds.

[223] viz. the elements.

[224] Reading *ouk ara amphotera arkhai*. Hayduck prints *ouk ara amphotera stoikheia*, 'so both groups are not elements', with no report of disagreement in the MSS. But this must be wrong: the thesis, 204,11-12, is that *genê* and *stoikheia* cannot both be *arkhai*, not that *genê* and *stoikheia* cannot both be *stoikheia*.

[225] The lemma in Alexander reads *pros de toutois ei eti kai malista* .... Ross and Jaeger print *pros de toutois ei kai hoti malista*, 'Further, if the kinds ... in the very highest degree ... .'

[226] The lemma reads *potera*, 'which group...?' Ross and Jaeger print *poteron*. Both readings find support in MSS of *Metaph.* At 204,26 Alexander uses *poteron* to paraphrase the passage.

kinds, those closest to particulars, those which he calls indivisible
species (*atoma eidê*). (By 'kinds' Aristotle now means species as
well.)[227]

[The case for highest kinds as principles]

Now if the universals are always principles to a higher degree than
things which are not in like manner universal – on account of its
30   being laid down at the outset that the universal is a principle – then
the highest and most common kinds would be principles. And thus
the highest kinds would be the principles of beings, and the
principles will be as numerous as the primary kinds. Assuming this,
Aristotle adds, 'Therefore One and Being will be principles and
substances; for they, most of all, are said of all things' [998b20-1].[228]
205,1   For if they should be predicated, as kinds, of all beings, they would
be principles and causes of beings (for this[229] is what the word
'substances' [998b21][230] signifies).

[The case against highest kinds as principles]

Having said these things, and having reduced [them] to this
argument (*logos*), that if the most generic and the most common
things are principles, then Being and One will be the principles of
5   all beings, since these are the most common, Aristotle next argues
and proves that One and Being are not kinds of beings, and that if
they are not kinds, it is clear that they are not principles either. But
thus[231] the same principle could not be [the principle] of all things
either, if it were not a common kind of those things – if the kind is a
principle; for it is posited that kinds are principles, and of these the
most common kinds.[232]
   Assuming this[233] as the opinion of certain thinkers, Aristotle

---

[227] i.e. species as well as genera.
[228] Alexander's citation gives a slightly different word order from that in MSS of
Metaph. The citation ends with *kata pantôn*, 'of all'. Most MSS of *Metaph.* extend the
text: *kata pantôn tôn ontôn*, 'of all beings', which Ross prints but Jaeger brackets.
Alexander uses *kata pantôn tôn ontôn* in his paraphrase at 204,34-205,1.
[229] i.e. causes.
[230] I adopt Hayduck's suggestion to read the plural *ousiai* in preference to the
singular *ousia* of the MSS. Alexander is not giving a general explanation of the term
ousia as meaning *aition*; he is not saying that 'substance' means 'cause'. Rather he is
explaining a particular occurrence of *ousiai* at 998b21, and saying that there
Aristotle says 'substances' but means 'causes'. The plural *ousiai* is found in MSS of
Metaph. and in Alexander's citation at 204,33.
[231] i.e. by the reasoning of the argument just mentioned: if (only) kinds are
principles, then something that is not a kind is not a principle.
[232] i.e. that the most common kinds are principles of the less common kinds.
[233] The thesis that Being and One are the principles of all things.

argues in this way against their view; he also spoke about this view a little earlier [998b9-11]. That Being and One are not kinds, then, he proves as follows. Every difference that divides a kind is both a being and a one. Therefore, assuming that One and Being are kinds, their differences will be, each of them, a one and a being. But if Being and One are found in each difference of Being, while Being is a kind and One is a kind, then the kinds would be predicated of their proper differences. But this, he says, is impossible.

For, [speaking] universally, the *species*[234] – that is, the species which belongs to a genus; 'species' is used in many ways, as was said a little earlier [203,14-23][235] – is not predicated of its proper difference, if the difference is taken by itself. For [i] the difference is predicated more extensively than the species (for example, rational and mortal [are predicated] more extensively than man); but it is impossible for that which is said less extensively to be truly predicated of that which is said more extensively. This is why Aristotle said 'of their proper differences' [998b25], meaning the equivalent of 'the differences by which they are constituted as species'.

[ii] Further, the species is a complex entity (*sunamphoteron*), while the difference is a part (*meros*) of the complex entity.[236]

[iii] Further, the difference is a portion (*morion*) of the species, insofar as each of the items included in a definitory formula (*logos*) is a portion of that thing whose essence (*ousia*) it joins in completing, and an anomoeomerous portion;[237] for in a definition, the kind does not mean the same as each of the differences. But such a whole is not predicated of its parts. Therefore the species is not predicated of its proper difference in either way.[238] For the kind does not include the species as parts in this way; for the species are not included in the definitions of the kinds.[239]

But neither are *kinds* predicated of their proper differences, when the differences are considered apart from the species and the species

[234] Literally 'neither the species'; but *oute*, 'neither', is not picked up until *oude* at 205,28, and so I have used the simple negative 'not'.

[235] 203,14-23 does not quite say that *eidos* is said in many ways, but it distinguishes two ways in which *eidos* is said.

[236] The unstated assumption is that the whole is not predicated of the part. If species stands to difference as whole to part, then species is not predicated of difference.

[237] i.e. the nature of the portion is not the same as the nature of the whole.

[238] The first way is if the difference is taken by itself, as in [i]; the second way is if the difference is considered as part of the species, as in [ii] and [iii].

[239] This sentence may be understood as replying to an unstated objection: does not the fact that kinds are predicated of their species indicate that species must be predicated of their differences? The answer is that the two cases are importantly different: kinds are defined without mention of their species, while the definition of a species includes its specific difference.

are not included in them. For example, when animal is predicated of rational, it is predicated of a rational *animal* (on this occasion this is what is meant by rational), whereas it is not predicated of the difference taken by itself without the species, for example, of

206,1 rationality. For differences[240] are certain qualities (*poiotêtes*); how would it be possible to predicate of them animal, which signifies a complex substance?

Hence neither[241] the species nor the kinds are predicated of their differences.

If this is the case, then, if Being and One are kinds, their differences are not beings, nor is each of them a one; that is, no

5 difference is either a one or a being; for they will all be [differences] of Being.[242] But this[243] is absurd. Therefore Being and One are not kinds. But if they are not kinds, then they are not principles, given that kinds are principles.[244]

The statement, 'It is impossible either for the species of the kind to be predicated in the case of their proper differences' [998b24-5] is equivalent in meaning to 'It is impossible either for the things called species to be predicated in the case of their proper differences (*oikeiai diaphorai*), that is, the differences that are exclusively theirs (*idiai diaphorai*)'. The [rest of the statement], 'or for the kind

10 [to be predicated] apart from species' [998b25-6][245] is either equivalent to 'or for the kind to be predicated of something else apart from its own species', or equivalent to 'for the kind to be predicated of its differences, unless the differences are taken as already being species and complex entities'.[246]

The argument appears to me to be rather verbal,[247] as indeed do most of the arguments that Aristotle mentions.[248] For, under

15 whatever kind we range the differences – for they must be from some kind, given that they too are among beings – it is necessary for the proper kind of those differences to be predicated of the

---

[240] i.e. differences taken by themselves.

[241] Accepting Hayduck's mild recommendation to read *oute ara* as at Asclepius 180,8, in preference to MSS *oute gar*, 'for neither'. The sentence states the overall conclusion of 205,15-206,1, not a piece of supporting evidence for the preceding argument.

[242] One might have expected Alexander to say 'of One and of Being'.

[243] viz. that these differences are neither beings nor ones.

[244] One might have expected 'given that principles are kinds'. But Alexander is staying close to Aristotle's wording in 998b28.

[245] Alexander has *aneu tôn eidôn*. Ross and Jaeger print the fuller *aneu tôn autou eidôn*, 'apart from its own species'. Alexander uses the fuller form in his explanation, 206,10.

[246] As in the example at 205,30-1.

[247] *logikôtera*; cf. n. 34.

[248] I am not sure how widely Alexander means this censure to extend; but see 210,20-1, and his concluding remarks at 236,26-9.

differences of that kind. For either it will be a kind but will not have differences, or the differences will be under the kind that they divide. For example, if all differences were under quality, it would be clear that the differences of quality itself would be under quality. And thus the kind would be predicated of its proper differences; for to say that 20 the other differences were qualities, while those of quality were not, but to place them under some other kind, would be contrived and absurd. So one would think that the differences in each kind are present in the same kind, that is, in the same category (*katêgoria*). And indeed, even if the kind that is proximate to particulars is not predicated of the difference, because it[249] is already something complex – something which takes place in the case of substances 25 alone; for from substance there comes also a certain kind of complex substance,[250] which cannot be predicated of the difference which is simply a difference of the kind – still the higher kind, being more common and simpler, *would* be predicated of the difference; for substance is common and [inclusive] of both simple and composed substances. Therefore, even if [the kind] animal should be a composed (*sunthetos*), i.e. a complex (*sunamphoteros*) substance, and on this account is not predicated of its difference taken by itself, still 30 substance will be predicated of it.[251] Now if substance is also predicated of that difference which divides [the kind] animal, then it is *eo ipso* proven that the kind which is divided by the difference is predicated of the difference. But such was the point in question.

But even if this[252] is true in some cases, still it is not impossible for some kind to be predicated of the difference that divides it. For, 35 whatever difference that divides substance is taken, it is necessary 207,1 that this difference be a substance.

The reason why it does not appear that the kinds are predicated, in an exclusive way, of their differences is the equivocal character of words. 'Piercing', for example, applies to colours and to flavours; so which will be predicated of it? But when its own proper kind has been combined with it, it is by that very fact a species.[253]

Having proven that Being and One are not kinds, Aristotle adds in 5 logical order: 'But if they are not kinds, then they will not be principles, if indeed the kinds are principles [998b27-8].'

---

[249] viz. the lowest kind or *infima species*.

[250] 'Complex substance' may suggest that Alexander means an individual such as Socrates. But here Alexander means a lowest kind or *infima species*; he is thinking of genus-difference composition, not of form-matter composition.

[251] i.e. of the difference.

[252] viz. Aristotle's thesis, that genus cannot be predicated of difference.

[253] It is understood that a kind is predicated of its species.

998b28 Further, the intermediates, taken together with their differences, will also be kinds ...

10 What Aristotle says now, he will appear to say, not only with an eye to whether the primary kinds are or are not principles but also in support of the view that the kinds are *not* principles. For [if the kinds are principles], the principles of each being will be infinitely many. For each of the differences present in the indivisible species, combined with the kind of which it is a difference, makes a kind. For each of the kinds intermediate between the primary kind and the indivisible species, combined with its proper difference, makes a

15 kind – even if this does not appear in some cases, because the kind of that thing has not received a name of its own. This is what is meant by 'some appear but others do not appear' [998b30]. Winged animal is a kind, just as animal is, even if it does not appear to have received a name. Or he meant 'some appear, but others do not appear' in the sense that, as he said in the first book of *On Animals* [*PA* 1.3] it is only the privative differences which, when combined

20 with kinds, do not produce species or kinds, for they do not convey [anything] definite either.

And this would be yet another absurd consequence for those who call One and Being a kind and then make species and definitions by dividing the kind into two. For the intermediates, which result from the combination of differences with kinds, must also become kinds and even species; but this does not follow for those who divide the

25 genera into two. Further, they are forced to divide by privation; but a privative difference, combined with a kind, does not make a species. So there are many kinds of the same indivisibles, and many principles, if Being and One are kinds and principles of beings.

In the phrase 'right down to the indivisibles' [998b29], Aristotle would be referring to the ultimate species, for these are no longer divided by differences.

Further, on this reasoning (*logos*),[254] the differences will be

30 principles no less than the kinds, for these too are common and are predicated of a plurality of things. If, then, the differences too are principles, then, because the kinds which are taken together with their differences are also common, the principles will be almost infinitely many – especially if one assumes the highest kind as a principle, for the differences of such a kind are even more numerous.

35 This seems to be unreasonable. And in fact those who posited the kinds as principles posited this at the outset in the belief that by assuming that which was common they were escaping from multiplicity. Aristotle has spoken in this fashion, supposing that it follows, for one who posits the primary kind as a principle, that he

---

[254] i.e. on the assumption that what is predicated is a principle.

also calls the other kinds that come after the primary kind
principles. But even if differences are said more extensively than 208,1
are the species which result from them, still they are not predicated
of them in an essential way (*en tôi ti estin*)[255] nor are they predicated
as kinds.

[The case for lowest kinds as principles]

999a1 But even if the One is more of the nature of a
principle ...

Having first argued that the highest kinds are to a higher degree 5
principles of beings, Aristotle now argues to prove that the species
(*eidê*) are principles to a higher degree than the kinds. For if the One
occupies the place of a principle, that which is to a higher degree one
would be to a higher degree a principle. But the One is undivided
(*adiaireton*). For that which is not divided, or is undivided, is a
principle to a higher degree – given that it is one to a higher degree.
But the species is undivided to a higher degree than the kind.
Therefore it is to a higher degree a principle. 10
    That species is undivided to a higher degree, Aristotle proves as
follows. That which is undivided is such either in respect of form
(*eidos*)[256] or in respect of quantity. Undivided in respect of form is
that which is not further divided to produce a form; such are the
indivisible species (*atoma eidê*). Undivided in respect of quantity is
that which is not divided by number, such as what is one in number
and particular; for each of these things, being one in number, is not
further divided into quantities which are many in number but like 15
it[257] in quality. For by divided 'in respect of quantity' [999a3]
Aristotle means divided 'in respect of number'. Of these undivided
things, the first in order and in nature is that which is undivided in
form [which is prior] <to that which is undivided in respect of
quantity>, while that which is undivided in quantity is prior to that
which is divided in respect of quantity.[258] Having given an account

---

[255] Or perhaps 'in the category of substance'.

[256] At 208,5-10 Alexander used *eidos* in the sense of species or *infima species*. In
208,10-18 he uses *eidos* in the distinct but related sense of form as opposed to
quantity.

[257] viz. the original whole.

[258] Hayduck prints *prôton ... to tôi eidei adiaireton †tou kata to poson
diairoumenou to de tôi posôi adiaireton* and notes corruption. He cites S *quam quod
per quantum, id est, quam individuum quanto*, which suggests that S read, or
understood, something like *tou kata to poson, toutesti tou tôi posôi adiairetou*. One
might perhaps get by with repositioning *de: prôton ... adiaireton, tou de kata to poson
diairoumenou to tôi posôi adiaireton*: 'the first ... is that which is undivided in form,
but that which is undivided in quantity is [prior] to that which is divided in respect of
quantity.' The structure of the sentence would be: A is prior, and B is prior to C. I

of this view, which comes from outside,[259] Aristotle then proves that
while the kinds are divided into species, the ultimate species (*eidê*)
20   are undivided in respect of form (*eidos*), which is why the ultimate
species would be principles to a higher degree: they are one to a
higher degree.

Having said that the kinds are divided into species, then, lest
anyone think he means that the indivisible species too are divided,
the way he has been speaking up until now,[260] Aristotle adds, 'For
man is not the genus of the particular men (*tines*)' [999a5-6] of
whom it is predicated and into whom it is divided. For man is
divided, but not into species (for it is not a kind) but only into
25   individuals (*atoma*), while a kind is divided both in respect of species
and in respect of individuals.

> **999a6** Further, in those cases in which there is[261] a prior and a
> posterior, it is impossible for that which applies to these things
> (*to epi toutôn*)[262] to exist as something distinct from these
> things.

Aristotle makes this argument too in support of the view that the
ultimate genera, that is, the indivisible species, must be termed
principles to a higher degree than the highest and most common
30   kinds. For the kinds that are predicated of the species are not even
anything at all distinct from the species of which they are
predicated. He proves this as follows. In cases where there is a prior
209,1   and a posterior, that which is predicated in common of these, as a
kind, is nothing distinct from the things of which it is predicated.
For example, if in the case of numbers two or three is the first of the
numbers,[263] there does not exist some further nature of number,
distinct from these numbers, two and three and those that follow, of
5   which it is predicated as a kind. Likewise in the case of figures, that

---

suppose, however, that Alexander wrote *prôton ... to tôi eidei adiaireton tou kata to
poson* (sc. *adiairetou*) *tou de kata to poson diairoumenou to tôi posôi adiaireton*, and
translate accordingly. The structure of the sentence would be: A is prior to B and B is
prior to C. Then someone, missing the point, struck out *tou de kata to poson* as
repetitious, setting up the corruption which Hayduck prints. Someone else went
further, striking out *diairoumenou* as well, paving the way for the interpretation we
find in S.

[259] i.e. from outside Aristotle's own position.

[260] Aristotle has been using *genê*, 'kinds', in the broad sense, as including lowest
species. But when he claims that kinds are divided into species, he is thinking of
kinds above the lowest species, not lowest species themselves.

[261] In Alexander *estin* comes right after the relative pronoun; Ross and Jaeger place
it at the end of the relative clause, as does Alexander in his paraphrase, 209,1.

[262] Or 'that which is over these things'. Aristotle means a common predicate such
as 'number' or 'figure'.

[263] Establishing that numbers are a case of prior and posterior.

which is predicated in common of the figures, as figure, is nothing distinct from triangle and square and the remaining figures, since in their case too triangle is first, then square, and the other figures in order.

Aristotle assumes this as being the view of those thinkers as well – the disciples of Plato – for they were the ones who posited the highest kinds as principles of beings, as he has related: One and Being, and the Great and the Small. For in cases where there is a prior and a posterior, they said that the common factor was not something distinct from the things of which it was predicated. This was, at any rate, the reason why they said that there was no Idea of these things either, as Aristotle relates in other places but especially in the first book of the *Nicomachean Ethics* [*EN* 1.6, 1096a17-19]. Assuming, then, as the view of these thinkers, that in these cases the common factor is not anything distinct from the things of which it is predicated (for it is not in the case of numbers or in the case of figures), Aristotle, speaking in his own name, adds that, if in these cases there exists no common factor distinct from the things of which it is predicated, <much less will there be in the case of the other kinds>.264

Either265 this is what Aristotle means, or he is speaking on the supposition that *all* kinds have a prior and a posterior, and that there is no difference266 between the very predicates in question267 and the other kinds, but that both the latter and the former are kinds in like manner.

If, then, in the case of those things which seem to be kinds in the highest degree, the common factor is not anything distinct from the things of which it is predicated, it could not be [distinct] in other cases, even if they do not have a prior and a posterior.

But this was the reason why they268 seemed to the Platonists to be

---

264 Following Hayduck's suggestion to supply the apodosis on the basis of S' *multo minus caeterorum genera*. That would reflect something like *polu hêtton epi tôn allôn genôn* (construction parallel to *epi toutôn*, 209,16), which I translate, or perhaps *polu hêtton ta tôn allôn genê* (closer to S). This suggestion fits the train of thought in 209,20-2.

265 Alexander is distinguishing two possible interpretations of Aristotle's argument. The first, already set forth, takes it as an argument *a fortiori*: if kinds are not distinct in cases of prior and posterior, then they are not distinct in other cases. The second, introduced here, takes it as an argument based on the assumption that *all* kinds are cases of prior and posterior. I suspect that *touto de êtoi* printed by Hayduck has suffered from corruption, as has the preceding phrase. One would expect *êtoi* to introduce the first of a series of disjuncts, but no second interpretation follows. I suspect that Alexander wrote *êtoi de touto ê* ... and translate accordingly.

266 Accepting Hayduck's suggestion *mê ousês tinos diaphoras* in place of MSS *mesês tinos diaphoras*, 'some intermediate difference'.

267 *en te tois autois katêgoroumenois*. Alexander means number, figure, and other obvious cases of priority and posteriority. *Pace* Hayduck, there is no need to suppose that these words are corrupt.

268 viz. the kinds number and figure. Alexander has returned to considering the

kinds and principles, that they thought that numbers and figures
were beings in the highest degree (*malista onta*), things whose kinds
would *be* in the highest degree (*malista einai*). Further, it is clearly

25   apparent that figure is predicated, as a kind, of figures and that
number is predicated, as a kind, of numbers. If, then, the common
factor in these cases is not a principle, then the common factor in the
other cases could not be a principle. For if the common factor, the
kind, is nothing distinct from the species of which it is predicated, it
could not be a principle; on the contrary, the species which are
predicated of individuals (*atoma*)[269] would be principles to a higher
degree. For in the case of individuals, one thing is not prior and

30   another posterior, so that the species which is predicated of these
would appear to be nothing distinct from the individuals. But if in
the case of figures or numbers, figure and number, the common
factors, are not principles – if, on the contrary, triangle [is the
principle of triangles] and two is the principle of the particular twos
– the same would hold in other cases as well, and the indivisible
species would be principles, not the common kinds.

   To what he has said already, Aristotle adds a proof that in all

35   kinds one thing is prior and another posterior.[270] For one mode of
prior is that which is better, as he showed in his division of the term

210,1   'prior' in the *Categories* [*Cat.* 12, 14b3-8]. But in all kinds one of the
species is better while another is inferior.[271] Therefore none of the
kinds is a principle; on the contrary, the indivisible species will be
principles to a higher degree, because of the individuals ranged
under them one is not primary and another posterior.

   In handling this aporia, Aristotle has exploited the equivocal

5   character (*homônumia*) of the word 'primary'. He uses the equivocal
character of 'primary' in order to prove that the kind is nothing
distinct from the things of which it is predicated.

   In the case of animals, at any rate, one is better and another is
inferior. God is something better and for this reason is also
something primary. Man, in turn, is a better animal than the other
animals and is also something primary. In colours, too, white is
better than the others; and in flavours the sweet is better.[272]

10   Having said these things in order to prove that the species, the
ultimate kinds, are principles to a higher degree than the things
which are common and most generic, Aristotle goes on to say, 'From
these considerations, then, it appears that those things which are

---

argument *a fortiori*.
[269] Here *atoma* are individual things, of which the indivisible species are
predicated.
[270] Alexander returns to the second argument to confirm the premise that all kinds
are cases of prior and posterior.
[271] It would be reasonable to insert 210,6-9 at this point.
[272] It would be reasonable to insert 210,6-9 at 210,1.

predicated of the individuals are principles to a higher degree than the kinds' [999a14-16].

[The case against lowest kinds as principles]

Next, in turn, Aristotle argues for the view that the indivisible species cannot be principles. The argument is as follows. The principle and cause of something must be distinct from the object whose principle and cause it is, and must be able to exist apart from   15
that whose cause it is. But nothing can exist in its own right as a separate thing, unless it is particular (*kath' hekaston*). For if someone should say that species exist, because they are predicated universally of the things, i.e. the particulars, under them, and [each species] is different from each of them, and for this reason should say that the species are principles, by this reasoning the kinds higher up will be principles to a higher degree than the species; for   20
they are common to a higher degree than the species and are predicated of more things.

Aristotle has argued this[273] very much on the basis of accepted opinion, and on a verbal level.

CHAPTER 4

[Aporia 8]

999a24 There is an aporia connected with these, the most difficult of all and most necessary to consider, to which the discussion has now turned.

Aristotle says that this is the most difficult aporia, and the most   25
necessary to determine (*diorizein*), to obtain knowledge of the principles, and in general for the proposed treatise. While it depends on the aporiae presented a little earlier concerning kinds and species, it is connected with the preceding aporia,[274] because in the preceding aporia we were inquiring whether, of things common, the more common was a principle to a higher degree, *or* that which was closer to the particular; and also because, when we assumed that   30
the principle had to be separate and subsist (*huphistasthai*) in its own right, we were denying that any of those things[275] was a

---

[273] The Greek is *tauta*, literally 'these things'. Alexander may mean his censure to extend further back than this last argument.

[274] The preceding aporia is aporia 7. The 'aporiae presented a little earlier concerning kinds and species' would seem to be the arguments about kinds as 'principles in aporia 6.

[275] viz. common things, kinds or species.

principle. Now the inquiry is whether this common factor, which we
call kind or species, exists as something distinct from the
particulars and individuals *or* not. Aristotle shows what absurdities
follow if one posits that they do not exist; and if one says that they do
35   exist, Aristotle will tell in turn the difficulties that follow from this
hypothesis [999a29-999b1].

[The case for the distinct existence of non-particulars]

Now if there be nothing in addition to particulars, science will be
211,1   done away with. For particulars are infinite,[276] and it is impossible
for knowledge and science and comprehension (*perilêpsis*) of the
infinite to develop. For knowledge and science of particulars seems
to develop, insofar as some one and the same thing is present in all
of them; for it is predicated of them universally, in common; if
5   this[277] did not exist, then neither could knowledge of these things
develop. But if there is science and knowledge, it will follow, overall,
that there exists, distinct from the particulars, something common,
in terms of which knowledge and science will be constituted
(*sunistasthai*); and this is the kind: either the ultimate kind which is
called species in the proper sense, or the primary kind, which is
kind.[278]

[The case against the distinct existence of non-particulars]

And that none of these things exists, Aristotle says, 'We have just
now worked through the aporia' [999a32],[279] referring us back to
10   what he said while inquiring whether species is a principle. For he
said, 'The principle, the cause, must exist as distinct from the
objects whose principle it is, and be able to exist in separation from
them; but why would anyone suppose something of this sort to exist
as distinct from the particulars?' [999a17-20].[280] But a little earlier
[999a6-12] it appeared to have been proven that that which is
predicated in common of certain things is nothing distinct from the
15   things of which it is predicated. For, having proven that this is
agreed in the case of figures and the case of numbers – because in

---

[276] i.e. infinitely numerous.

[277] viz. the common predicate or common factor.

[278] i.e. *genos*, 'kind', without qualification.

[279] i.e. we have settled the point by working through the aporia. Here *diaporein*
involves not only setting forth the problems but also coming to some sort of
conclusion.

[280] Ending as it does here the citation might appear to be a rhetorical question. In
Aristotle the question continues: 'unless because it is predicated universally and of all
things?' Alexander appears to have that in mind in the comment immediately
following.

them there is a primary and a posterior – Aristotle went on to say that if in these cases there will not exist anything common distinct from the particulars, then it will not exist in other cases either; for if it did exist, it would exist most of all in those cases.

[The case for the distinct existence of non-particulars resumed]

999a32 Further, if there is indeed something distinct from the composite, when something is predicated of matter ...

By composite (*sunolon*) Aristotle means the particular which is 20
sensible, a complex (*sunamphoteron*) of matter and form; this is his more customary way of indicating the particular and the compound (*sunkekhumenon*).

The clause 'when something is predicated of matter' [999a33-4] may indicate the *whole*, the composite. For there is some whole, at the point when something is predicated of matter, that is, when it supervenes on matter; this is the form: for matter becomes a body by 25
taking form. Or he now means by 'matter' the *subject*, which he has called a composite. When something is predicated of the sensibles, which are wholes and are, as items of matter,[281] subjects for what is predicated, it is this[282] which is predicated of them.

What he means is as follows. Even if it be granted that the universal exists, that is, the kinds and species – for these are the things predicated of the substance in the sense of matter, that is, the 30
individual substance (*atomos ousia*) – granted that they exist as distinct from the individuals whose kinds and species they are, do these universals exist as distinct from *all* the individuals (does there exist, in the case of all individuals, whether works of nature or products of art, something common distinct from those things?), *or* does there exist something common distinct from *some* individuals, but nothing common distinct from other individuals? Having mentioned these [alternatives], which follow from the initial hypothesis, Aristotle next adds, '*or* distinct from none' [999b1], which negates the hypothesis; for, if it were found that a common 212,1
factor could not exist as distinct from any of the particulars, <then neither could there exist anything> separate <as distinct from particulars>.[283]

Having added these [alternatives], Aristotle begins with the last (if ... as distinct from none), and shows what absurdities follow, if the common factor is not to exist at all as distinct from any of the

---

[281] *hulai*, literally 'matters'.
[282] viz. form.
[283] Accepting Bonitz' conjectural supplement, on the basis of S: <*oud' an dunaito ti para ta kath' hekasta einai*> *khôriston*.

5   particulars. For there will be no intelligible object. On the contrary, all
beings will be sensible; for such[284] are the wholes, the things composed [of matter and form], and it is posited that there exists nothing
else distinct from these. But if there does not exist something intelligible, neither will there be science of anything; for it is in terms of
common factors, that is, of intelligibles, that the sciences are framed –
unless someone wished to say that sense-perception is science; for [on
that view] all things will be objects of science, and so known, [but] not
according to what is termed science in the proper sense.

10   Aristotle adds that there will be nothing eternal or unmoved, 'for
all the sensibles perish and are in motion' [999b4-5], that is, in flux
(*rhusis*). He is arguing on the basis of accepted opinion, and in line
with the views of those who thought that all sensibles were generated
(*genneta*) and perishable (*phtharta*). Plato, most of all, was of this
view. For even though he supposed that the world would not perish,

15   he still said that it was, in terms of its own nature, perishable.[285] That
it followed,[286] given that the world is generated, that the world would
be perishable, belongs to another view [than Aristotle's]. Aristotle's
view is that all sensibles are in motion, but not that they are all
perishable; for he considers the body that has the property of circular
motion to be completely ungenerated and imperishable. But at
present, as I said,[287] he is arguing on the basis of accepted opinion.[288]
For those who think that all sensible things are material (*enula*)[289]

20   and in continuous flux, also think that they are perishable.

Having assumed that if there is not to be something distinct from
the sensibles nothing will be eternal, Aristotle adds, as a consequence
of this, 'But if nothing is eternal, then neither is it possible for there to
be becoming (*genesis*). For it is necessary for that which [a thing]
becomes to be something, and for that from which it comes to be [to be
something], and of these the ultimate is ungenerated, if, that is, [the
process] comes to a halt, and it is impossible for becoming to take
place (*gignesthai*)[290] from non-being' [999b5-8]. [He says this] to

284 Accepting Bonitz' conjecture of plural *toiauta* for singular *toiouton*.
285 At *Cael.* 1.10 Aristotle ascribes this view, or something close to it, to Plato. J.L.
Stocks, in a note to his Oxford translation of the passage, cites *Timaeus* 31; see also
32c, 38b, and especially 41a-b on the point that the heaven is of its own nature
perishable but guaranteed not to perish.
286 Or perhaps, if we supply the particle *an*, 'it would follow ...'.
287 212,18; 225,2 and 229,14 are the only passages in the commentary on *Metaph*. 3
where Alexander speaks in the first person singular.
288 The passage shows that an *endoxon*, 'accepted opinion', need not be *universally*
accepted.
289 I prefer 'enmattered' to 'material' as a translation for *enulon*, and to reserve
'material' for *hulikon*; but here 'enmattered' might seem to attribute hylomorphism to
the Presocratics or to Plato.
290 The present infinitive *gignesthai* would connote the *process* of coming to be, in a
way that the aorist *genesthai* would not; cf. Aristotle's description of instantaneous

prove that if there is not something eternal, neither will there be 25
becoming; and if there is no becoming (*genesis*), neither will there be
things generated (*genêta*); and if there are no things generated,
neither will there be sensibles. From which it follows that, if only
sensible things exist, then even sensible things will not exist.

That if there is not something eternal neither will there be
becoming, Aristotle proves in the following way. If something comes
to be, it is necessary that there exist something that [it] is coming to
be,[291] that is, that which the thing coming to be[292] is coming to be,[293]
and, different from this, that from which it is coming to be.[294] For 30
example, if a man is coming to be, there must exist, i.e. exist
potentially,[295] both [i] that *which* a man is coming to be (for, if man
were not already in existence, a man could could not come to be)[296] –
so man, which [it] is said to come to be, must exist as something – and
in addition [ii] that *from which* this man comes to be (for everything
that comes to be, comes to be from what is unlike itself; for if it *were* it,
it could not be *becoming* it); this is the subject, matter. Of these 35
subjects from which things that come to be come to be (there are a
number of proximate subjects, for one of the subjects is a proximate 213,1
subject to another), of these subjects, he says, it is necessary that the
ultimate subject be eternal (primary matter is the ultimate subject),
for, when we break down the proximate matters of the things that are
coming to be, we stop at that ultimate matter.

That it is necessary for that ultimate matter to be eternal, Aristotle 5
proves from [the fact] that if there is not some ultimate eternal
subject, from which becoming takes place, it will follow either that
one thing comes to be from another, to infinity, or that there is
becoming from non-being; but both of these are impossible. For if
every subject that is assumed has come into being,[297] it must have

---

events as *genêta … aneu tou gignesthai*, *Metaph.* 5.3, 1027a29-30. Ross, following the
MSS of *Metaph.*, prints *genesthai*. Jaeger prints *gignesthai* with Alexander.

[291] The Greek is present tense, *gignetai*, and might be rendered 'is in process of
coming to be', to underline the progressive force of the present.

[292] The Greek is the present participle *gignomenon*, and might be rendered 'the
thing that is in the process of coming to be'.

[293] The Greek is *ho gignetai to gignomenon*. This is the *terminus ad quem* of
becoming.

[294] viz. the matter which is a *terminus a quo* of becoming.

[295] *kai dunasthai einai*, literally 'and be able to exist'. For this use of *dunasthai*, cf.
216,10. Alexander here interprets the existence of the *termini* of becoming as a
potential rather than an actual existence. 999b5-8, however, speaks of the *termini* as
eternal and ungenerated, and says nothing about potential existence. Cf. 215,18,
proüparkhon pôs.

[296] In the context of this argument, the point of Aristotle's example is not the
obvious one, that every human being has to have a parent, but the less obvious points
that the humanity which one attains must somehow pre-exist one's attainment of it,
and that this pre-existent humanity exists independently of particulars.

[297] The Greek is perfect tense, *gegone*.

come into being either from another subject or from non-being (if it
10 has come into being, but not from a subject). But either way it is
impossible. For it is not possible for becoming to take place from
non-being; for this was the common view of those who said anything
about nature, that nothing comes into being from non-being; and it
is evidently absurd and impossible to say that something comes into
being in this way. But neither is it possible to go straight on to
infinity, with one thing a cause of another and one thing serving as
15 subject for another, as Aristotle proved in the previous book, Alpha
Elatton [*Metaph.* 2.2]. Now if neither of these is possible, then either
there will not be becoming, or the primary subject will be eternal
and ungenerated. So it follows, from the view that nothing is
eternal, that neither is there becoming.

The words 'and of these' [999b7] may be meant not only in
reference to the matter, which is that from which [something] comes
to be, but also in reference to the thing that [it] is coming to be.[298]
For it appears, in things that come to be according to nature, that
20 like comes to be under the agency of like. For example, man begets
man, so that if some man is coming to be, there must [already] be
man: the man producing and begetting. It is necessary in these
cases as well for there to be an eternal productive cause, and
Aristotle himself, after speaking about matter, tries to prove that
the thing that [the thing coming to be][299] is coming to be must be
eternal.

999b8 But further,[300] if there is becoming and if there is
25 motion, it is necessary that there be a limit.

This argument too is directed to showing that there is some
principle of becoming, which is a primary and ungenerated subject,
and that coming to be does not go on to infinity, one thing coming to
be from another.[301]

The argument is in effect as follows. If there exists a limit of every
motion and every becoming, there is a principle of these things.
30 For it is necessary that that which has a limit also has a principle.

---

[298] The Greek is *epi tou ginomenou.* One might at first think to translate 'in
reference to the thing that is coming to be', i.e. as a reference to a particular that is
coming to be. But neither Aristotle nor Alexander supposes that particulars that
come to be are eternal. The point is rather that every instance of becoming requires
an eternally existing *terminus ad quem: touto ho gignetai to gignomenon*; cf. 212,29;
also 215,1-2. The supplement '[it]' is an attempt to put this point across.

[299] I supply, for the reasons outlined in the previous note.

[300] Alexander's lemma reads *eti de kai.* Ross and Jaeger omit *kai.*

[301] Ross, *Aristotle's Metaphysics* I.241, on 999b8-12, points out that the argument is
not another argument to prove that generation has a beginning, but rather an
argument to prove that generation has an end. But Alexander still uses the term
hupokeimenon, 'subject', 213,27; and cf. his summary at 214.11-12.

For if there were no principle – if, on the contrary, becoming or motion went on to infinity – then becoming and motion could not have any end (*telos*). But every becoming and every motion has an end, as Aristotle assumed in the words, 'for neither is any motion infinite' [999b9-10] – a point which has been proven elsewhere,[302] on account of the fact that every motion is from something to something; for that which is increasing has some limit to its increase, and likewise that which is changing in quality, and likewise that which is perishing. But just as there is a limit of every motion, so too there is a limit of becoming. For nothing which is incapable of coming to be comes to be. In fact this too has been proven; for that which is incapable of coming to be does not come to be either. For example, the diagonal[303] *does* not become commensurate with the side, because it *cannot* become commensurate, and cannot reach this as an end. But something cannot come to be which does not have a limit of becoming – something which, on the contrary, goes on to infinity in becoming, so that it does not come to be at all. Hence everything that *is* becoming *can* become; and that which can become can [still] become even if it is becoming.[304] But 'it is necessary that there be a first moment when that which has come to be (*gegonos*) has come to be' [999b11-12]. For when that which has come to be *is*, it has stopped coming to be; this has been proven in *Physics* 6 [*Phys.* 6.5]. But if there is a first moment when it has come to be, then there is a limit of everything that comes to be. It was for the sake of making this point that Aristotle used the expression, 'It is necessary that there be a first moment when that which has come to be has come to be' [999b11-12]. Hence there is also a principle of everything that comes to be and is in motion. But if this is so, becoming does not go on to infinity, one thing coming to be from another. But if that is not the case, there is some ultimate eternal subject.

The argument appears unclear because Aristotle has omitted that [premise] which logically belongs after the [premise] that every movement and becoming has a limit, viz. that things which have a limit also have a principle.[305] Having omitted this, as something

3

214,1

5

10

15

---

[302] Presumably a reference to *Metaph.* 2.2. Cf. *Phys.* 8.8, 261b27-265a12, where Aristotle admits and discusses an infinite circular motion.

[303] i.e. the diagonal of a square. The Greek is *diametros*. Translated 'diameter', it might suggest a circle; but Alexander is thinking of a line drawn from one angle of a square to the opposite angle.

[304] Reading, with Hayduck, *to de dunamenon genesthai k'an genoito*, supplying in thought *dunatai genesthai* from the preceding parallel clause, and taking *k'an genoito* as adversative. Becoming takes time; a *gignomenon* still in process of becoming is capable of further becoming; hence the supplement. Contrast the *gegonos*, which has come to the term of its becoming, and cannot become further.

[305] Alexander's claim is not that this premise follows from the former, but that it is the premise to be supplied to make Aristotle's argument complete; to get from

that obviously followed, he simply proved that there is a limit of every movement and becoming. (Even circular movement has a limit, for it comes to be from the same to the same; and the infinity (*apeiria*) of this movement consists in its becoming the same movement all over again, not in its being a different movement at different times.)

**999b12 Further, if indeed matter exists on account of its being
20   ungenerated,[306] it is much more reasonable that essence
(*ousia*)[307] should exist.**

Having proven that there is some ultimate eternal subject – for this is what he expresses in the words, 'further, if indeed matter exists on account of its being ungenerated' [999b12-13]; for it [would be] impossible for there to be becoming, if there were no such thing. (In fact, if matter went on to infinity, nothing could come to be from
25   matter, because matter would never stop coming to be, one matter coming to be from another, the [one] matter dissolving that which it received from the other,[308] but not coming to be present in it.)[309]

---

premise All A are B (every movement has a limit) to conclusion All A are C (every movement has a principle), supply premise All B are C (everything that has a limit has a principle); All B are C does not follow from All A are B, but it logically 'fits' after it.
306 The Greek is *dia to agenêtos einai*; on this the MSS of *Metaph.*, Alexander and Asclepius are agreed. But it is not clear to me why the MSS give the nominative *agenêtos* rather than the accusative *agenêton*.
307 Or 'substance'.
308 viz. the previous matter.
309 Reading *ekluousês tês hulês ta ek tês allês all' ouk enginomenês* with Hayduck, but departing from Hayduck's view that the passage is corrupt. The context is the step-by-step build-up from simpler or less formed matter to complex or more formed matter. Each subsequent level of matter should come to be present in the previous level of matter, preserving its determinations, but adding others. Alexander's point is that this build-up does not work if new matters go on coming to be to infinity. The breakdown occurs because the infinite coming to be of matters would require each new matter to shed or dissolve (*ekluousês*) the features received from the previous matter, instead of coming to be present in that matter (*ouk enginomenês*), i.e. taking root in it, retaining its features and building on them. In brief: infinite coming to be of matter implies that matter is not retentive of determination. Hayduck seems to depend on a different interpretation, found in S: *excludente materia quae ex alia nondum genita generari debeant*, 'as matter would exclude properties which would have to be generated from other matter, matter not yet generated'. If there were an infinite coming to be of matter, then at any point in the process, matter would be incomplete, because it would lack features that could only come from types of matter not yet generated; as there would always be more types of matter remaining to be generated, matter could never be actually complete, could never have its full complement of features. In brief: infinite coming to be of matter implies that matter never receives full determination. It is not clear how S's 'non-reception' or 'incompleteness' interpretation could be squared with the words *ekluousês ... ouk enginomenês*; if S is correct then Hayduck has reason to consider these words corrupt. But on the 'non-retention' view sketched above there is no need to regard these words

Having proven, then,[310] that the primary subject must be ungenerated, and that becoming (*gignesthai*) does not go on to infinity, one thing coming to be from another, Aristotle now proves that the form, which comes to be in the matter, must be eternal as well, thereby proving and establishing that there will be some unitary eternal essence (*ousia*).[311] For if there is a nature of matter,[312] then it is more reasonable for the essence to be this   30 nature which the matter receives. This is what Aristotle expresses by saying, 'whatever that matter comes to be' [999b14]. By essence (*ousia*) [999b14] he means the form (*eidos*). For that according to which each thing has being, is essence. For matter, having received form, presents that which comes to be[313] from it as having come to   215,1 be,[314] that is, as that which it receives and which it becomes.

That it is reasonable, then, for the form too which the matter receives to pre-exist, being eternal, Aristotle proves as follows. Just as it was impossible for anything to come to be if the subject did not exist, so too it would be impossible for there to be becoming (*genesis*),   5 if that which the subject receives did not exist. Aristotle says this in the words, 'for if neither the latter nor the former[315] is to exist, nothing at all will exist' [999b14-15], which is equivalent to, 'for if *both* did not exist, the matter and the form, both eternal, nothing at all could come to be'. Aristotle expresses that this is what he means, saying, 'It is necessary that there exist something distinct from the composite: the shape, the form' [999b16], meaning by the composite (*sunolon*) that which has come to be, which is complex   10 (*sunamphoteron*) and sensible. Saying that *each* of the two must exist, the two from which the composite must exist (the matter, and the shape or form, as we said; for he says, 'If neither the latter nor the former' – meaning the form and the matter – 'is to exist, nothing

---

as corrupt.

[310] MSS ALM give a longer version: *eti eiper hê hulê esti dia to agenêtos einai, deixas hoti*, 'further, if indeed matter exists on account of its being ungenerated, having proven that ...'. This is mainly an unnecessary repetition of 999b12-13, already cited at 214,22; but *eti*, 'further', suggests the beginning of a new argument; and the relation of this protasis to the rest of the sentence is awkward. I follow Hayduck in accepting the shorter *deixas oun hoti* on the basis of S, with Brandis and Bonitz. The phrase resumes the exposition begun at 214,21 but interrupted by the long parenthesis.

[311] Or perhaps 'substance'. I favour 'essence' here in the light of the explanation at 214,32.

[312] i.e. if matter, itself without determinate nature, comes to have determinate nature.

[313] *gignomenon*, present participle, indicating that which is in the process of coming to be.

[314] *gegonos*, perfect participle, indicating that which has come to be; cf. 215,9.

[315] In Alexander's citation 'the former' is neuter, *ekeino*. At 999b15 Ross and Jaeger print the feminine, *ekeinê*. Citing this text again at 215,12 Alexander uses the feminine.

at all will exist' [999b14-15]), Aristotle continues, 'but if this is
impossible' [999b15], that is, if it is impossible for nothing to exist, 'it
is necessary that there exist, distinct from the composite' [999b16]³¹⁶

15   – that is, from that which is composed, which is form in matter – 'the
shape, the form' [999b16]. He rightly assumes that, as matter [exists
as eternal], there must also exist some eternal form – not that the
form which comes to be in the matter must be this;³¹⁷ it is rather the
productive form which, if it is like the form that is produced, would be
in some manner pre-existent.³¹⁸

[The case against the distinct existence of non-particulars resumed]

Assuming from the argument the [conclusion] that the form, like the
matter, must pre-exist, in order for the composite composed of both to

20   come to be from them as pre-existent, Aristotle raises a further
aporia, which he proposed to face when he began this aporia, when he
said, 'whether, if there is [anything distinct from particulars], it must
be distinct from *all* things' [999a34].³¹⁹ For if one posits that the form
which comes to be in matter pre-exists and is eternal, in the case of
which beings and things which come to be will he say that the form

25   pre-exists as eternal, and in which cases not? For it is not possible to
say this in the case of *all* things that come to be. Aristotle mentions
the things that come to be by way of art, about which it is absurd to
say that the form which, under the agency of the artisan, comes to be
present in matter, pre-exists and is eternal. These remarks may also
be meant, and raised as an aporia, in reference to the Ideas, but they
may simply be meant in reference to the enmattered form, in logical
continuity with the aporia.³²⁰

---

³¹⁶ Here Alexander omits *ti*, 'something', found in MSS of *Metaph.* and in his own
citation at 215,8 above.

³¹⁷ viz. the form in question.

³¹⁸ As Alexander sees it, Aristotle maintains the pre-existence of form in the parent
or agent, not the pre-existence of a form which later comes to be in the offspring or
product. Alexander judges the success of the argument in the light of Aristotle's
actual views about generation and form. In a dialectical work such as *Metaph.* 3,
however, Aristotle sometimes argues, on the level of plausibility, for a conclusion at
variance with his own position.

³¹⁹ i.e. supposing that there exist some things distinct from particulars, the
question arises whether this is true in all cases, whether it is necessary to posit
non-particular existents corresponding to each and every kind of particulars; cf.
above 211,28-212,2.

³²⁰ i.e. with the present aporia as it has developed to this point, with reference to
matter and form as necessary conditions for coming to be, but without any reference
to the Ideas.

999b20 In addition to these points, whether there is to be one   30
essence (*ousia*)[321] of all things, for example, of men; for are not
all things whose essence is one one thing?[322]

Aristotle deals with this aporia too, in addition to the preceding:
whether – given that the forms too, like matter, pre-exist – there is
numerically one form and numerically one essence for all men, *or
many*, as many as there are particular men. For, if one posits that   35
there is numerically one form, then there will come to be, from the
matter that receives that form, one man. But if there are as many   216,1
forms as there are particular men, that is unreasonable; for how will
those forms of man, taken in separation from matter, differ from one
another? For the differences between particular men are material.[323]

Aristotle raises further aporiae: how matter receives these forms,
already pre-existing and existing in some way or other;[324] and how   5
each of the sensibles (which are wholes, composed of both these
factors) comes to be and is: are these factors combined, or blended,
or mixed? Or what is the manner in which the matter, by receiving
the forms, becomes the things that it becomes? He has also dealt
with these aporiae elsewhere, inquiring what it is that unifies and
holds together the form in matter; there he says that it is the
potential character of matter[325] which becomes the cause of
[matter's] grasping form and [of the form's] remaining in matter   10

[321] Or 'substance'.

[322] Reading *ou gar hen hapanta hôn hê ousia mia* with Hayduck but punctuating
the phrase as a question. Translated as indicative, the text yields the startling 'for not
all things whose essence is one are one thing'. Ross and Jaeger print *all' atopon· hen
gar panta hôn hê ousia mia*, the directly opposite sense, 'but this is absurd; for all
things whose essence is one are one'. As Hayduck's and Ross's apparatus reveal, the
majority of MSS of *Metaph.* give the same reading as Alexander's lemma. It is
possible that Alexander's lemma has suffered contamination; but it is not necessary. I
suspect that Aristotle originally wrote *ou gar hen hapanta hôn hê ousia mia* as a
question, that Alexander's MS of Aristotle read these words, and that Alexander
understood them as a rhetorical question, and so I translate. Other readers, I suspect,
understood Aristotle's words as a statement and adopted countermeasures, such as
deleting the negative *ou* and relocating *gar*.

[323] *hulikai*, i.e. due to matter.

[324] Reading, on Hayduck's suggestion in his apparatus *ta proüparkhonta êdê kai
hopôsoun onta eidê*. In his text Hayduck prints *ta proüparkhonta †eidê ê hopôsoun ta
eidê*, noting corruption. This would yield 'pre-existing or forms however they exist',
taking *ê hopôsoun* as opening an *alternative* to the pre-existence of forms. But the
aporia, how to get form and matter together, is acute precisely on the assumption
that form *does* pre-exist its involvement with matter. Hayduck's suggestion takes *kai
hopôsoun* as leaving open the exact *mode* of pre-existence. This leaves the aporia
intact. Hayduck reports MSS A¹LMF as reading *ta eidê holôs oun ta eidê*, which
would yield something like 'so the forms in general'. I miss the point of this; Hayduck
reports A² as deleting it.

[325] The Greek is *to dunamei* [sc. *einai*] *tês hulês*. I have not found a perfect match
with any text in Aristotle. Cf. *GC* 1.3, 317b13-33, 319b3-5; 1.4, 320a2-7. See also the
remark of H. Bonitz, *Index Aristotelicus*, s.v. *hulê* 3, 785a46: '*hulê idem est ac
dunamis*' as well as the following references.

while matter is changing[326] into that which, up to that point, it has been potentially;[327] and clearly this takes place with some pre-existing productive cause.

[Aporia 9]

999b24 Further, one might also raise this [328] aporia concerning the principles: for if they are one in form ...

15 This aporia logically follows on the earlier aporia: whether the form (*eidos*) is numerically one or more than one. But it may also have reference to the Ideas, because Aristotle mentions One Itself and Being Itself. Or the aporia could be about the principles in general, for the principles are beings in the proper sense; that is why he adds the 'Itself' to them.[329] So, if the aporia is a general one, it may also have an application to the things that are called subjects.

The aporia Aristotle faces concerning the principles is whether
20 each of them – whether one supposes the principles to be one or more than one – whether they have[330] unity [only][331] according to form (*eidos*)[332] or numerically. For example, if matter is one, is it one

---

[326] Reading *kai menein en autêi eis touto metaballousêi*, and understanding *to eidos* as subject of infinitive *menein*. Hayduck reports the MSS as reading *kai menein en autêi eis touto metaballousan*. But then dative *autêi* and accusative *metaballousan* both seem to refer to matter. Hayduck emends *en autêi*, 'in it', to *en hautêi*, 'in itself'. That would yield 'and of matter's remaining in itself while changing...'. But the point is not that matter remains in itself; and potentiality would not explain how matter remained in itself. The point is rather the receptivity of matter to form; potentiality is invoked to explain the fact that form remains in matter. The remedy is to understand *to eidos* as subject of *menein*, to retain *autêi* with the MSS, and to emend accusative *metaballousan* to dative *metaballousêi* to agree with *autêi*. This is what I translate.

[327] *edunato*, literally, 'was able', 'was capable'. For this use of *dunasthai*, cf. 212,30.

[328] *touto aporêseien*; Ross and Jaeger print *tode aporêseien*.

[329] The use of *auto* as prefix or suffix originates with Plato. But unnamed 'he' in Alexander is generally Aristotle, and Aristotle does use the *auto* terminology in 999b26. Alexander's point is that *autoen*, 'One Itself', *autoon*, 'Being Itself', may be taken as Platonic references, but that they may also be taken more generally, *koinôs*, because Aristotle may be using the *auto* prefix to designate, not Forms in particular, but principles in general.

[330] The original subject is singular, but the parenthetical remark is followed by a plural verb.

[331] In aporia 9 to be one in form is to be one *merely* in form, as opposed to being one in number.

[332] Taken by itself *eidos* may be translated 'kind', 'species', or 'form'. Ross uses 'kind' in his translation of this aporia, but I have used 'kind' to translate *genos* in aporiae 6 and 7 above. 'Species' is tempting, but in 216,36-217,11 it becomes clear that the aporia concerns the generic level as well as the specific level. Alexander's usage at 217,15-16 ('things cannot be one even in *eidos* unless they have some common *eidos* which is numerically one'), and a desire to translate *eidos* so far as possible in one way throughout this aporia, lead me to favour 'form'.

in number or in form? And if form is one, is it so in number or in form?

[The case against principles as one merely in form]

Now if each of the principles is one in form but many in number, there will be, Aristotle says, nothing numerically one among the principles of things that come to be. But if none of the principles is numerically one, then neither could any of the things composed out 25 of the principles be numerically one. For things composed out of that which is one not in number but [only] in form, are one in form, not in number. For if things composed out of what is numerically one are one in number, it is clear that the things which derive their existence from [something which is] one in form will possess unity in like manner as those things[333] do.[334]

Aristotle adds an absurdity that follows from this: that neither One Itself nor Being Itself – the very things which those who said 30 the Ideas were principles placed among the principles – will be numerically one. But if One Itself is not numerically one, while all things are one by participation (*metousia*) in this One, then none of the other things, which have their existence by relation to it, could be numerically one; for, being assimilated to that which is one in form, they themselves would possess unity in like manner. So there will be nothing that is numerically one, if not [any] of the things that come to be in relation to something is numerically one, nor the One 35 Itself, the principle, nor any other of the principles either.

Aristotle adds to this that there will be no science either, if there 217,1 is not something which is numerically one. For the sciences come about by one thing's being taken as over (*epi*) many things, as he said shortly before [999a26-9].[335] For the sciences are framed in terms of what is common, and what is common is proven to be numerically one. For what is common – the species (*eidos*) which 5 applies to those things, or the kind (*genos*) – will not be one [only] in form (*eidos*)[336] or kind (*genos*),[337] in the way that the things under what is common are one with each other, in form or in kind;[338] for that way things will go on to infinity. For example, if animal is to be

---

[333] viz. those things which are one in form. But the plural *ekeinois* is unexpected and should perhaps be changed to the singular *ekeinôi*, 'that thing', with *henos* as antecedent; cf. 216,34.

[334] i.e. will have the real but limited unity possessed by a group of things which are one with one another in form but not numerically one.

[335] Aristotle's earlier argument spoke of an object of science as distinct from (*para*) particulars, not as over (*epi*) them.

[336] i.e. in specific form.

[337] i.e. in generic form.

[338] i.e. it will be numerically one instead.

one, possessing its unity according to the common form, those [factors] too[339] according to which animals are one will, if they are one [only] according to form, be in like manner numerically many, and thus things will go on to infinity.[340] But [in fact] each of the things

10 that are common is numerically one. But if the sciences have these things as objects, things which are numerically one, and if nothing is numerically one, [i.e.] if the principles possess their unity [only] in form, then science would be done away with.

For if someone says that that which is over the principles is numerically one – since it has been supposed that [the principles are] one according to form – he would be saying that the principles no longer possess unity [only] in form. For that form, which is one in

15 number, is a principle to a higher degree than the things under it, and it is no longer one in form but rather one in number.[341]

Further, things cannot be one even in form unless they have some common form which is numerically one. For if things which are numerically many have community (*koinônia*) with one another according to something which is not numerically one,[342] these things could no longer be the same [even] in form.

One can understand the words, 'And how will there be scientific

20 knowledge, if there is not to be some one over all?' [999b26-7] as directed to those who posited the Ideas. For they said that the only way there would be science was if the Ideas existed; for the sensibles are infinitely many and in continuous flux, and for this reason are not objects of science either;[343] but distinct from sensibles and particulars there is the Idea, which, being one in number and taken as over

25 many, becomes the immovable and eternal cause of science. But this

---

[339] viz. the relevant generic forms.

[340] The members of the genus animal are one with one another in generic form, but this generic form must itself be numerically one, not merely generically one. If this form were only generically one, its generic unity would be due to some further generic form, and so on to infinity. The point is that talk about things as being one in *form* supposes the *numerical* unity of that in virtue of which the things are one in form.

[341] 217,12-15 formulate an objection and a reply. Objection: principles *can* be one merely in form, provided there is something over the principles, and that something is one in number. Reply: the objection is self-cancelling, because the so-called principles are not really such; the one above the 'principles' is the real principle.

[342] Reading *ei ekhei kata ti koinônian allêlois, ho mê esti kat' arithmon hen*, in line with Hayduck's suggestion in his apparatus. Hayduck prints †ekhonta an koinônian allêlois, ha mê esti ta kat' arithmon hen, noting corruption. A more drastic emendation would be *ei mê ekhei kata ti koinônian allêlois, ho esti kat' arithmon hen*, 'if they do not have community with one another according to something which is numerically one'. Presumably this is what Alexander meant; that is not to say that it is what he wrote.

[343] Alexander's interpretation runs together two Platonic arguments. The first: particulars are not objects of science, because they are infinitely many. The second: sensibles are not objects of science, because they are in flux.

view is done away with, if even those Ideas do not possess numerical unity.

[The case against principles as one in number]

999b27 But if [the principles] are one in number and each of the principles is one ...

Having proven what an absurdity follows, if the principles are said to be, each of them, one [only] in form, Aristotle now argues in turn in support of the view that the principles cannot possess numerical unity either. He focuses the argument in turn on the principles which are called elements (*stoikheia*),[344] things from which a 30 product comes to be by combination, as in the case of letters (*stoikheia*); and he proves, in the case of things termed principles in this way, that if each of them is numerically one, beings will be no more numerous than the elements. For, as syllables which are the same as one another according to form turn out to be numerically infinite – because the letters, by combination of which they are produced, can be taken as numerically infinite while being the same 35 in form – so, if the letters are not numerically many, if on the contrary there is numerically one *a* and one *b*, then it is necessary for the combination of these very letters to result in one syllable, and 218,1 it will not be possible, if *b* is one in number, to get hold of any more syllables containing *b* besides the syllable *ba*.[345] For in general, *b*, if it is one being, is no longer present in any other thing besides the syllable *ba*. So, as is the case with syllables and their letters – that[346] if the letters are numerically one, they will not be more 5 numerous [when combined] in syllables, but rather exactly as numerous as they are by themselves – so too, he says, will it be the case with beings, if their principles are one thing, each of them numerically one.

Aristotle has explained what one in number is, that it is the particular, and what the universal is, that it is that which is taken as common, over the particulars, that is, species and genus.

But having said, 'So, just as, if the elements of speech were 10 definite in number, the letters (*grammata*) that are written would also be the same in number as their elements (*stoikheia*)'

---

[344] Taken generically, *stoikheia* are 'elements'; taken specifically, they are 'letters', i.e. letters of the alphabet. The overall thesis of the argument is about elements in general, while the evidence adduced has to do with letters and syllables.

[345] The token *ba*, not merely the type *ba*. There will be exactly as many token letters as there are type letters.

[346] Beginning the parenthesis at *ei hen* rather than at *ou pleiô* as in Hayduck.

[1000a1-3],[347] Aristotle did not express the corresponding [clause][348] 'so it will be in the case of beings and of the number of beings'. (For there will be nothing else distinct from the elements; that is, beings will be no more numerous than elements.) He left this conclusion to
15 be supplied, considering it to be obvious. For if earth and each of the four elements is one in number, and if they are present in some particular body, it is clear that it would be impossible for any other body to be derived from them. The argument is exceedingly verbal and dialectical.

[Aporia 10]

1000a5 An aporia which is no less than any other has been left unresolved both by present day thinkers and by earlier thinkers.

20 This aporia, which, Aristotle says, requires to be straightened out but has been left unresolved by his predecessors, has also been mentioned, like the previous aporiae, in the presentation of the aporiae at the beginning of the book. It is as follows. He inquires whether the principles of perishable (*phtharta*) and of imperishable (*aphtharta*) things are the same. For, if they are the same, what is the cause of the fact that, while all beings derive from the same
25 principles, some beings are perishable and others imperishable? Here Aristotle cites Hesiod and the mythologists of old, who supposed that all things come from the same principles, which are eternal and imperishable, and simply asserted, what seemed plausible to themselves, that[349] some things are imperishable while others are perishable, but neglected us [and failed] to instruct and to persuade us.[350] For, supposing that the principles are eternal and
30 divine, and that all beings derive from them and have come to be from them, they assert that some beings, having tasted ambrosia and nectar, became gods, while those that did not taste are perishable. A first [problem] is that they speak of ambrosia and

---

[347] Alexander's citation ends *ên an kai ta grammata tosauta ta graphomena hosa autôn kai ta stoikheia.* Ross and Jaeger print *anankaion ên an tosauta einai ta panta grammata hôsper ta stoikheia,* 'it would be necessary for all the letters to be just the same in number as the letters'. Alexander's citation lacks *anankaion,* 'necessary', and its infinitive; and it explains *grammata,* 'letters', as *ta graphomena,* 'those which are written', in contrast to the elements of speech mentioned earlier in the sentence.

[348] i.e. the principal clause of the sentence; cf. Ross, *Aristotle's Metaphysics* I.242.

[349] Following Brandis's suggestion, *pithanon einai to ta men ...,* Hayduck prints *pithanon einai tou ta men ...,* 'that which persuaded them of the fact that ...'.

[350] i.e. they recognised the existence of perishables as well as of imperishables, but failed to explain how this diversity was compatible with their exclusive affirmation of imperishable principles.

nectar, divinising fluids[351] perhaps obvious to themselves, but *not* to us or to anyone else. A second problem is that they speak of the very application (*prosphora*) of these things without explanation, in a manner quite unobvious; for why did [the imperishables] come to   219,1 taste of these things that are the causes of their immortality? For if they taste them for the sake of pleasure, then the nectar and the ambrosia contribute nothing to their existence; hence they would not, on account of tasting them, be immortal. But if the tasting of these things contributes to their existence, it is clear that they are   5 nourishment for them; but how is it possible to say that things which are nourished, and would not exist unless nourished, are eternal?

[Critique of Empedocles' system of principles]

Having mentioned these views of Hesiod and the other mythologists (*theologoi*), Aristotle declines to examine their opinions seriously, as they are speaking myths, and pulling together and contriving falsehoods by way of myths. The phrase, 'those speaking subtly in mythic form' [1000a18-19] is equivalent to 'those who do violence   10 to the truth by way of myths'. He proceeds to those who appear to speak about these things with [some use of] demonstration, and says that we must examine and find out from these thinkers the cause (*aitia*)[352] [of why], if all things have come to be from the same principles and elements, some of the things that derive from them are eternal and imperishable, while others are perishable. For, he says, if they do not give some cause of this, and if their view does not have some other aspect of reasonableness to it, then it is clear that   15 the principles of all things could not be the same.

Aristotle says that even Empedocles, who appears to speak the most consistently of all the natural scientists (*phusiologoi*), does not [do this]. For he introduces one element as the cause of becoming (*genesis*) and of existence (*einai*) – for Friendship (*philia*) is such a thing for him – and another as the cause of perishing (*phthora*) – for Strife (*neikos*) is such a thing. Only [this is] not [the whole story];[353] on the contrary, it appears that for him in many cases Strife includes the cause of becoming as well, and Friendship the cause of

[351] The Greek is *namata*. But MSS of *Metaph.* followed by Ross and Jaeger give at 1000a13 *onomata*, 'names' or 'terms'. But nectar is, and ambrosia can be, a fluid; and it is hard to see how names or terms can be *theopoia*, divinising. This latter term is not found in aporia 10, and Bonitz' *Index* cites no instance anywhere in the Aristotelian corpus; one wonders where Alexander picked it up.

[352] Or perhaps 'explanation'; but 'cause' figures several times in the ensuing discussion of Empedocles' theory of elements.

[353] In the Greek this clause is simply *ou mên*; the supplements are my attempts to fill in the ellipsis, in line with what follows.

20   perishing. Aristotle shows how Empedocles, despite seeming to
      speak consistently, does not escape the aporia. For Empedocles
      posits among the principles even Strife, which is, for him, the cause
      of perishing; this is why, on his view, all the things that come to be
      perish (as opposed to some things perishing but not others). This
      statement of his seems to be consistent, that all things that come to
25   be, being from the same principles, likewise all perish, not that some
      perish while others remain and are eternal (he supposes that only
      the elements are imperishable, that is, the four bodies and Strife
      and Friendship). In this way Empedocles seems to leave behind
      some cause of why the things that perish perish, and to speak
      consistently with himself, assigning one cause as cause of becoming
      and another as cause of perishing. But insofar as he says that this
30   very Strife also begets, that is, that it turns out to be a cause of
      becoming and not only of perishing, and as he takes Friendship to be
      a cause of perishing, for it is not [only]354 a cause of becoming –
      for355 it is out of the One (which he calls God and Sphere), which
      came to be under the influence of Friendship, that all the beings, on
      his view, come to be, under the influence of Strife, except God,
      meaning the Sphere, which he also calls One, as is made clear in the
      verses he presented – speaking this way he could no longer speak
35   consistently.356 For he could no longer maintain that one thing is
      the cause of perishing and another thing the cause of becoming – the
      feature which made his view appear reasonable.

220,1   **1000a27 But this too [Strife] would appear to beget no less ...**

      That is, [it would appear to be] generative and productive. To 'For
      from the One come all things, and from this the other things, except
      God' [1000a28-9]357 we must add the things that come to be under

      354 Following the Latin translation S, which gives *non tantum*, 'not only', and in
      line with *ou ... monon* at 219,30, à propos of Strife. Hayduck prints *ou gar geneseôs*
      'for it is not [a cause] of becoming'. But the following lines make it clear that
      Friendship *is* a cause of becoming.
      355 One would expect at this point an explanation of why Friendship is not, or not
      only, a cause of becoming, or of why Friendship is a cause of perishing. As it stands,
      however, the sentence explains that Friendship is a cause of becoming.
      356 Empedocles' alleged inconsistencies appear to be two: positing Strife as a cause
      of becoming, when he had initially posited Strife as the cause of perishing; and
      positing Friendship as a cause of perishing, when he had initially posited Friendship
      as the cause of becoming. Empedocles could of course reply that the perishing of the
      Sphere is the becoming of individual things, and that there is no inconsistency in
      Strife's being the cause of both. Likewise, that the coming into being of the Sphere is
      the perishing of individual things, and that there is no inconsistency in Friendship's
      being the cause of both.
      357 Translating Hayduck's *ek gar tou henos hapanta kai ek toutou ta alla esti plên
      theos*. Hayduck's use of single quotation marks rather than widely spaced letters
      suggests that he believes that Alexander regards the whole phrase as a quotation

the influence of Strife. Having cited the verses which express Empedocles' view that Strife, which he included among principles as productive of *perishing*, is the cause of the *becoming* of all things, 5 'things which were, and things which are' [1000a29], Aristotle says that it is clear, even apart from these verses, that on Empedocles' view Strife is generative. For if Strife were not [found] among beings, he says, all things would be one and could not be differentiated or come to be. For the admixture of Strife is the cause of the fact that the 10 One (*to hen*),[358] the product of Friendship, does not perdure among beings. For, when all things come together and become One, it is then, he says, that at the very end Strife is separated from them, as cause of the existence (*ousia*) of different things, things which in separation from Strife can be unified.[359] It is for this reason, Aristotle says, that Strife is also present, on Empedocles' view, in all other things, just as each of the other elements is; for this is how they would be differentiated, and [each would exist] in its proper nature. Only in the 15 One, the God, is Strife not present, so that this alone does not have Strife as the cause of its being; but all other things do.

Having related how Empedocles' statements are inconsistent with one another, and having mentioned that on Empedocles' view it is only in God that Strife is not present, and so it is not the productive cause of God, Aristotle criticises Empedocles on the ground that in this respect he makes God less conscious (*aphronesteros*)[360] than 20 other things. For, according to Empedocles, all other things will think, because they include in themselves all the principles, and because thought (*noêsis*) of like comes by like. Whereas God will think other things, because he too includes in himself the elements of the other things, but will not be thinking of Strife, since Strife is not present in him at all.

One might raise the aporia, how Aristotle means the statement that on Empedocles' view God turns out to be less conscious, since he 25 does not think all things; for in this respect God would be unconscious (*aphrôn*) on Aristotle's own view as well. But Aristotle says some-

---

from Empedocles. But the phrase does not scan. Ross and Jaeger print *exô tou henos· hapanta gar ek toutou t'alla esti plên ho theos*, 'apart from the One; for all the other things are from this, except God'. The words 'apart from the One' thus form part of the preceding clause, and the words are Aristotle's paraphrase of Empedocles, not a direct citation from Empedocles.

[358] The context is the Empedoclean cosmic cycle, specifically the extreme phrase in which the four elements have all come together to form the Sphere or One.

[359] i.e. without Strife these things would be liable to be reduced to the One, with consequent loss of their diversity.

[360] Alexander uses this word here and at 220,25, and he may have read it in his MS of Aristotle. Ross and Jaeger print *hêtton phronimon* 'less aware', at 1000b4, with no indication of divergence in the MSS.

where that there are some things, such as evils, that it is better not
to think.[361]

Or perhaps Empedocles' view is that the God is less conscious in
this respect, that he does not seek to share in the other things;[362]
for, despite having himself come into being from the elements (apart

30   from Strife), and thinking of nothing else of higher dignity than the
elements from which he and other things come, he does not think of
the elements.[363] But [on Empedocles' view] all the elements
think, but God alone, though derived from them, is incapable of
thinking.[364]

Further, God will be thinking of all the material elements, but not
of all the productive elements as well, which are of higher dignity
than the material.[365] Aristotle says elsewhere that according to
Empedocles only Strife is imperishable.[366]

35   Having raised this aporia from outside his own position[367] in
response to Empedocles, Aristotle returns to prove Empedocles'
inconsistency with himself, insofar as he does not retain Friendship

221,1 as the cause of becoming or Strife as the cause of perishing, but on
the contrary makes each of these no more a cause of each effect than
the other, by making Strife a cause of becoming and Friendship a
cause of perishing. He goes on to say that Friendship causes
perishing, and tells how: it is clear that by bringing all things into
One it destroys the things that were in existence before this
convergence.

---

361 cf. *Metaph.* 12.9, 1074b25-35. On this interpretation, God is *aphronesteros* in
the sense of not knowing bad or inferior things; we might call this the 'better not to
think about it' interpretation.

362 Reading with Hayduck *pleonektôn tôn allôn*, the reading of MSS LF. Hayduck
reports A as reading *pleon ek tôn*.

363 Taking *ginomenos* as concessive and reading *tôn stoikheiôn ou noei* with
Hayduck. Bonitz raised the possibility of reading *tôn stoikheiôn ou pleon noei*, 'does
not think any more of the elements'. I am not sure what led Bonitz to advance this
suggestion.

364 On this interpretation, God is *aphronesteros* in the sense of not paying attention
to other things; we might call this the 'God couldn't care less' interpretation. But the
interpretation is almost overwhelmed by two objections to the resultant position: (i) it
is odd for God not to think of the elements, given that they are God's constituents and
that God has nothing better to think about; (ii) God turns out to be less conscious
than the elements themselves.

365 This seems to be an objection to a version on which God would think the four
material elements but not the productive elements, Friendship and Strife, or at least
not Strife.

366 The eternity of Strife argues for its high status and hence for its worthiness to
be an object of divine thought. I have not found in Empedocles a statement to the effect
that *only* Strife is imperishable.

367 Alexander means the aporia about God's thinking, not the larger aporia about
the principles of perishables and of imperishables. The aporia about God's thinking
comes from outside Aristotle's position in the sense that it is based on Empedoclean
assumptions which Aristotle does not share.

But if Strife is no more a cause of perishing than is Friendship, in 5
this respect too it would be plausible that God for Empedocles is less
conscious[368] than other things. For on Empedocles' view, there is no
special evil in Strife such that it would be reasonable for God not to
think of it alone.[369] For God does not thereby[370] suffer privation of it,
despite being a synthesis,[371] as he would if Friendship or something
else were supposed not to be present in him.[372] Hence[373] God will not 10
think of Strife, not on the ground that it is reasonable for him not to
think of it, but rather because he is incapable of so doing, because he
does not come from Strife.

Aristotle criticises Empedocles for not telling the cause why at
times Friendship dominates[374] while at other times Strife dominates
the whole. For it is not sufficient to say 'Thus it is by nature' [1000b13]
and 'Thus it is necessary'.[375] For one can say this in the case of all
things that come to be and are; but to say that a thing 'is thus by 15
nature' is not to answer the question about its cause.

[The case against all principles' being imperishable]

Despite making these criticisms of Empedocles, Aristotle says that he
alone spoke consistently to this degree at least, [that he held] that
things that come from the same principles are all in like manner
perishable, *not* that some are perishable and others not, which [latter
position] seems to contain an inconsistency: how, on the view of those
who say that all things come from the same [principles], are some
things, from the same [principles], imperishable, and others
perishable?

[The case against perishable principles]

Having raised an aporia, in response to those who supposed that the 20

---

[368] i.e. less conscious because not thinking of Strife.

[369] Taking the negation as applying to the whole sentence, both initial assertion
and result.

[370] viz. by not including Strife.

[371] Accepting Hayduck's suggestion to read *sunthesis tis ôn* in place of MSS *auto
sunthesis tis*. On God as synthesis of elements, cf. 219,31-4; 220,10.15.22-3.28-32.

[372] i.e. God will not include Strife, but that lack is not a privation, because Strife is
not part of God's nature.

[373] Reading *oukh hôs eulogon ara* for *oukh hôs eulogon gar*. This sentence does not
give a reason for the preceding; it states a consequence of the preceding: the absence
of Strife from God precludes God's thinking of Strife. The passage offers a third
interpretation of Empedocles' position; we might call it the 'God cannot think of what
is not in God' interpretation.

[374] Deleting *ton theon* in line with A²S: as accusative it can only be in apposition to
tên philian; but God is the synthesis of the elements, not the synthesising Friendship.

[375] The Greek is *houtôs anankê*; cf. Aristotle's *hôs anankaion*, 1000b16.

principles of all beings were the same, Aristotle next raises aporiae in response to those who suppose that the principles of imperishable things and the principles of perishable things are different. He begins by raising this aporia: whether the principles of perishable things are also perishable, *or* imperishable. If, then, they are perishable, it is clear that they will come from the same things as

25 those into which they perish (for they do *not* perish into non-being). For the things into which each thing perishes are the things from which it has been constituted. Therefore there will be principles of the principles. But if so, they[376] will not be the principles; on the contrary, those from which they come will be the principles. But it is impossible for there to be principles of principles; for principles do not come into being from principles, whether they come to a halt at some point, or proceed to infinity. For, if they come to a halt, those principles at which the perishing stops would be the principles of the

30 supposed principles, and would in addition be eternal, as has been proven – or else, if perishing comes to a halt at non-being, there would be becoming from non-being. But if principles go on to infinity, that into which each perishing principle perishes will be its principle. More than this: there will be no principle at all; for this has been proven in the previous book [*Metaph.* 2.2].

35 Or else the statement, 'Therefore it happens that there are other prior principles of principles' [1000b26-7] follows from the

222,1 statement, 'both if it comes to a halt and if it goes on to infinity' [1000b27-8]. For on each of these [alternatives] it follows that there are principles of principles. After which Aristotle might say, 'But this is impossible' [1000b27]; but, placed as it is between the other two statements, it has rendered the text rather unclear.[377]

1000b28 Further, how will perishable things exist, if their
5 principles are done away with?

The meaning is, if perishable things come to be from perishable principles, how could these perishable things still come to be, once their principles have perished? For once the principles have perished, it would no longer be possible for the things which come from the principles to come to be.

The meaning would be as follows. How will perishable things be

---

[376] viz. the principles originally supposed, which now turn out to depend on further principles.

[377] 1000b26-8 runs 'Therefore it happens that there are other prior principles of principles; but this is impossible, both if it comes to a halt and if it goes on to infinity'. Alexander's point is that the sense would be more clearly expressed by a different order: 'Therefore it happens that there are other prior principles of principles, both if it comes to a halt and if it goes on to infinity; but this is impossible.'

perishing and coming to be, if their principles do not exist?[378] For   10
things which come to be and perish come to be and perish by virtue
of having principles, from which and under the influence of which
they come to be and into which they perish; perishing is [the process
of] being broken up into those things <from which the thing [in
process of] perishing came to be>.[379] How then could [things]
perish, if those things by dissolution into which they are to perish
did not exist?

[The case against deriving both perishables and imperishables from imperishable principles]

But if someone says that the principles of imperishable and of   15
perishable things are imperishable, he faces in turn the aporia: how
and on account of what do imperishable things come from these
imperishable principles *and* perishable things come from these
same imperishable principles? 'For this', Aristotle says, 'is not
reasonable, but rather is either' completely[380] 'impossible, or it
requires much argument' [1000b31-2] to prove that this is
reasonable. An aporia remains, practically the same as the
preceding.[381]

In addition, Aristotle says that no one at all has claimed[382] that   20
there are different principles for perishable things and for
imperishable things; all suppose them to be the same for perishable
things and for imperishable things. But as they suppose the first
aporia [as settled] – how both perishable and imperishable things
come to be from the same principles – they dismiss it and remove it
from consideration.[383] This is the meaning of the expression, 'They   25

---

[378] After this sentence Hayduck prints, in brackets, the reading of MS M: *ho
edeikhthê akolouthêsai ei phthartai eien hai arkhai*, 'which has been proved to follow,
if the principles are perishable'. The nominative *ho*, 'which', is a conjecture of Bonitz.
MS M of Alexander gives the dative *hôi*, 'on which it has been proved to follow...'.
Brandis follows M. Neither the version with the nominative nor the version with the
dative seems to advance the argument, and Hayduck reports that the clause is
lacking in MSS ALFS.

[379] Accepting Hayduck's supplement, on the basis of LF and S: *ex hôn gegone to
phtheiromenon*.

[380] *pantelôs*. Ross and Jaeger cite no evidence for *pantelôs* in MSS of *Metaph*.
Hayduck prints it in regularly spaced letters, rather than in the widely spaced letters
he uses for citations, indicating that he thinks Alexander inserted the word into his
citation, not that he read it in his MS of Aristotle.

[381] i.e. the immediately preceding problem about the positing of perishable
principles, not aporia 9 about whether principles are one in number or one merely in
form. The two aporiae are the same in that they both come to absurd conclusions, not
in the sense that the absurd conclusions are the same.

[382] *eirêkenai*. Ross and Jaeger report that its occurrence here led Bonitz to
conjecture *eirêken* at *Metaph*. 1000b32 in place of MSS *enkekheirêken*.

[383] Reading *aphairousi*, as Hayduck suggests, on the basis of Asclepius 200,4-5, in
place of corrupt *aporousi*; the one thing these people do *not* do is to raise or face the

swallow [it]' [1001a2], as is clear also from the following phrase, 'assuming this to be a small point' [1001a2-3]. For, as they supposed it to be a small point, and not involving an aporia, that the same principles should be the principles of all things, they produced no discussion of the aporia.

Or else he said 'They swallow [it]' [1001a2] in place of saying that they try to produce a comfortable conviction, by way of certain things that seem to them plausible – as he had said about Hesiod 30 and the mythologists of old, and about Empedocles too, who, 223,1 while producing all things out of the same principles, set up one as the cause of becoming, another as the cause of perishing – as though supposing [they were facing] nothing great or difficult.

On Aristotle's view, however, the principles of eternal things and the principles of perishable things are not the same. And among perishable things not all the principles are eternal – for form is not eternal – while matter is eternal, only not immune to change 5 (*apathês*), but rather subject to change and alteration.

[Aporia 11]

1001a4 The most difficult point of all to consider, and the most necessary to attain knowledge of the truth ...

The aporia which Aristotle says is most difficult and most necessary for the knowledge of the truth is the following: whether Being (*on*) 10 and One (*hen*)[384] are substances[385] (*ousiai*) of beings (*onta*), that is, whether they are principles simply by being this, Being and One – not by being present in some other being and manifesting this nature[386] in the things of which they are predicated, *or* whether there is some other nature, underlying them as subject, which is the principle and substance of beings; [in the latter case] one must inquire what it is: whether it is fire or air or some other thing, or even several things, with One and Being present in those things as in subjects.

15 That the inquiry is necessary is clear, from the fact that some thinkers have expressed themselves in the former way on these matters, and some in the latter way, and from the aporiae which Aristotle will go on to raise, and because in the consideration of

---

aporia.

[384] Or perhaps 'Unity'. Aristotle and Alexander are speaking of the Pythagorean-Platonic first principles. I have not used the definite article with One, partly to maintain parallelism with Being, partly to avoid Neoplatonic overtones, but principally to keep in view that the Platonic One, as understood by Aristotle, is first and foremost a predicate, and is a principle because it is a predicate.

[385] Or perhaps 'essences'.

[386] viz. being, unity, conceived of as attributes of things.

truth the inquiry concerning Being is of the highest importance, and because the possibility of numbers' being said to be the principles and elements of beings depends on [the resolution of] this issue. The inquiry into this point is, then, most necessary for the knowledge of the truth, but the judgment (*diakrisis*) about these matters is also most difficult. For knowledge of the intelligibles and of the primary causes and beings is most difficult.

Aristotle himself explains the question, 'whether One and Being are substances of beings' [1001a5-6] in the words '[whether] each of them is not some other thing, but one thing is One, the other Being' [1001a6-7]. The expression is equivalent to 'whether, since Being and One are among beings, they are beings as substances, *or* as accidents of substance'.[387]

Having said that some [thinkers] conceived of One and Being in this way, as certain natures existing in their own right, while others conceived of them as accidents of certain other natures – like the difference, of course, which he also pointed out in the first book of the *Physics*,[388] concerning the infinite: some [thinkers] posited a certain nature of the Infinite Itself (as the Pythagoreans did too, for the even number is such a thing for them), while others said that the infinite is an accident of something – having said this, Aristotle goes on to relate who held the latter view about these things and who held the former view.

The phrase 'Or [whether] one must inquire what in the world One is and what in the world Being is, on the supposition that some other nature is [their] subject' [1001a7-8] is equivalent to 'Or [whether] one must inquire what is subject for One and for Being, on the supposition that they are accidents of those things but do not express their essence (*ousia*)'.[389]

Now Plato and the Pythagoreans said that these things [One and Being] are not present in something else as in a subject, that, on the

20

25

30

35

224,1

---

[387] Are these really equivalent? As Aristotle first expresses it, the question seems to be whether Being is purely being, not something else, whether One is purely one, not something else. Thus Ross renders 1001a6-7 'whether each of them, without being anything else, is being or unity respectively'. This suggests that the point of *oukh heteron ti*, 'not some other thing', is the pure or unmixed character of One and Being. But as Aristotle goes on to explain himself, the question seems to rather to be 'whether each of them is not something which some other thing is', i.e. whether each of them is not an attribute of something else. The issue is whether One and Being exist in their own right, as substances do, or whether they exist as attributes of other things. That is how Alexander seems to understand the phrase here. At 225,10-32 he offers four distinct explanations of it.

[388] The reading of ALFS and Asclepius 203,21-2. Hayduck points out that the reference is actually to *Phys.* 3.4. Is this just a mistake to be corrected? Or did Alexander think of our *Phys.* 3 as the first book of the *Physics*?

[389] Or perhaps 'substance'. The main issue of the aporia is whether One and Being are *ousiai* in the sense of substances.

contrary, their nature is [to be] subject and their essence³⁹⁰ is [to be] this very thing (*auto touto*), One and Being. The phrase 'on the supposition that [their] essence is to be One Itself (*auto to hen*) and some Being (*on ti*)' [1001a11-12]³⁹¹ is equivalent to 'on the supposition that the essence of One and of Being is the same, and that it

5   is the same thing to be one and to be a being'. That Plato said that the One is a certain substance, and Being [a certain substance], is clear from the fact that he even called Being Itself and One Itself Ideas.³⁹²

But the natural scientists, among whom Empedocles is included, supposed something else [as subject] for Being and One, and said that they are present in those things. Empedocles, as though reducing the One to something more familiar, supposes Friendship as subject, and

10 predicates One of it – since on his view Friendship is the cause, for all things, of the fact that each of them is one thing, for it collects and combines them. Others of the natural scientists put Fire [as subject] for One and Being, as did Heraclitus, others Air, as did Anaximenes, and others something else. For each of them supposed a principle and cause of beings, and predicated One and Being of this. But even those who held that the elements of beings were a plurality also held that

15 each of these was some one thing and a being.

[The case for One and Being as substances]

Having recounted and presented the conflicts in views about the principles, Aristotle next begins the aporia. And first he faces [this side of] the aporia: if one does *not* say that One and Being are substances. This is what the text 'If one does not posit that One and Being are some substance (*tina ousian*)' [1001a20-1] expresses. The meaning is the same even if it is written 'he means substance of

20 something (*tinos ousian legei*)'.³⁹³ For Being is predicated most

³⁹⁰ Or perhaps 'substance'.
³⁹¹ Reading with Hayduck *hôs ousês tês ousias auto to hen einai kai on ti*. The distinctive point in the citation would be the explicit use of the Platonic *auto*, 'Itself', terminology. Hayduck thinks that Alexander may well have read *hôs ousês tês ousias tautou tou heni einai kai onti*, 'on the supposition that the substance of one and of a being is the same'. Ross and Jaeger print *hôs ousês tês ousias autou tou heni einai kai onti*, 'on the supposition that its substance is to be one and a being'. As their apparatus indicate, the witnesses to the text of *Metaph.* are quite divided, and conjectures are numerous. The supplement '[their]' is not meant to suggest that Alexander read *autôn*, or that Aristotle wrote it; but neither would I rule out those possibilities.
³⁹² That Plato spoke of One and Being as Ideas would show that he regarded them as substances. It would not imply that he identified them as the same substance. But Alexander thinks of One Itself and Being Itself as two names for a single Idea; cf. *in Metaph.* 63,12-14.
³⁹³ Hayduck takes *legei*, 'he means', as part of the citation, and Ross and Jaeger, who print *tina ousian*, include *tinos ousian legei* along with other variants in their apparatus of *Metaph.* But it is hard to fit *legei* into Aristotle's sentence at 1001a20.

[widely] of all things. For man is predicated only of men, and likewise animal is predicated of certain determinate things, but One and Being are predicated of all beings. Therefore, if the things that are most universal are not substances[394] and not beings, then none of the other universals could exist.

He states [the condition] 'But if there is not some One Itself (*autoen*)[395] and Being Itself' [1001a22-3] in place of 'For if it is not possible to assume One and Being as genera of beings, and as predicated of them in that way' – that is, not as equivocal terms, as he has shown elsewhere [*Cat.* 5, 3a33-3b5]. He says 'substance of something (*tinos ousian*)' [1001a20][396] in place of 'being the substance of something, and being predicated, in the [category of] substance, of whatever anything is predicated'.[397] [If the condition is not fulfilled], then only particulars will exist, not universals. But Aristotle has proven that this is absurd [999a24-999b8];[398] for neither will there be sciences, nor will there be anything intelligible; on the contrary, all things will be sensible; and there will not be anything eternal either.

Aristotle now goes on to say that number will not be a substance, as separated and existing in its own right, as the Pythagoreans and Plato hold, if One is not some substance. And he tells the reason: a number is a combination of units (*monades*), and the unit is the same thing as One; therefore, if One is not a substance, then neither are the units; but if the units are not substances, then neither is number; hence number will be an accident, not a substance – given that One is not some substance but rather an accident of something else.

The expression 'just what One is' (*hoper hen*) [1001a26-7] is equivalent to 'One in the proper sense' (*kuriôs hen*) or 'under One as genus'; for One is predicated of the unit.

Aristotle said this [conclusion] as one that would appear absurd to

25

30

35

225,1

Perhaps Alexander knew of a MS that read *tinos ousian*, or even *tinos ousian legei*. But perhaps he knew of a marginal comment *tinos ousian legei*, 'he (*sc.* Aristotle) means substance of something', and *gegrammenon* means written in the margin of a MS rather than in the text itself.

[394] Reading plural *ousiai* as suggested by Bonitz on the basis of S.

[395] Ross, Jaeger print *hen auto*. There is no obvious difference in meaning.

[396] Here Alexander seems to adopt the reading, or interpretation, *tinos ousian*, 'substance of something', which he earlier mentioned as alternative to *tina ousian*, 'some substance'.

[397] For every predicate φ, One and Being are predicated of φ. But by the rule of *Cat.* 2, 1b10-12; 5, 3b4-5, anything predicated of a predicate φ is also predicated of any subject of which φ is predicated. Hence for any subject x of any predicate φ, One is predicated of x and Being is predicated of x. One and Being are predicated of every predicate, and so they are predicated of every subject of every predicate.

[398] Aristotle's arguments for this point extend further, to 999b16 and include arguments not mentioned here. For Alexander's discussion of the arguments cited here, see 210,35-213,23.

those who say that number is a certain separated substance; for it does *not* appear absurd to Aristotle himself, though it did, as I said, to those who held that view; for the man[399] who says that the mathematicals are intermediate substances placed number, too, among these substances.

[The case against One and Being as substances]

Next Aristotle argues to the effect that One and Being are not
5   substances in their own right. First he posits and proves that it follows for those who say that there is a One Itself and a Being Itself – that is, those who say that One and Being are not accidents of other things but rather beings in the proper sense – that they [must] say that One and Being are substances (*ousiai*), and that their being (*einai*) consists in being One and in being Being. For the phrase 'for their substances[400] to be One and Being' [1001a27-8] expresses that these[401] are the substances of One and of Being, but that neither
10   being One nor being Being is present in any other thing. In proof of this Aristotle says 'For no different thing is predicated universally' [1001a28-9],[402] which is [i][403] equivalent to 'For [the predicates] One and Being are not some beings different from their subjects of which they are predicated universally; on the contrary, as being these very things, One and Being, they are predicated of them'.

[ii] Or as follows: 'For it is not something different that will be
15   predicated of substance, but rather these things, Being and One, so that everything whatever that is substance would be One and Being, not as being something else [which also is one and a being], but rather [itself being] this very thing.'[404] As, when the predicate man [is predicated] of men, the things of which it is predicated are men, not some other thing, so for the things of which Being and One

---

[399] viz. Plato.

[400] *ousias autôn*. Ross and Jaeger print the singular *ousian autôn*, 'their substance'.

[401] viz. Oneness or Unity, Being or 'Being-ness'.

[402] 'Universally' is *katholou*, the reading of MSS and Alexander, which Ross prints. Jaeger, crediting Bonitz, prints *kath' hou*, 'of which'. This yields 'For it is no other thing of which they are predicated universally', i.e. One and Being are predicated of themselves. Cf. *kath' hôn* in Alexander's explanation, 225,12.

[403] I number the four explanations of *ou gar heteron* ..., 1001a28-9. Each insists on a certain identity, and denies a corresponding sort of difference or non-identity. In [i] One and Being are identical with the subjects of which they are predicated (Bonitz' and Jaeger's *kath' hou* would fit this better than Alexander's *katholou*). In [ii] One and Being are identical with the very essence of the subjects of which they are predicated. In [iii] the predicates One and Being are identical with the Ideas One and Being. In [iv] the entities One and Being are identical with the predicates One and Being; this identity is so strong that the entities One and Being admit of no other predicates than One and Being.

[404] That is, One and Being. If Being and One are predicated of something, they express that thing's essence, which is precisely to be a being, a one.

are predicated in the [category of] substance: the substance of these things will be Being and One, if Being and One are certain substances; for water, or fire, is not predicated of beings in such a way that we would say that this was their substance; but Being and One are so predicated. But if these things, being substances, are predicated of beings universally, then the substance of these things of which they are predicated would also be One Itself and Being.

[iii] The statement 'But if there is some One Itself and Being, it is necessary that their substances (*autôn ousias*)[405] be One and Being' [1001a27-8] can be understood as a reply to those who call One and Being Ideas. For those who hold that One Itself is an Idea and Being Itself is an Idea must hold that One and Being are the substance of these things. For Being Itself and One are predicated universally of beings, not as being some different beings;[406] for [if they were different] they would no longer be One Itself and Being Itself; on the contrary, these things exist precisely as One and Being, predicated universally of other things.

[iv] Or as follows: 'For no different thing is predicated universally, but rather these things themselves' [1001a28-9]. That is, 'For no different thing is predicated universally of One Itself and Being Itself, in such a way that they would belong to that nature[407] which is signified by that which is predicated universally of them; on the contrary, One and Being are these very things that are predicated of them.'

1001a29 But now, if there is to be some One Itself and Being Itself,[408] there is a great aporia over how there will be any other thing distinct from these.

Having proven that for things of which Being and One are predicated their substance will be Being and One, which are certain substances, not accidents of substances, Aristotle says that it becomes an impassable difficulty (*aporon*)[409] to prove that anything else exists distinct from One and Being. For, as Parmenides said, that which is distinct from Being is non-being. This[410] was the One, so that whatever is distinct from the One will not exist. For the same thing turns out to be distinct from Being, if indeed it is also distinct from the One. (This [is said] on the supposition that Being and the

20

25

30

35
226,1

5

---

[405] Ross, Jaeger print *ousian autôn*, 'their substance'.
[406] There is no difference between the Idea One and the one that is predicated, between the Idea Being and the being that is predicated.
[407] i.e. the nature of that different thing
[408] *ti auto hen kai auto on*. Ross and Jaeger print *ti auto on kai auto hen*.
[409] The difficulty is spoken of as an obstacle which one cannot get past. In ordinary English one might speak of such a difficulty as insuperable.
[410] viz. Being, according to Parmenides.

One are the same.) Therefore there will not exist many things. For
the many things are distinct from the One; <but things distinct
from the One were distinct from Being, and things distinct from
Being do not exist>.[411] This is the result, if Being and One are
substances, and if they are not said equivocally: all beings will then
be One, and this One will be the only Being, just as Parmenides
said.

10   **1001b1 It is difficult either way; for [both] if One is not a
        substance and if One Itself is [a substance],[412] it is impossible
        for number to be a substance.**

Having proven previously that if One is not a substance, then
neither will number be a separated substance – for number is a
combination of units, and units are not substances – Aristotle now
15   says that even if One *is* a substance, not even on this alternative can
number be a substance, for it does not exist at all. For there will
exist nothing distinct from One Itself; for that which is distinct from
One is not one, just as that which is distinct from Being is not being.
     Assuming that, if there is something distinct from One, it will not
be One but many, Aristotle proves that it is impossible for many to
exist, by assuming that the many are formed by combination from
many units, which cannot exist; for [if they did exist] they would be
20   distinct from the One. But if several units did not exist, number
could not exist either.[413] For it is necessary that every additional
unit[414] be distinct from One Itself, the substantial One; but a
substance distinct from the One could not be a one. But if several
units did not exist, number could not exist either; for all beings are
either one or many, but it is impossible for the many to exist,
because the many would come from many units, and there cannot be
25   [units] distinct from One Itself – for that which is distinct from One
is not a one, just as that which is distinct from Being is not a being.
But if it is not possible for the many to exist, number could not exist
either; for the many are a plurality (*plêthos*) of units.
     The statement '[There is] the same aporia as that concerning
Being' [1001b4] makes the point that the same aporia will be met

---

[411] Accepting the suggestion of Hayduck, who indicates corruption, to change
Alexander's singular *to de para to hen*, to plural, and to supply a lacuna, by reading *ta
de para to hen para to on ên, ta de para to on ouk esti*, on the basis of Asclepius
205,22-3.
[412] *an te êi to autoen*. Ross prints *an te êi to auto hen*, yielding the same sense; cf.
Aristotle's Metaphysics I.245. Jaeger prints *an te êi ti auto hen*, 'and if there is some
One Itself'.
[413] This sentence is practically a doublet of the sentence at 226,22-3. Here it
interrupts the train of thought; there it is perfectly in place.
[414] *pollên monada*.

with concerning One as concerning Being. For, as that which is distinct from Being is not a being, so that which is distinct from One is not a one. This is made clear by the question 'For from what will there be another One distinct from One Itself?' [1001b4-5].[415] For it is necessary that there not exist anything else, distinct from One, from which the other One might come. For as, given that Being is substance, there turned out to be no other substance, because that which is distinct from substance is not substance, so, if One is also substance, everything which is distinct from it[416] will be neither a being nor one. But if this [is the case], many will not exist either. For each of the many is a one – for the many, and number, come from ones (*henades*) – and if these things did not exist, many could not exist, nor could number exist.

Or as follows.[417] If there is a One Itself, then, if there are to be numbers, there must also come into being another one. But this thing which *comes to be* one necessarily comes to be [one] when it *is not* one;[418] so it will be from not-one. So what will this 'not-one' be? For if all beings are either one or many, and if the many come from ones – from which [something] does not *come to be* one[419] – then there could be nothing from which the [additional] one comes to be.

[A criticism of One drawn from Zeno]

1001b7 Further, if One Itself is indivisible, then, according to Zeno's axiom, it would be nothing.

In addition to what has been said, Aristotle raises a [further] aporia concerning One: if it is in all respects indivisible and without magnitude, how can it be a principle of magnitude (*megethos*)? For according to Zeno it will be nothing. For Zeno – he refers to Zeno the Eleatic, the acquaintance of Parmenides – took it as an axiom that something which is capable neither of making something larger when added to it nor of making it smaller when subtracted from it is not anything at all. But One Itself is such a thing.

Now Zeno took this as an axiom on the supposition that every being is a magnitude, a body; for on his view there is no other kind of magnitude in reality (*hupostasis*), capable of being increased or of increasing [something], apart from body. 'For this is being in every respect' [1001b11]. That is why such a magnitude, added in any

---

[415] Taking *auto* with preceding *to hen* rather than with following *allo hen*.

[416] Accepting Hayduck's suggestion, drawn from Bonitz, of *ekeino*, accusative singular, in place of *ekeinôn*, genitive plural.

[417] The phrase introduces an alternative explanation.

[418] A thing cannot become what it already is; if it is becoming something, then it is not yet that something.

[419] They cannot come to be one, because each of them already is one.

20   way, increases [a thing], while other [kinds of] magnitudes do not increase the whole simply by being put together with it; [it matters] *how* [they are put together], as they are not magnitudes in the proper sense or in their totality. The line and the plane, for example, only increase [lines or planes] when put together at their limits. For example, a surface, put together [with another surface] along a line which is itself a limit of the surface, increases the surface; but not if put together [with another surface] surface to surface and breadth

25   to breadth; for it coincides [with the other surface], because depth cannot come from the combination of surfaces. Likewise the line, which is a magnitude, if combined with a line at a point (*sêmeion*) which is its limit, makes the whole line longer; but if combined line to line, it coincides and does not increase [the line], because breadth is not filled up by line. Now each of these,[420] even if it is not a being in the proper sense, is still a being in some sense, insofar as it

30   increases beings. But on Zeno's view the point (*stigmê*) and the unit are no longer beings at all, since they are in every respect without magnitude, for they are not capable of causing increase.

[A Problem: the derivation of magnitudes from One]

Having mentioned Zeno's view as one that utterly does away with

228,1   the One, Aristotle goes on to say that even if Zeno's argument is crude – it says that nothing exists but magnitude alone; [this is crude] for something can exist even if it is indivisible; for the indivisible is not in every respect deprived of [power] to cause an increase; one can reply to Zeno that 'while it does not make[421] a thing larger, it does make it more numerous' [1001b15-16]; and in this way both the One and the indivisible cause increase; so that in

5   this way One Itself does not fall short of being something, inasmuch as it contributes to an increase – still, he says, it is worthwhile to raise that aporia,[422] how, from such a One, or from several such Ones, does magnitude comes to be. For this is like saying that a line is composed of points. He says this in opposition to those who suppose that numbers are the principles and elements of all things, for [on their view] numbers turn out to be principles even of

10   magnitudes; these were the Pythagoreans.
      He next raises a further aporia against the view of Plato, who supposed that One and something else not-One (that is, some number) are the principle of number and of the other things. This is expressed in the phrase 'and [from] another thing which is not One' [1001b20-1]. This was Inequality (*anisotês*), i.e. the indefinite Dyad

---

[420] i.e. surface, line.
[421] *poiei*. Ross and Jaeger print *poiêsei*, 'will make'.
[422] Reading infinitive *aporêsai* in place of future indicative *aporêsei*.

(*aoristos duas*), which he called Great and Small (*mega kai mikron*); he said that first of all number was generated from these – with the indefinite Dyad being made definite by the One and becoming two – and then the other things were generated.

Aristotle raises the aporia, how, from the coming together of the One and the indefinite Dyad, there come to be on the one hand number, on the other hand magnitude[423] (for on Plato's view it is not only the numbers that come from those [principles], but magnitudes as well). For if Inequality, the indefinite Dyad, being the same nature, is the principle of numbers *and* of magnitudes, how is it possible for any magnitude to come to be from the combination of One and this Dyad? For these are such as to generate *number*.

Or, if one says that first number comes to be from these [principles], and that then in this way, from number, magnitudes come to be, it is worthwhile demanding an answer [to the question], how could magnitude come into being either from a combination of numbers or from a combination of number with Inequality? For it is an impassable difficulty how things without parts could be productive of magnitude. (The statement 'if indeed the not-One was Inequality[424] and was the same nature' [1001b23-4] is equivalent to 'if indeed, on his [Plato's] view, the not-One was Inequality and, being the same nature, was on his view the principle both of numbers and of magnitudes'.) For how could it be possible for both numbers and magnitudes to be generated from the same principles?

CHAPTER 5

[Aporia 12]

[The case for numbers and geometrical entities as substances][425]

1001b26 An aporia connected with these is whether numbers and bodies and points are certain substances or not.[426]

Having shown, through the aporiae he raised, that numbers will not be substances, Aristotle next raises – in addition to the aporiae already discussed – the aporia, whether numbers and bodies and

---

[423] *to men arithmos ... to de megethos.* Hayduck cites Asclepius 208,6-7 as giving *pote men arithmos ... pote de megethos*, 'at one time number ... at another time magnitude'; that would fit the sequence set forth by Alexander at 228,20-1.

[424] *anisotês.* Ross and Jaeger print *hê anisotês*, which is found in Alexander's paraphrase, 228,25-6.

[425] As posed, the aporia is whether numbers and geometrical entities are substances or not; but the arguments presented in the aporia concern geometrical entities, and numbers appear to be forgotten.

[426] Ross and Jaeger include *kai ta epipeda*, 'and plane figures', between the mention of bodies and the mention of points.

229,1   points (and clearly surfaces and lines [are meant] as well) are
        substances or not. For if these things are not substances, then there
        could not be any substance at all. For what substances will there be?
        Things such as qualities (these he called attributes and
        motions),[427] and relatives, and conditions [1001b29-30] (which
        are themselves also qualities) are not substance. And the ratios
5   (*logoi*) [1001b30] (this is what he calls numbers) are not themselves
        substances, even if they do belong to substances. Aristotle means
        the statement 'they do not seem to signify the substance of anything'
        [1001b30-1] as the equivalent of 'they are not substances'.

        Likewise the other things listed under the ten categories are not
        substances;[428] for they are all said 'of some subject' [1001b31-2],
        that is, are present in some subject,[429] and have some other thing as
10   their subject, and do not function as subjects themselves; nor can
        any of them be exhibited as being a subject in its own right. By
        'substance' (*ousia*) [1001b31] Aristotle here means 'being' (*on*).

        Having said these things, Aristotle then posits it as evident that
        the simple bodies are substances in the highest degree; and, having
        separated from these their qualities and their other attributes, as
        being accidents of bodies, he assumes that the body that is the
        subject for these (I mean for the attributes) is substance – a body
15   which exists in three dimensions (*trikhêi diestôs*). Having made this
        assumption, Aristotle then proves that this body is a substance to a
        lesser degree, in a certain respect, than its proper limits. For surface
        is substance to a higher degree than body, and line is substance to a
        higher degree than surface, and point is substance to a higher
        degree than line.

        Then, in addition to these considerations, Aristotle will use the
        fact that these are not substances to do away as well with the claim
        that body is substance, employing the commonplace argument from
20   greater and lesser degrees. For if those things which are substances
        to a higher degree are not substances, then the things which are
        substances to a lesser degree than those could not be substances
        either.

        That body is substance to a lesser degree than these,[430] he proves

        [427] Reading *pathê te kai kinêseis* in place of Hayduck's *pathêtikas kinêseis*, 'affective
        movements'. 'Affective movement' is unusual terminology; and, as the point is to give
        a fairly complete list of obvious non-substances, there is no reason for Aristotle to
        mention a specific type of quality. Alexander makes no effort to explain it. Ross and
        Jaeger print *pathê kai hai kinêseis* at 1001b29.
        [428] Alexander is careless in speaking of the ten categories rather than of the nine
        non-substantial categories.
        [429] In *Cat.* 2 Aristotle distinguishes with some care between being present in a
        subject and being said of a subject; here Alexander appears to blur the distinction –
        unless *toutestin*, 'that is', is simply corrective.
        [430] viz. surface, line, point.

first by an argument of the following kind. The things by which something is defined[431] and given its form are substance to a higher degree than that which is defined by them; for the things which define something are beings to a higher degree, substances to a higher degree, than that which is defined and given its form – at least this is why Aristotle himself asserts that form *is* to a higher degree than 25
matter. But body is defined by surface and line and point. So these are substances to a higher degree than body.

Secondly, he uses an argument of the following kind. When one member of a pair can exist in its own right apart from the other, while the other cannot, that which can exist in its own right is substance to a higher degree. But of the limits of body and the body itself, the limits can exist apart from the body, but the body cannot exist apart from its 30
limits. Hence the limits of body are substances to a higher degree than the body.

(Aristotle did very well to add '*seems* to admit of existing' [1002a7]; for it is not possible for any of these things to exist in reality (*hupostasis*) apart from body, any more than it is possible for the body 230,1
to exist without them – though it is possible for them to exist by way of thought (*epinoia*) and reason.)[432]

For it is not possible to conceive of body without a surface, or of surface without a line, or of line without a point – for these items are included in the definitions of those things: body is said to be that which has length, breadth and depth; surface that which has length 5
and breadth; and line that which has length without breadth, and points as limits – but a point is conceived of even apart from a line, and a line apart from a plane, and a plane without body.

To confirm the position that these things are substances to a higher degree than body, Aristotle adds the views of his predecessors. The more ancient of these, who did not yet speak about beings with 10
mastery,[433] supposed that the substances of beings, their principles, were corporeal. Those who came after them, and so seem wiser, such as the Pythagoreans and Plato, asserted that the principles were numbers, on the supposition that these are substances to a higher degree than bodies. Aristotle means 'so that the principles of bodies would also be the principles of beings' [1002a10-11] as equivalent to 'so that they[434] said that the principles of bodies were beings in the 15

---

[431] *horizetai*. Alternatively, 'is delimited'.

[432] This comment interrupts the explanation of the second argument; it would fit better at 230,7.

[433] *epistasia*. The word seems to have overtones of *epistasthai*, 'to know, to understand', but also of *epistênai*, 'to be over, to be master'. I have adopted 'mastery' in an effort to do justice to both. At *Metaph.* 14.2, 1089b25 an *epistasis* appears to be a problem, something that makes one stop.

[434] The earlier thinkers, the corporealists.

proper sense', because they were the principles of beings, i.e. of bodies.

[The case against geometrical items as substances]

Assuming this,[435] Aristotle then says that if none of these things[436] is substance, then nothing else could be substance. For bodies could not be substances (they are substances to a lesser degree than these things), and even less[437] could the accidents of body be substances. But that these things are not beings, that is, not substances, he

20   proves in turn as follows. If point and line and plane are beings and substances, it is clear that their reality (*hupostasis*) is also in bodies; and if in bodies, in these bodies.[438] But none of these things is present in sensible bodies. For it is not possible to discover in sensibles a point such as we define a point to be, or a line such as we define a line to be. For it is not possible to assume, in a sensible body, a length that is altogether separated from breadth, and

25   likewise not possible to assume a surface apart from depth. If, then, they were beings and substances, they would be present in sensible bodies; for these are the only things in reality; but if they are not [in bodies], they could not be substances either.

Aristotle also proves that these things are not in reality from the fact that these things are attributes (*pathê*) and dimensions (*diaireseis*) of bodies, <that is, that it is in terms of these that the dimensions of bodies>[439] come into being. But the dimensions of the

30   body are not subjects or certain beings on the basis of their proper nature; for they are attributes, and attributes are not substances. For in respect of breadth[440] a body is cut by a line; in respect of depth, by a surface; in respect of length, by a point.[441]

In addition, Aristotle proves that they, that is, surface and line and point, are not present in bodies, as follows. It is by thought (*epinoia*) that these things are said to be present in bodies; for it is

[435] viz. that points, lines, surfaces are substances to a higher degree than bodies.

[436] viz. points, lines, surfaces.

[437] Taking *eti mallon* as reinforcing the negation.

[438] viz. the sensible bodies of this world.

[439] Following Hayduck in positing a lacuna and supplying *toutesti kata tauta tas tôn sômatôn diaireseis* from Asclepius 213,3-4. It has been suggested to me that 'divisions' might be a better translation of *diaireseis* than 'dimensions'.

[440] Reading *kata men gar to platos* in place of Hayduck's *kata mentoi to platos*, 'in respect of breadth, however'. The adversative 'however' seems out of place in a sentence that *supports* the claim that points, lines, surfaces are properties of bodies.

[441] More precisely: in respect of depth a body is cut by a surface; in respect of breadth a surface is cut by a line; in respect of length a line is cut by a point. This must have been what Alexander meant, but I do not contend that it is what he originally wrote, because I cannot imagine how that could have been corrupted into the text we have.

not by virtue of reality (*hupostasis*), i.e. the ability to exist in 231,1
separation. Making use of this, he says that it is possible to assume
any figure whatever and any surface whatever as being in like
manner in a body. For example, it is possible, by thought, to assume
both the figure of Hermes and the figure of Apollo as present in the
unworked stone – and in like manner the figure of someone else. But
in the cube as well, the half of the cube exists, by thought, and the 5
surface that divides the cube in two can be assumed as present in the
depth [of the cube] – and likewise any surface whatsoever. So, if all
figures and surfaces are in body in like manner, that is, by thought,
and if they are not, by virtue of the fact that they can, as assumed by
thought, come to be in body, present in body, then neither could
anything else be present in body. Therefore, if the figure of Hermes is 10
not present in the stone, then neither is the figure that the stone
appears to have; and if the surface that divides the cube in two is not
present in the cube, then neither is the surface that the cube appears
to have.

The fallacy in the argument lies in the assumption that all figures
are present in the subject in like manner, both those present
potentially and those present actually. The persuasiveness of the
fallacy derives from the fact that those things actually in the subject
seem to be present in it by thought, like those potentially in the
subject; this is because they are not separate. As in the case of 15
surface, so in the cases of line and point and unit (for the unit is a sort
of point). For in these cases too it is possible in like manner, by
thought, to say that any of these whatever is present in the body that
is subject, and then, assuming some of those things that are [present
in it] potentially, and proving that they are not present in the body
(for that which is present in something potentially is not yet present
in it), to prove that even the things that seem to be actually present in 20
body are not present in it.

Having proven by way of these [arguments] that surface and line
and point and unit are not substance, Aristotle draws, as following on
the points proven, the conclusion that not even body will be
substance, body which is defined by these. He has proven not only
that these things are not substances, but that they are not beings at
all. The statement '[if]442 these things are not and are not certain
substances' [1002a27] is equivalent to '[if] these things are not beings 25
and are not certain substances'.

1002a28 For, besides the preceding, the consequences concerning becoming and perishing also turn out to be irrational.

---

442 I understand 'if' on the basis of *ei* at *Metaph.* 1002a26.

The following argument also proves, for Aristotle, that the limits of
body (which he proved to be substance to a higher degree than body)
30   are not substances. For substances which previously did not exist
proceed into existence by way of becoming (*genesis*), and likewise
substances which previously existed pass into non-existence by way
of perishing (*phthora*). Therefore becoming and perishing precede
the existence and non-existence of sensible substances. But these
things[443] exist at one moment and do not exist at another moment,
without becoming or perishing.[444] Therefore they are not
232,1   substances.[445] The statement 'it is instantaneous (*hama*): at one
moment it is one,[446] while they are in contact; at another moment it
comes to be[447] two,[448] when they are divided' [1002b1-2] indicates
[that it comes to be two] apart from becoming. For when [bodies] are
in contact, directly and instantaneously, there is one [point, line,
surface]; but when they are divided, directly and instantaneously
there are two [points, lines, surfaces], with no becoming preceding.

That they exist at one moment, and do not exist at another
5   moment, apart from becoming and perishing, Aristotle proves as
follows. When bodies are in contact with each other, and in turn
separate from each other, at one moment surface is one and line is
one and point is one, all at once one – for when they are in contact,
the limits of the two are one, because they coincide – but when they
are separated, they are in turn all at once two. Therefore at one
moment the surface and the other things[449] exist, when the bodies
are not in contact with each other, while at another moment they do
10   not exist, when the bodies are in contact – and this apart from
becoming or perishing. For it is *not* that the point, which is by its
own nature indivisible, has been divided into two, in such a way that
this division would be the becoming of the other point; on the
contrary, the point which previously did not exist, [now] exists,
without becoming.

The same reasoning applies to the line and the surface. For it is

---

[443] viz. surface, line and point, the limits of body.

[444] It may seem odd to speak of coming into existence without becoming, or of
ceasing to exist without perishing; but Alexander's point is that these things come to
be and cease to be instantaneously, that they do not go through a *process* of becoming
or a *process* of perishing. Cf. 232,27-33.

[445] The assumption is that things which come to exist or cease to exist
instantaneously cannot be substances. By contrast, things which come to exist
through a process of becoming and things which cease to exist through a process of
perishing are substances.

[446] i.e. one point, line, surface.

[447] *gignetai*. Ross and Jaeger print plural *gignontai*.

[448] i.e. two points, lines, surfaces.

[449] viz. the line, point resulting from the separation.

not possible to divide a line in respect of width, so that in this way 15
one line would *become* two lines, by a dissolution of the contact; nor
is it possible to divide a surface in respect of depth.

Aristotle adds that everything that comes to be comes to be from
some subject;[450] but as for these things,[451] it is impossible for anyone
to say from what subject they come to be. Therefore, if everything that
comes to be comes to be from some subject and from matter, and if
nothing functions as subject for these things, then they do not come to
be. But if the items mentioned exist at one moment and do not exist at 20
another moment, without becoming, then they are not <sub-
stance>.[452]

Further, as is the case with the present instant (*to nun*), which is
the limit of time, so it will be the case with point and line and surface.
For all these items are in like manner either limits (one of body, one of
surface, one of line, one of time) or a dimension (for it is in respect of
these that the things in question are divided). If, then, it is necessary 25
that they all have in them in like manner the [characteristic of]
existing at one moment and not existing at another moment – given
that they are of the same nature – then the present instant exists at
one moment and does not exist at another moment, and is different at
each different moment, apart from becoming and perishing. For
every becoming [takes place] in time, and likewise every perishing.
Therefore the present instant as well, if it came to be, would first have
come to be in time and, as coming to be in time, it would be divisible
into parts and would occupy some interval (*diastêma*). For of that 30
which is coming to be in time, one part has [already] come to be while
another part is [still] coming to be; for it is in terms of the parts of time
that the parts of the thing that is coming to be come to be. Further,
every thing that comes to be has some subject, as Aristotle has said
already, but nothing functions as subject for the present instant.

Therefore, if the present instant exists at one moment and does not
exist at another moment, apart from becoming, this will also be true
of the items mentioned earlier;[453] but if so, they are not substances.

---

[450] In the text of *Metaph.* as we have it, Aristotle does not explicitly say this, but
proceeds directly to the rhetorical question found in 1002b4-5.

[451] viz. point, line, surface.

[452] Supplying *ousia*, as Hayduck suggests on the basis of S and Asclepius 215,29;
and cf. 231,33 and 232,34.

[453] viz. point, line, surface.

CHAPTER 6

[Aporia 13]⁴⁵⁴
[The case for the Ideas]

233,1   **1002b12 But in general one might raise the aporia, why we must also seek for certain other things of this kind,⁴⁵⁵ distinct from the sensibles and the intermediates, for example, the Forms that we posit.**

The aporia is, how it is reasonable to seek for and to posit certain other causes, distinct from the sensible substances and the
5   intermediates (that is, the mathematicals), as do those who claim that the Ideas exist. In support of this view, Aristotle presents the considerations which make it reasonable.

Now, if the reason why [they posit the Ideas] is this, that the mathematicals, even if they differ from sensible things in other respects (by being eternal and immovable, as Aristotle said earlier [*Metaph.* 1.6, 987b14-18]),⁴⁵⁶ none the less do not differ from
10   sensibles in this respect, that there are among them many things of the same form (for, as Aristotle said in his discussion above [999b24-1000a4], [they are not] numerically one, nor is each of them numerically one; on the contrary, each is one in form but many in number) ... .⁴⁵⁷ But if all such particulars are like one another, then none of them could be the substance⁴⁵⁸ or the element of the others. Therefore, if neither the principles of these⁴⁵⁹ nor the principles of the sensibles are determinate (*aphôrismenai*) in number, there will
15   be no principles of beings, determinate in number, nor will there be among principles any substance that is one in number and definite (*hôrismenê*) – unless there exist certain other substances, distinct from sensible substances and from mathematical substances, substances such as they claim the Ideas are. For none of the principles will be a substance that is one in number, if the sensible and the mathematical are one [only] in form, and if there is no other substance distinct from these.
20   Further, even the principles of beings will not be substances, if each of them is not one in number. For things which are universal have their being in the manner of accidents, as Aristotle will say further on.⁴⁶⁰

---

⁴⁵⁴ Aporia 13 was not announced in the listing of aporiae in *Metaph.* 3.1.
⁴⁵⁵ *all' atta toiauta.* Ross and Jaeger print *all' atta,* 'certain other things'.
⁴⁵⁶ This is presumed in aporia 5, 997b19-20, 998a14-15.
⁴⁵⁷ The long protasis trails off without an apodosis.
⁴⁵⁸ *ousia.* Alternatively 'essence'.
⁴⁵⁹ viz. the mathematicals.
⁴⁶⁰ I have not found an Aristotelian text that says in so many words that universals

Having said 'there will be no substance one in number as a principle' [1002b24],[461] Aristotle adds 'and in form' [1002b24],[462] either meaning 'in nature' and 'in reality' or meaning that there will not exist a principle that is one in number *and* a principle that is one in form. For only the principle which is one in form will exist – which is not even a principle in the proper sense (*kuriôs*), since it has its existence (*einai*) in, and is conceived of by derivation from, these things of which the principles are said [to be principles].

A better text would have been 'there will be no substance one in number *but rather* in form'.[463] For this pulls together the preceding remarks and the following statement 'nor will the principles of beings be such and such in number, but rather in form' [1002b24-5].

Given, then, that if there does not exist some *substance* distinct from mathematical and sensible substances, there will not exist any definite substances;[464] but that thus there will not exist any *principles* of substances either, in the proper sense and definite[465] – it appeared necessary to posit certain other substances, each of which would be a substance in the proper sense: substances having their being and unity not by participation (*metousia*) in something or in the

---

have their being in the manner of accidents. Perhaps Alexander is thinking of *Cat.* 5, 3b10-23, where secondary substances or substance universals are spoken of as some sort of quality, or perhaps he is inferring, from the argument of *Metaph.* 7.13, that no universal is a substance, that every universal is therefore some sort of accident. Cf. 234,30-4 and 236,3-7.

[461] *hôs arkhê*. These words are not found in the text of *Metaph.* as reported by Hayduck, Ross and Jaeger.

[462] *kai tôi eidei*. MSS of *Metaph.* give *kai eidei*, 'and in form', which Jaeger brackets. Ross prints *all' eidei*, 'but rather in form', in line with Alexander's suggestion at 233,26 and his paraphrase at 234,24.

[463] *all' eidei*.

[464] i.e. substances definite in number.

[465] Reading *houtô de oude arkhai ousiôn kuriôs tines kai hôrismenai*. The basic idea in 233,28-31 is: if there are no substances definite in number, then there are no principles definite in number. For the notion of principles definite in number, cf. 234,23-30. Hayduck prints the reading of A¹ and notes corruption: *houtô de †oude arkhai ousôn ousiai kuriôs tais kai hôrismenai*. This might be translated 'but thus, even given that there are principles, there will not be substances in the proper sense even for the definite principles (substances?)'. But why should the preceding denial that there are any substances definite in number be followed by such a condition as 'even given that there are principles'? And what is the point of speaking of substances to or for principles (or to or for substances – the feminine participle could have either substances or principles as antecedent)? Bonitz, according to Hayduck, proposed *houtô de oude arkhôn ousôn ousiai kuriôs tines kai hôrismenai*, 'but thus, even given that there are principles, there will not be any substances in the proper sense and definite'. The change from *tais* to *tines* and the change from dative to nominative are improvements. But on Bonitz' version (if there are no substances definite in number, then, even if there are principles, there are no substances definite in number) the argument does not advance. My suspicion is that *arkhai ousiôn* was corrupted to *arkhai ousôn*, then to *arkhôn ousôn*, then to *arkhôn ousôn ousiai* as the now-missing nominative was supplied.

manner of an accident (that which is one in form is one in the manner of an accident, but not in the proper sense).

[The case against the Ideas]

234,1 But if this is the reason why one is to posit that there are certain substances of this kind, Aristotle reminds us of the difficulties which he showed followed on the hypothesis of the Ideas [*Metaph.* 1.6, 1.9, 3.2, 997b5-12]. The sense (*nous*) of what he says is as follows. He brings up the elements[466] of syllables, proving how in their case the principles, the things predicated in common of something, are not definite in number but rather in form. For the common *a* is the

5 principle of the particular *a*'s, and it is one in form, not in number; likewise for the other letters. As in the case of the elements, so too man in the case of particular men,[467] and likewise in the case of the other sensibles.

Having said that 'the principles of the letters in this world[468] are not definite in number but in form' [cf. 1002b17-19],[469] since, however, in the case of the syllable that is determinate,[470] for

10 example, this particular syllable *ba*, its principles and elements, this particular *b* and this particular *a*, are determinate in number, Aristotle brings up the following point as well. He proves that while it is possible, in the case of syllables assumed in this way,[471] and in the case of all other products of combination, to assume the principles as being determinate in number,[472] still it is the common factors which are in turn the principles *of* these principles. For example, the *a* in this particular syllable and the *a* in that particular syllable have as their principle the *a* that is predicated in common.

15 Having proven in the case of the elements that that which is common and one in form turns out to be their principle, Aristotle says that this is likewise the case with the intermediates, meaning the mathematicals. For among them, as among the elements, the particulars assumed are many, even infinite, and the same as one another in form. But if these things, which are distinct from the

---

[466] *stoikheia*, also 'letters'.

[467] i.e. man, the principle of particular men, is one in form, not in number.

[468] *entautha*, literally 'here'.

[469] Hayduck prints these words in widely spaced letters, as a citation; I gather his reason is the introduction by *eipôn* without a connective such as *hoti*. The citation corresponds to the content of 1002b17-19, but the phrasing and word order are rather different, and the texts of Ross and Jaeger include *pantôn*, 'all', modifying *grammatôn*, 'letters'.

[470] i.e. determinate in number.

[471] i.e. assumed as particular or token syllables.

[472] e.g. the principles of the particular syllable *ba* are particular or token *b* and particular or token *a*, definite in number.

particulars,[473] are the same as one another in form – Aristotle speaks in like manner in the case of natural [particulars] and in the case of mathematical [particulars], for the reasoning in the two cases is the 20 same – and if there is not to be some other substance, one in number (or of whatever kind those who believe in the Ideas wish to posit), then 'there will not be a substance one in number and in form' [1002b24],[474] that is, there will not be some formlike substance (*eidikê ousia*) which is numerically one, and hence neither will the principles of beings be numerically definite, such and such in number, but rather [only] in form.

But if this is necessary, that the principles of beings be definite in 25 number – for [only] thus they will be substances; for that which is common is not substance in the proper sense, which is why it is not a principle or an element either – it will appear that those who supposed the Ideas were moved by necessity to arrive at their position. And indeed, even if they do not say this explicitly, because they do not articulate their view to any great extent, still this appears to be what led them to suppose the Ideas as the principles of beings: 30 the need for the principles to be substances and to be definite.[475] For that is the sense in which their principles turn out to be substances: substances in their own right, differing from the other things which have their unity [only] on the level of form, and [existing] not in the manner of accidents, as the things which are common seem to do (for the existence of things which are common is not in its own right, but rather in the manner of an accident).

Having said these things, and having brought in the further point that it is reasonable for the principles of beings to be of this kind, 235,1 Aristotle goes on to remind us of the aporiae raised against this position, and in general against the view that each of the principles is one in number. For it has been said [999b31-1000a4] that [on this view] there will be nothing else distinct from the principles; for it has been proven that things whose principles are definite in number are equal in number to their principles; therefore there will not exist 5 other things distinct from the principles. But he would remind us too, and even more importantly, of the aporiae raised against the Ideas in the first book [*Metaph.* 1.6, 1.9].

[Aporia 14]
[The case against principles in actuality]

---

[473] i.e. from the mathematical particulars.

[474] *kai eidei*. Ross prints *all' eidei*, 'but in form', in line with Alexander's paraphrase at 234,24 and his suggestion at 233,26 above. Jaeger prints *kai eidei* but in brackets.

[475] i.e. definite in number.

1002b32 Very close to these points is the matter of working through the aporia, whether the elements are in potentiality or in some different manner.

This aporia is quite verbal. Aristotle inquires whether the elements
10 and the principles of beings are in potentiality *or* in actuality; the latter is what is meant by 'or in some different manner' (*tina heteron tropon*) [1002b33-4]. For if they are in actuality – he has expressed this, in turn, in the words 'for if in some other way' (*allôs pôs*) [1002b34] – there will be principles of principles, as he says, and there will be something prior to the principles. But this is absurd; what will be prior? That which is in potentiality. For on the same ground, that which is in potentiality seems to be primary relative to
15 actuality; therefore the potentiality of a cause and principle in the way of actuality will be a thing prior to the principle – the principle which is in the way of actuality. For that which is potential need not, by that very fact, be in actuality. Therefore, if the relation is not reciprocal – if, on the contrary, potentiality precedes that which is in actuality, and is present in everything, while actuality is not by the same token present in everything that is potential – then potentiality will be prior.[476]
20 He expresses himself quite briefly, linking 'for potentiality is something prior to that cause' [1003a1] to 'that which is potential need not all be in that manner' [1003a2], that is, be in actuality. He says '[prior] to that cause' [1003a1] in place of '[prior] to that principle', namely, the principle in the way of actuality. With the statement, 'for potentiality is something prior to that cause' [1003a1] he assumes that if something is in actuality, prior to this it had the [status of being] in potentiality.

[The case against principles in potentiality]

25 But if someone is going to posit that the elements are in potentiality and not in actuality, it will follow from this that it is possible for nothing at all to exist. For that which does not yet exist is capable of <not>[477] existing; therefore the principles, if they are in potentiality, are also capable of not existing. But if they did not

---

[476] The argument pretends to reduce the thesis, that the principles are in actuality, to absurdity. The absurdity is that there would be something prior to the principles. The argument reduces the thesis to absurdity only by focusing on one sense of priority, the sense in which potentiality is temporally prior to that actual thing whose potentiality it is, to the exclusion of other and weightier senses of priority. This, I think, is why Alexander criticises the argument as merely verbal.

[477] Supplying a negative so as to read *dunatai gar* <*mê*> *einai* in place of Hayduck's *dunatai gar einai*, 'is capable of existing', which is true enough but beside the point of the argument. An alternative would be to supply <*kai mê einai*>.

exist, neither would the things that derive from them.

That even non-being is capable of being, Aristotle proves as follows. If that which is coming to be *is not*[478] – this he expresses in the words 'for, while non-being comes to be' [1003a4-5] – and if that which is potential comes to be, then that which is potential *is not*. He 30 took his second premise from the statement 'none of the things that is incapable of being comes to be' [1003a5]; for this is equivalent to saying that that which is in potentiality, that which is potential, is what is coming to be.[479]

[Aporia 15]
[The case against principles as universals]

In addition, Aristotle in turn recalls the aporia already stated earlier, namely, whether the elements and the principles of beings 236,1 are universal, some sort of things that are common, *or* whether they are particulars [998a20-998b14]. And he adds another aporia distinct from the one stated at that point. If, he says, the principles have their existence as universals, they will not be substances. For substance is a subject, an individual thing (*tode ti*);[480] but none of the things that are common is a subject or an individual thing, but 5 rather a 'such' (*toionde*);[481] for the genera and species even of substances do not signify an individual thing; rather they 'restrict quality to [the category of] substance', as he said in the *Categories* [*Cat.* 5, 3b20].[482] But that that which is common does not express an individual thing, he proves as follows. If someone says that that which is common is an individual thing and is subject to exhibition (*ekthesis*)[483] and proof, then Socrates, the individual substance (*atomos ousia*), will be numerically many animals – for Socrates himself is both animal and man – given that [the common things] 10 man and animal are individuals, things in their own right, and are subject to proof and exhibition. For Socrates is a man, and to be Socrates and to be a man are not the same thing. But [the same is true of] animal as well; for Socrates is an animal, which [animal]

---

[478] *ouk esti.* Alternatively, 'does not exist'.

[479] Summarising and formulating in the affirmative a step that Alexander leaves in the negative: that which is potential comes to be; that which comes to be *is not*; hence that which is potential *is not*; (but that which is potential can be) ; hence that which *is not* can be.

[480] Or 'this something'.

[481] Or 'a certain kind of thing'.

[482] As framed in *Cat.* 5, 3b10-23, the contrast is between *tode ti* and *poion* or *poia tis ousia*. The contrast between *tode ti* and *toionde* is found at *Metaph.* 7.13, 1039a1-2 and 15-16.

[483] According to Alexander *in Metaph.* 124,9-125,4 *ekthesis*, 'exhibition' or 'exposition', was a Platonic method of reducing sensible multiplicities to higher and higher unities.

was itself supposed to exist and to have existence in its own right; for it too is universal. But this is absurd.

[The case against principles as particular]

15 'But if [the principles] are not universal ...' [1003a13]: this is the conclusion towards which Aristotle argued, when he said 'Socrates will be many animals' [1003a10-11].[484] Or the meaning is this: 'if, on the contrary, someone were to think that the universal is such as to signify, not a 'such' but rather an individual, a substance, and that it is such as the things that are made manifest by exhibition.' And so he says that that which is predicated in common is 'also exhibited' [1003a10];[485] and the universal is such a thing. This is why Aristotle
20 now appropriately shifts to the other side of the aporia, and says as follows: 'but if [the principles] are not universal ...' [1003a13]. The meaning is, that if someone says that the principles are not universal, but rather particular and indivisible, Aristotle says once again that there will not be science of them; for science is of universals.[486] Therefore either there will be, once again, other principles, universal, *of* the principles, if there is to be science of
25 them, and then once again universals will be principles; or else there will not be principles as objects of science.

The aporiae presented in Beta contain arguments [drawn] from accepted opinions (*endoxa*) and [conducted] on the level of plausibility (*kata to pithanon*). And indeed, it is impossible for people to argue for opposed positions, except by using [merely] verbal arguments; nor, for that matter, could the aporiae be solved, if this were not the case.

---

[484] *zôia*. Ross prints it. Jaeger, reporting a doubt by Christ, brackets it.

[485] *kai ekthesthai*. This is the reading of the MSS of *Metaph*. Ross, following Richards, prints *kai hen thesthai*, 'and to posit as one'. Jaeger reads *kai <dei> ekthesthai*, 'and must be exhibited'. Jaeger cites Alexander's discussion of 992b10. This is found at 123,19-126,37; 124,9-125,4 are most relevant to determining the meaning of the Platonic *ekthesis*.

[486] At 1003a14-15 Aristotle says that science is *katholou*, 'universal'. But to say that universality is characteristic of science is not quite the same as saying that the objects of science are universals.

English-Greek Glossary

The Glossary lists key terms in the English translation, and supplies the Greek words which they represent. It is also an aid to locating terms in the Greek-English Index. The attempt has been made to limit the Glossary to terms of philosophical interest, in contrast to the more inclusive policy followed in the Greek-English Index. In some cases a family of cognate terms is represented by one or two leading members. Abbreviations: (n) = noun; (v) = verb; (tr) = transitive; (intr) = intransitive; (a) = adjective.

able, be: *dunasthai*
abstraction: *aphairesis*
absurd: *atopos*
accepted opinion: *to endoxon*
accident, be an: *sumbainein*
accident: *sumbebêkos*
accidental cause: *kata sumbebêkos aitia*
account: *apodosis, logos*
account, give an: *historein*
action: *praxis*
activity: *energeia*
actuality: *energeia*
actually: *energeiâi*
add a further argument: *prosepikheirein*
add: *epipherein, prostithenai*
addition: *prosthêkê*
admit: *anadekhesthai*
advance (n): *euporia*
affective: *pathêtikos*
affective attributes: *ta pathêtika*
affirmation: *kataphasis*
air: *aêr*
akin: *sungenês*
analytic: *analutikos*
angle: *gônia*
animal: *zôion*
anomoeomerous: *anomoiomerês*

aporia: *aporia*
aporia, face, raise, state, deal with: *aporein*
aporia/aporiae, work through: *diaporein*
appear: *dokein, phainesthai*
application: *prosphora*
apprehension: *antilêpsis*
argue: *epikheirein*
argument: *epikheirêsis, logos*
art: *tekhnê*
articulate (v): *diarthroun*
artifact: *tekhnêton*
artisan: *tekhnitês*
assimilated, be: *homoiousthai*
assume: *hupotithesthai, lambanein*
astronomy: *astrologia*
attribute: *pathos*
audible: *akoustos*
axiom: *axiôma*
axiom, take as an: *axioun*

based on, be (geom.): *anagraphesthai*
be: *einai*
become: *gi(g)nesthai*
becoming: *genesis*
beget: *gennan*
begin: *arkhesthai*

197

begin by facing aporia, apo-
    riae: *proaporein*
Being (Platonic): *on*
Being Itself: *autoon*
being (ens): *on*
being (esse): *einai*
being of: *to einai* (+ dat)
belong: *huparkhein*
body: *sôma*
breadth: *platos*
broken up, be: *analuesthai*

can: *dunasthai*
capable: *dunatos*
category: *katêgoria*
cause: *aitia, aition*
certitude: *pistis*
chance, matter of: *tukhôn*
change (n): *metabolê*
change (v): *metaballein*
change (v) in quality: *alloiousthai*
changeless: *ametablêtos*
circle: *kuklos*
circular motion, having property of:
    kuklophorêtikos
clear: *dêlos*
colour: *kh:ôma*
combination: *sunthesis*
combine: *sunkrinein*
combined, be: *suntithesthai*
come into being (also): *pros-*
    gignesthai
come to a halt: *histasthai*
come to be: *gi(g)nesthai*
come together: *sunerkhesthai*
common: *koinos*
community: *koinônia*
comparable: *analogos*
complete, most: *teleiotatos*
complex (form + matter): *sunam-*
    photeros
complex entity: *to sunamphoteron*
composed: *sunthetos*
composed, be: *sunkeisthai*
composite: *sunolos*
composition: *sunthesis*
compound: *sunkekhumenon*
comprehension: *perilêpsis*
conceive of: *dianoeisthai, epinoein*
conceived of, be: *noeisthai*
concern oneself with: *kataginesthai,*

    pragmateuesthai
conclusive: *sullogistikos*
concord: *sumphônia*
condition: *diathesis*
confirm: *pistin pherein, pistousthai,*
    sunistanai
confirmation: *bebaiôsis, pistôsis*
connect: *sunaptein*
consequence: *akolouthon*
consequent (log): *to deuteron*
consider: *theôrein*
consideration: *theôria, theôrêma*
consistent: *katallêlos*
constituents: *enuparkhonta*
constituted, be: *sunistasthai*
contact: *haphê*
contact, be in: *haptesthai*
contemplation, object of: *to*
    theôrêtikon
continuous: *sunekhês*
contradiction: *antiphasis*
contrariety: *enantiotês*
contrary: *enantios*
contribute: *suntelein*
contribute to an increase: *sun-*
    auxanein
convergence: *sunodos*
counteract: *anelittein*
curved: *peripherês*
curvilinear: *peripherogrammos*
customary way: *ethos*

deal with: *dialambanein*
define: *horizein*
defined: *horistos*
definite: *aphôrismenos, hôrismenos*
definition: *horos, horismos*
definition, object of: *horistos*
definitory: *horistikos*
demonstrate: *apodeiknunai*
demonstration: *apodeixis*
demonstrative: *apodeiktikos*
density: *puknotês*
deny: *anairein*
depend: *artasthai*
deprived, be: *stereisthai*
depth: *bathos*
deserving: *axios*
determinate: *aphôrismenos*
determine: *diorizein*
dialectic: *hê dialektikê*

dialectical: *dialektikos*
differ (in fact): *diapherein*
differ (in opinion): *diapheresthai*
difference: *diaphora*
different: *allos, heteros*
differentiated, be: *diakrinesthai*
difficulty: *duskolia*
dimension: *diairesis*
discover: *heuriskein*
discovery: *heuresis*
discuss: *poieisthai logon*
discussion: *logos*
dissolve: *apoluein, ekluein*
dissolved, be: *dialuesthai*
distinct from: *para*
disturbed, be: *sunkeisthai*
diverse: *diaphoros*
divide: *diairein*
divine: *theios*
divisible into parts: *meristos*
division: *diairesis*
do away with: *anairein*
do away with as well: *sunanairein*
do geometry: *geômetrein*
doctrine: *dogma*
Dyad (Platonic principle): *hê duas*

earth: *gê*
eclipse: *ekleipsis*
effort: *ephesis*
element: *stoikheion*
end: *telos*
enmattered: *enulos*
enumerate: *exarithmein*
equal: *isos*
equivalent (in meaning): *isos*
equivocal: *homônumos*
equivocal character: *homônumia*
error, be in: *pseudesthai*
essence of: *to einai* (+ dat)
essence: *ousia, ti ên einai*
essential, essentially: *kath' hauto,
    kath' hauta*
essential accident: *kath' hauto
    sumbebêkos*
essential property: *kath' hauto
    huparkhon*
establish: *kataskeuazein*
eternal: *aïdios*
even (math.): *artios*
evident: *enargês, phaneros*

evident, make: *endeiknusthai*
evil (a): *kakos*
evil (n): *kakia*
examine: *episkeptesthai, exetazein*
example: *paradeigma*
exhibited, be: *ektithesthai*
exhibition: *ekthesis*
exist: *diistanai, einai, huphistanai,
    huphistasthai, sunistanai*
existence: *to einai, ousia*
explain: *exêgeisthai*
extension: *diastasis*
extensively, more: *epi pleon*

fallacy: *paragôgê*
false: *pseudês*
figure (geom): *skhêma*
figure (syllogistic): *skhêma*
final: *telikos*
final cause: *kata to telos aitia, hôs
    telos aition*
fire: *pur*
flux: *rhusis*
follow (logically): *akolouthein*
following (logically): *akolouthos*
force: *bia*
form: *eidos*
Form (Platonic): *eidos*
form (log): *tropos*
form (of motion, of place): *skhêma*
form, be given: *eidopoieisthai*
form, same in: *homoeidês*
formal: *eidikos*
formlike: *eidikos*
formula: *logos*
Friendship (Empedoclean prin-
    ciple): *philia*
function as subject: *hupokeisthai*

generated, be: *gennasthai*
generated: *gen(n)êtos*
genus: *genos*
geometrical proposition:
    diagramma
geometry: *geômetria*
go on: *anienai, badizein, proienai*
go right through: *diienai*
goal: *skopos*
god: *theos*
good: *agathos*
Good Itself: *autoagathon*

grant (in argument): *didonai*
grasp (n): *lêpsis*
grasp (v): *lambanein*
Great (Platonic principle): *to mega*

happen: *sumbainein, tunkhanein*
harmonics: *hê harmonikê*
health: *hugieia*
Health Itself: *autoügieia*
Heaven Itself: *autoouranos*
heaven: *ouranos*
Horse Itself: *autoïppos*
how much? how many? *posos*
human being: *anthrôpos*
hypothesis: *hupothesis*

Idea (Platonic): *idea*
immaterial: *aülos*
immediate (premise): *amesos*
immortality: *athanasia*
immune to change: *apathês*
imperishable: *aphthartos*
impossible: *adunatos*
in (its, their) own right: *kath' hauto,*
    kath' hauta
in many ways: *pollakhôs*
in three dimensions: *trikhêi*
inconsistency: *anomologia*
increase (n): *auxêsis*
increase (v tr): *auxanein*
indefinite: *aoristos, apeiros*
indemonstrable: *anapodeiktos*
indicate: *endeiknusthai*
individual: *atomos, tode ti*
indivisible: *adiairetos, atomos*
induction: *epagôgê*
Inequality (Platonic principle):
    anisotês
infinite: *apeiros*
inquire: *zêtein*
inquiry: *zêtesis*
inseparable: *akhôristos*
intelligible: *noêtos*
intermediate: *emmesos*
intermediates (Platonic): *ta metaxu*
intersect, be made to: *histasthai*
interval: *diastêma*
introduce: *epagein*
irrational: *alogos*
Itself: *auto* (prefix/suffix)

join in completing:
    sumplêroun
judgment: *krisis, diakrisis*

kind (n): *genos, eidos*
kind, same in: *homoeidês*
know: *eidenai, epistasthai, gig-*
    nôskein, gnôrizein
knowable: *gnôstos*
knowledge: *gnôsis*
known: *gnôstos, gnôrimos*

length: *mêkos*
letter (of alphabet): *gramma,*
    stoikheion
like: *homoios*
likewise: *homoiôs*
limit: *peras*
limited: *peperasmenos*
line (geom): *grammê*
Line Itself: *autogrammê*

magnitude: *megethos*
make: *poiein*
make clear: *dêloun*
man: *anthrôpos*
manner: *êthos, tropos*
material: *hulikos*
mathematical: *mathêmatikos*
mathematicals (Platonic): *ta*
    mathêmatika
matter: *hulê*
mean (geom): *mesos*
mean (v): *sêmainein*
meaning: *to legomenon*
medicine: *hê iatrikê*
metaphysics: *meta ta phusika*
mind: *nous*
mixed, be: *kerannusthai,*
    mignusthai
mixture: *sunkrisis*
mode: *tropos*
modification: *pathos*
moon: *selênê*
mortal: *thnêtos*
motion: *kinêsis*
move (v tr): *kinein*
multiplicity: *plêthos*
music: *hê mousikê*
must, one: *dei*
myth: *muthos*

mythologist: *theologos*

natural: *phusikos*
natural inclination: *rhopê*
natural philosophers: *hoi phusikoi*
natural philosophy: *hê phusikê*
natural scientist: *phusiologos*
nature: *phusis*
nature, be by: *phuein*
necessary, be: *dein*
necessity: *anankê*
negate: *anairein*
negation: *apophasis*
non-being: *mê on*
nourishment: *trophê*
number: *arithmos*
numerically: *kat' arithmon, kata ton arithmon*
numerically one: *hen kat' arithmon*

object (n): *pragma*
object of science: *epistêtos*
odd (math): *perittos*
one: *heis*
One (Empedoclean, Platonic): *hen*
One Itself: *autoen*
one in form: *eidei hen*
one in number: *arithmôi hen*
one, a: *henas*
opinion: *doxa*
opposed, be: *antikeisthai*
opposites: *antikeimena*
optics: *hê optikê*
order: *taxis*
order, in logical: *akolouthôs*

part: *meros, morion*
participation: *methexis, metousia*
particular, particulars: *to kath' hekaston, ta kath' hekasta*
pattern: *paradeigma*
perfection: *teleiotês*
perish: *phtheiresthai*
perish along with: *sumphtheiresthai*
perishable: *phthartos*
perishing: *phthora*
perpendicular: *kathetos*
philosopher: *philosophos*
philosophy: *philosophia*
place (n): *topos*
place toward which: *poi*

plane, plane figure: *epipedon*
plausible: *pithanos*
pleasure: *hêdonê*
plurality: *plêthos*
point (geom): *sêmeion, stigmê*
point out: *deiknunai*
posit: *tithesthai*
posited, be: *keisthai*
positing: *thesis*
position: *thesis*
possessor of science: *epistêmôn*
possible: *dunatos*
possible, be: *endekhesthai, eneinai, hoion te einai*
posterior: *husteros*
potential: *dunatos*
potentiality: *dunamis*
potentially: *dunamei*
practical: *praktikos*
pre-exist: *proüparkhein*
precede: *proêgeisthai*
preconception: *prolêpsis*
predicate (v): *katêgorein*
premise (log): *protasis*
present (v): *ektithesthai, parekhein, parekhesthai, tithenai*
present in, be: *enuparkhein*
present instant, the: *to nun*
presentation: *ekthesis*
primary: *prôtos*
principle: *arkhê*
principle, of the nature of a: *arkhoeidês*
prior: *proteros*
privation: *sterêsis*
produce: *poiein*
product: *ergon*
productive: *poiêtikos*
proof: *deixis*
proper: *idios, kurios, oikeios*
proper sense, in the: *kuriôs*
propose: *prostithesthai, protithesthai*
propose to oneself: *prokeisthai*
proposed: *prokeimenos*
proposition, geometrical: *diagramma*
prove: *deiknunai*
proximate: *prosekhês*
pull together: *sunagein, sunistanai*

qualification, without: *haplôs*
quality: *poiotês*
quantity: *poson*

raise a further aporia: *prosaporein*
rarity: *manotês*
ratio: *logos*
rational: *logikos*
rationality: *logikotês*
reality: *hupostasis*
reason (faculty): *logos*
reason (why): *aitia*
reasonable: *eulogos*
reasoning: *logos*
receive: *dekhesthai*
receptive: *pathêtikos*
recount: *histbrein*
rectilinear, rectangle:
    euthugrammos
reduce: *anagein, epagein*
refute: *anairein, elenkhein*
relate: *historein*
relative: *pros ti*
remain: *menein*
remainders (math): *kataleipomena*
right (geom): *orthos*

say: *eirein, legein, phanai, proeipein*
science: *epistêmê*
see: *horan*
seem: *dokein*
sense, sense-perception: *aisthêsis*
sensible: *aisthêtos*
separate (v tr): *khôrizein*
separate (v intr): *diistasthai*
separate (a): *khôristos*
separation: *diakrisis, khôrismos*
shape (geom): *skhêma*
share (v): *koinônein, metekhein*
show: *deiknunai*
side: *pleura*
signify: *sêmainein*
simple: *haplos*
simply: *haplôs*
Small (Platonic principle): *to mikron*
solid: *stereos*
solution: *lusis*
solve: *luein*
sound (n): *phônê*
speak: *eirein, legein*
speak consistently: *homologein*

species: *eidos*
species, be constituted as:
    eidopoieisthai
speech: *phônê*
sphere (geom): *hê sphaira*
Sphere (Empedoclean): *ho sphairos*
spherical: *strongulos*
square: *tetragônon*
squaring: *tetragônismos*
star: *astron*
status: *logos*
stereometry: *stereometria*
Strife (Empedoclean principle):
    neikos
subject to alteration: *alloiôtos*
subject to change: *pathêtos*
subject: *hupokeimenon*
subsist: *huphistanai, huphistasthai*
substance: *ousia*
suffer privation: *stereisthai*
sun: *hêlios*
Sun Itself: *autoêlios*
supervene: *epigi(g)nesthai*
suppose: *hupolambanein, hupoti-*
    thesthai
surface: *epiphaneia*
syllable: *sullabê*
synthesis: *sunthesis*

text: *lexis*
that for the sake of which: *to hou*
    kharin
that-for-the-sake-of-which: *to hou*
    heneka
theological science: *hê theologikê*
theological: *theologikos*
theorem: *theôrêma*
theory: *doxa*
think, think of: *axioun, noein,*
    oiesthai
this something: *tode ti*
thought: *dianoia, epinoia*
time: *khronos*
tool: *organon*
touch (v): *haptesthai*
treat of: *pragmateuesthai*
treatise: *pragmateia*
triangle: *trigônon*
Triangle Itself: *autotrigônon*
true: *alethês, hugiês*
truth: *alêtheia*

type: *tropos*

ultimate: *eskhatos*
understand: *akouein, manthanein*
undivided: *adiairetos*
ungenerated: *agen(n)êtos*
unify: *henoun*
unit: *monas*
unitary: *monadikos*
unity: *to hen*
universal: *katholou*
universally: *katholou*
unlike: *anomoios*
unmoved: *akinêtos*
use: *khrasthai*
useful: *khrêsimos*

valid (log): *hugiês*
verbal: *logikos*
view: *doxa*
visible: *horatos*

water: *hudôr*
whole: *holos*
wisdom: *sophia*
wise: *sophos*
wish: *boulesthai*
without breadth: *aplatês*
without magnitude: *amegethês*
without parts: *amerês*
without qualification: *haplôs*
word: *onoma*
world: *kosmos*
worthy: *axios*

Greek-English Index

This index lists the principal Greek terms that occur in Alexander's commentary on *Metaphysics* 3, together with the meaning or meanings given to them in the translation. The aim of the index is to enable a reader to find out how the translator has rendered this or that Greek term, and to provide a representative, if not always complete, list of citations for terms that may be of philosophical interest. Readers seeking a complete list of occurrences for a given term, or seeking information about the occurrence of words not included in this index, may wish to bypass the *Index Verborum* in Hayduck's *CAG* edition and to access the *Thesaurus Linguae Graecae*. Readers seeking fuller information may wish to consult, besides the indexes to the translations of Alexander's commentaries on *Metaphysics* 1 and 2, Liddell-Scott-Jones, *A Greek-English Lexicon*, H. Bonitz, *Index Aristotelicus*, and M. Kappes, *Aristoteles-Lexikon*. In Alexander's commentary on *Metaphysics* 3 some verbs appear in the middle or the passive but not in the active voice; some adjectives appear in the comparative or superlative but not in the positive degree; some words appear in specialised or technical senses but not in their ordinary or primary senses. The entries in the index have been tailored to reflect this situation. Cognate terms are grouped together, and thus the listing of terms does not always follow strict alphabetical order. Page and line references in the index are to Hayduck's edition of the Greek text.

adiairetos, undivided: 208,8-10; indivisible: 227,9; 228,2.4; 232,11

adunatos, impossible: 188,32.34; 205,14; 211,1; incapable: 213,36

aêr, air: 224,12; Air (Presocratic principle): 180,2

agathos, good: 175,12.13; 181,36.38 (see *ameinôn, aristos, auto-agathon, beltion*)

agein, lead (v): 234,29; focus (argument) 217,29

agen(n)êtos, ungenerated: 181,32.35-6; 212,17.23; 213,16.27

agnoein, not know: 172,27; 173,19; 195,36; not realise: 200,20

aïdios, eternal: 197,7; 199,35; 212,10

aisthêsis, sense(s): 198,26.28.30; sense-perception: 212,8

(accounts): 176,26
apodosis, account: 185,9
aitias apodosis, to answer the
    question about the cause:
    221,14
apoluein, dissolve
apoluomenês tês haphês, by dis-
    solution of the contact: 232,15
apophainesthai, express oneself:
    223,15-16
apophasis, negation: 185,7; 188,23
apoplêroun, make up ... complete
    (sensible nature): 201,8
aporein, face an aporia, aporiae (see
    n. 3): 171,13-172,29, *passim*;
    173,6.12.13; 190,21;
    222,15.24? (see n. 383) ; raise
    an aporia: 191,2; 194,11;
    220,24.34; 223,16; 228,31.32;
    state an aporia: 183,15: deal
    with an aporia: 216,8
aporeisthai, (of an aporia) be
    faced: 180,7; 187,16; be raised:
    235,2.6; be presented: 236,26;
    be met with, 226,28; be
    settled: 222,23
aporoumena, points of aporia:
    172,24-5.30; 173,10
êporêmena, points of aporia:
    172,13.17
axion aporêthênai, the aporia
    deserves to be faced: 175,24
pôs êporêtai, how the aporia has
    developed: 172,31
aporeisthai dunamena, possible
    aporiae: 173,20.26
dunatai aporeisthai, the aporia
    could be: 216,16-17
koinôs aporoumenê, (if) the
    aporia is a general one: 216,18
aporia, aporia (see n 3): 172,6;
    172,27-173,4, *passim*; 179,25;
    180,17; 190,21; 194,10.14;
    196,4; 197,30; 219,21; 221,22;
    222,26.28; 224,16; 225,34
aporos, matter of aporia: 172,15;
    insuperable difficulty: 226,1
apotrôgein, swallow (v): 222,24-5.28
argos, unworked: 231,3
aristos, best: 183,12 (see *agathos*,
    beltiôn)

arithmos, number: 176,29;
    178,20; 198,20; 208,13.15;
    224.31.33.35; contrasted with
    megethos, 228,16-28
*kat' arithmon, kata ton arith-
    mon*: numerically:
    215,33.34.35
arkhê, principle: 174,10; 175,1.5.5-
    6; 177,26; 180,19-20; 181,33;
    181,34; 186,8.9; 218,22;
    221,27; 234,5
tên arkhên (adverbial), at all:
    182,27; 221,33; 226,15;
    227,15; 231,24
arkhesthai, begin: 182,10; 212,3;
    215,21; be the beginning of:
    186,11
arkhaios, of old: 178,5; 218,25;
    222,30
arkhikôtatos, most suited to rule:
    184,17
arkhitektonikos, most archi-
    tectonic: 184,17.22
arkhoeidês, of the nature of a
    principle: 208,4
artasthai, depend: 172,13; 203,17;
    210,27; 223,18
artios, even (math.): 176,29; 223,30
asaphesteros, rather unclear: 222,3
astrologia, astronomy: 198,5.17;
    200,4-5
astrologikos, astronomical: 200,13
astrologos, astronomer: 198,8;
    200,12
astron, star: 198,6.8.10
athanasia, immortality: 219,2
athanatos, immortal: 219,4
athroizesthai, be gathered: 193,9
athroôs, all at once: 232,7.8
atomos, indivisible (of species):
    204,28; 207,12-28, *passim*;
    209,33; (of principles): 236,22
atomos ousia, individual sub-
    stance: 211,30; 236,9
atoma, individuals: 178,1;
    209,28.29.30; 209,29;
    210,3.11; 211,31
atopos, absurd: 179,12; 191,6
to atopon, absurdity: 184,7;
    191,31; 195,28.30; 201,12
atopôteros, more absurd: 201,11

aülos, immaterial: 171.9;
178.20; 179,1
autoagathon, Good Itself (Platonic):
182,6.20.21
autos, self
　autos, without expressed ante-
　　cedent = Aristotle: 171,10.11;
　　172,18; 173,28; 177,3.4.20;
　　178,12; 206,13; 208,21
　autos without expressed ante-
　　cedent = Plato: 204,7
　autoi without antecedent = Pla-
　　tonists: 197,8; 199,26
　auta, things (letters, elements)
　　themselves, 218,6
　auto, Itself (prefix or suffix indi-
　　cating a Platonic Idea or
　　Form: 197,8-14, *passim*;
　　216,17
autoêlios, (combine diaeresis & long
　mark?) Sun Itself: 198,15
autoen, One Itself: 216,16.29.35;
　224,6; 227,16
autogrammê, Line Itself: 199,13
autoïppos, Horse Itself: 197.9
autoon, Being Itself: 216,16.29;
　224,6
autoouranos, Heaven Itself: 198,15
autothen, directly: 182,8; immedi-
　ately: 188,21-2
autotrigônon, Triangle Itself:
　199,12-13
autoügieia, Health Itself: 197,10;
　199,9.11.15
auxanein, increase (v tr): 227,18-24,
　passim; 228,3.4
　auxanesthai, be increased,
　　increase (v intr): 213,34;
　　227,18
　auxêsis, increase (n): 213,34
　auxêtikos, capable of causing
　　increase: 227,31
axiôma, axiom: 175,7.9.14; 179,20;
　187,17; 227,10
axios, deserving, worthy
　axion aporeisthai, the aporia
　　deserves to be faced: 175,23;
　　176,1
　axion prosaporeisthai, a further
　　aporia deserves to be faced:
　　179,22

axion aporêsai, worthwhile
　to raise aporia (conjectural,
　see n. 422): 228,6
axion zêtein, it deserves inquiry:
　177,32; worthy of inquiry?:
　204,26
axion apaitein: worthwhile
　demanding an answer: 228,23
axioun, think: 181,12; 236,17;
　take as an axiom: 227,13.16

badizein, walk: 173,19; go on (to
　infinity): 222,1
bathos, depth: 230,5.31
bebaiôsis, confirmation: 182,31
beltiôn, better: 182,25; 209,36;
　210,1 (see *agathos, ameinôn*)
bia, force: 201,28
biblion, book: 218,22; 221,34
boulesthai, wish: 182,6; 197,23;
　212,8; 234,21
brakhus, short
　pro brakheos, shortly before:
　　217,2
　brakheôs, briefly: 235,19

deiknunai, prove: 172,28.29;
　173,28; 177,8.14; 179,12;
　182,19; show: 186,20; 190,16;
　192,23-6; point out: 223,28
　deiktikos, that proves: 176,35;
　　193,24; able to prove: 189,18
　hôn deiktikon, in proof of this:
　　225,10
　deixis, proof: 200,10.13; 202,16;
　　236,8.11
　hupo deixin piptein, be exhi-
　　bited: 229,10
dein, be necessary
　dei, one must: 171,13; 172,3; one
　　has to: 173,7; 188,27
　to dein, the need: 234,30
　deisthai, have need: 188,25;
　　require: 222,18
　deontôs, as (they) ought: 172,5
dekhesthai, receive: 214,30.32
dêlos, clear: 183,29; 196,21
　dêlon hoti, it is clear that: 218,16;
　　that is: 198,3
　dêlôtikos, that indicates: 189,9;
　　which would signify: 197,28;

that expresses: 204,15; 225,9
hôn dêlôtikon, this is made clear: 226,29
toutou dêlôtikon, this is expressed: 228,12
dêloun, make clear: 175,8; 176,3; 178,30; 182,12; 189,33; convey: 207,20; manifest: 223,11; express: 223,36
dêlousthai, be made manifest: 236,18
desmos, knot: 172.25.27.28.33
deuteros, second
to deuteron, the consequent (log): 187,32-3
diagramma, geometrical proposition (see n. 209): 202,12
diairein, divide: 206,17; 231.10-11; 232,1.3.11.14
diaireisthai, be divided: 177,25.29; be distinguished: 203,22
diairesis, division: 203,19; 232,12; dimension: 230,28.29; 232,24
diairesei, by dividing: 207,22
khreia tês diaireseôs, need of dividing: 199,3
kata tauta hai diaireseis, in respect of these things are divided: 232,24
diairetikos, that divides: 205,11; 206,35
diakrinesthai, be differentiated: 220,8.14
diakrisis, separation: 178,10; judgment: 223,20
diakritikos, piercing: 207,2
dialambanein, deal with: 176,20; 177.1.11; 187,26; 191,11
dialektikos, dialectical: 177,22
ho dialektikos, dialectician: 177,1
hê dialektikê, dialectic: 173,28-174,3 *passim*
dialektikôs ekhein, be dialectical: 218,17
dialuesthai, be dissolved: 202,10; 222,14
diamartanein, err
diêmartêmenôs hupolambanein, hold erroneous views: 172,5

dianoeisthai, conceive of: 223,26
dianoia, thought: 172,27-173,3, *passim*
diapherein, differ (in fact): 175,22.23.29; 180,7
diapheresthai, differ (in opinion): 223,28
diaphora, difference: 200,30; 203,7.9; 205,10-208,1, *passim*
diaphoros, diverse: 172,7; different: 175,19; 191,17
diaphônia, conflict: 224,16
diaporein, work through aporia/ aporiae: 172,9.11-12; 173,9; 174,2,15.22.31; 180,33; 211,9; 235,7
diarthroun, articulate (v): 234,28
diastasis, extension: 201,8.9.27
diastêma, interval: 232,30
diathesis, condition: 229,4
didaskein, teach: 188,25; instruct: 218,28
didaskalia, instruction: 185,6
didaskalikos, capable of teaching: 184,19
didonai, give: 186,1; 199,20; grant (in argument): 186,33; 211,18
diienai, go right through: 201,23
diistanai, (act) exist: 229,15; (mid) separate (intr): 232,6
dikha, in two: 231,11
diorizein, determine: 184,12.29; 210,25
dogma, doctrine: 197,1.8
dokein, seem: 174,11.12; 186,15; 202,33; 203,27; 218,27; 222,29; appear: 175,8; 196,11; 207,1.10.15; 219,10; 233,31; 234,27
tisin edoxe, some have thought: 172,21; 177,10
enargôs dokein, be clearly evident: 209,24
doxa, opinion: 172,7; 187,17; 191,29.30; view: 174,17; 200,38; 203,3; 219,7; 227,31; 228,10; 233,7; theory: 196,23; 197,3
duas, Dyad (Platonic principle): 203,31; 228,13-18, *passim*

dunamis, potentiality:
235,15.18.19
  dunamei, in potentiality:
  235,7-32, *passim*; potentially:
  231,13.14.18.19; in a potential
  way: 180,13; in effect: 181,2;
  203,3; 213,28
  dunasthai, be able (can, may):
  171,14; 186,25; 212,30;
  231,1.8; be potentially: 216,10
  ison dunasthai, be equivalent (in
  meaning): 186,22
  dunatos, possible: 212,22;
  potential: 235,16.18.21;
  235,30; capable: 235,28
duskherês, difficult
  ta duskherê, difficulties: 234,1
duskolia, difficulty: 196,29.31
dusleptos, difficult to grasp: 197,35
duslutos, difficult: 223,2

eidenai, know: 172,31; 183,2.4.5;
185,4
eidos, kind: 174,16-31, *passim*;
  176,1; 179,6; 181,7-18,
  passim; species: 204,28;
  207,12-28, *passim*; 208,6.19;
  form: 171,9; 177,28; 178,18;
  179,5; 181,22; 183,30.31;
  184,1; 208,11.19; 214,28;
  215,29; (Platonic) Form (=
  idea): 176,4.15; 178,27; 233,3
  eidopoieisthai, be given form:
  229,22.24; be constituted as
  species: 205,21
  eidikos, formal: 179,14; 181,21;
  186,4; formlike: 234,22-3
eikotôs, appropriately: 236,19
einai, be, exist, 171,5, *passim*; be
  possible: 200,9; 234,12
  to einai, being (esse), existence:
  180,6; 192,14; 199,31-2,
  passim
  to einai (+ dat), the being, essence
  (of): 203,21; 236,12
  to ti esti, what (a thing) is: 177,18;
  185,14.23-4; 194,26
  en tôi ti estin, in an essential way
  (see n. 255): 208,2
  to ti ên einai, essence: 193,27;
  194,2; 195,29; 196,28

to on, being (ens): 177,12,
  passim
to on, (Platonic) Being: 204,33-
  207,27, *passim*; 223,9-226,29,
  passim
to on hêi on, being as being:
  177,12
to mê on, non-being: 212,24;
  213,7-12, *passim*; 221,25;
  235,28
to mêpô on, that which does not
  yet exist: 235,26
mê an onta, things which would
  not exist: 219,5
to dunamei on, that which is
  potentially: 231,19
to malista on, that which in the
  highest degree is, 183,12
ta onta, beings, things that are:
  176,29, *passim*
eiôthenai, be commonly: 176,25
eirein, speak: 175,30; say: 181,19;
  235,3
  rhêthêsetai, (the issue) will be
  raised: 199,23
  eirêmenon, statement: 174,12-
  13.25; 220,17; phrase: 172,1
eisagein, introduce: 219,17
ekei, there (in text): 174,26
ekleipsis, eclipse: 185,30.31
ekluein, dissolve: 214,25
ekpheugein, escape: 207,35; 219,20
ekpiptein, fall short: 228,5
ekthesis, (initial) presentation:
  194,10-11; 196,4; 202,8;
  218,22; exhibition (see nn.
  483, 485): 236,8.11.18
ektithesthai, (mid) present: 174,17;
  187,8; 224,15; (pass) be exhibited: 236,19
elattôn, less
  ep' elatton, less extensively:
  205,18
elenkhein, refute: 183,28; 200,19
emmesos, intermediate: 177,20
emperiekhesthai, be included:
  177,18-19
enantios, contrary: 176,32; 187,1
  to enantion, the opposite side of
  the argument: 183,15
enantiotês, contrariety: 176,32;

177,19; 187,1
enargês, evident: 229,12
enargôs dokein, be clearly evident: 209,24
endeiknusthai, make evident: 183,6; 191,5; indicate: 195,3
endekhesthai, be possible: 175,10; 183,21; 188,8.9; 228,1-2
endein, be missing: 193,32
endoxos, accepted
to endoxon, accepted opinion: 176,34; 236,26
kata to endoxon, on the basis of accepted opinion: 210,21; 212,12.18
endoxôs, on the level of accepted opinion: 177,2
eneinai, be possible (can): 183,2; 184,20; 189,31
energeia, activity: 182,18; actuality: 235,14-23, *passim*
energeiâi, actually: 231,13.14.20; in actuality: 235,10-24, *passim*
kat' energeian, in the way of actuality: 180,14; 235,15.16.23
engignesthai, come to be present: 214,26; 215,27
entautha, here (in text): 196,23; in this world: 234,7
enulos, enmattered: 178,18-34, *passim*; 198,14; 215,29
enuparkhein, be present in: 235,18
ta enuparkhonta, constituents: 177,25; 202,5.17
eoikenai, be like
eoikenai tuphlou poreiais, walk like blind men: 173,9
epagein, introduce: 191,31; reduce (to absurdity): 193,12-13
epagôgê, induction: 202,32
epanabainein, go up
ta epanabebêkota genê, the kinds higher up: 210,19
epanienai, return: 180,34; 220,35
epanô, above (in text): 233,11
epekhein, have (status): 200,27; occupy (place): 208,7
epharmozein, apply: 197,12; have an application: 216,18; coin-

cide: 227,24.27; 232,8
ephesis, effort: 175,12
ephiesthai, strive: 182,18
ephexês, next: 190,21
hai ephexês gôniai, the resultant angles: 195,11
ephistanai, set up: 223,1; intersect: 195,13; (of discussion) turn to: 210,23-4
epienai, proceed: 184,20
epigi(g)nesthai, supervene: 211,24
epigraphein, entitle: 171,6
epikheirein, argue (see nn. 19, 74): 174,2.29-30; 181,2; 188,14.16; 190,19.24-5; 202,32.34; 204,9.12; 205,5; 208,5.6; 210,12; 212,12.18; 217,28; 225,4; 236,15.27-8
touto epikheirein, make this argument: 205,28
epikheirein deiknunai, try to prove: 213,23
epikheirêsis, argument: 181,25.26; 187,27; 203,3.14; 204,12; 210,13; 215,18-19; 229,21; 231,28; 236,26.28
epikheiretikê, that argues: 176,35
epikratein, dominate: 221,11
epimimnêskesthai, mention: 219,7
epinoein, conceive of: 198,16
epinoia, thought (esp abstractive): 199,22: 230,34-231,17, *passim*
epipedon, plane: 195,5.8; plane figure: 180,26
epiphaneia, surface: 227,22.23.24; 231,11
epipherein, add: 176,4; 186,27; go on (to say): 186,21; make a further point: 187,4; supply: 218,14; indicate: 173,1; 183,19
epipheromenon, following statement: 233,27
episkeptesthai, examine: 173,10; 177,22; 178,16
episkopein, preside: 195,28
epistasthai, know
to epistasthai, scientific knowledge: 184,5; 217,19
epistasia, mastery: 230,9
epistêmê, science: 171,5.12; 172,3;

174,9.32; 183,17 (cj); 212,8.9;
236,24
epistêmôn,possessor of science:
183,20.23
epistêtos, object of science:
181,26.27.28; 183,17 (but see
n. 93); 212.8; 236,25
epitassein, ordain: 184,24
epitunkhanesthai, hit on: 202,2
epizêtein, raise a question: 193,16
epizêteisthai, be the object of
inquiry: 171,5
epos, verse: 219,34; 220,4.6
ergon, product: 183,31.33; 220,9
eskhatos, ultimate: 204,27; 207,28;
208,19.20; 213,2-5, *passim*
ethos, customary way: 211,21
êthos, manner: 196.22
eulogos, reasonable: 175,25; 187,3;
190,24; 191,3.19-20; 219,14
eulogôs, reasonably
eulogôs dokein, seem reasonable:
203,27
eiê an eulogôs legôn, it would be
reasonable for him to say:
174,30
eulogôteros, more reasonable:
204,9; 214,30
euporein, advance
euporêtai (impers pass), (the
inquiry) has advanced: 173,15
euporia, advance (n):
172,12.16.17
eutelestatos, most complete and
perfect: 182,34
euthugrammos, rectilinear (plane
figure): 195,17; rectangle:
185,32-186,1, *passim*
euthuôria, straight course or
direction
kat' euthuôrian, direct series:
174,19; straight on: 213,14
euthus, straight: 195,10-11
exairetos, special: 221,6
exakouesthai, be meant: 205,32
exarithmein, enumerate: 171,13;
187,16
exêgeisthai, explain: 177,17;
197,25; 218,7; 223,21-2
exetazein, examine: 177,23; 194,18;
219,7-8.11

exô, outside: 196,9; 200,38
exôthen, from outside (one's position): 208,18; 220,34; on
different grounds: 190,20

gê, earth: 185,31
genesis, becoming: 212,22.25;
219,17.19; 231,26-232.33,
passim (see n. 444); coming
into being: 202,24; (plural)
instances of becoming: 186,3
gennan, beget: 213,20.21; 219,30;
(pass) be generated: 228,14.28
gen(n)êtos, generated:
212,12.15.26
gennêtikos, generative: 220.2.7;
such as to generate: 228.20
genos, kind (see n. 204): 178,2;
202,4-210,19, *passim*; genus:
192,24-193,19, *passim*; genus
(= category): 195,35; classification: 175,26
genikôtatos, most generic: 205,3;
210,10
geôdaisia, surveying: 199,1.6.8
geômetrein, do geometry: 182,28
geômetrês, geometer: 195,7
geômetria, geometry: 181,17;
182,24; 190,3; 195,5; 199,6
geômetrikos, geometrical: 190,4
geuesthai, taste (v): 218,30-219,4
geusis, tasting: 219,4
gi(g)nesthai, come to be, come into
being, come about, come:
182,26; 192,17; 203,15;
212,28-213,13, *passim* (see nn.
290-2); 220,21; 232,16-32,
passim (see n. 444); become:
211,25; 226,2; 228,15; turn out
(to be): 192,2-3; 220,25; 226,4;
228,9; 234,15.31; take place:
206,25; 212,24; occur: 200,25;
involve: 182,17; develop:
211,2.3.5; be derived (from):
175,6; be directed (to): 213,26
gi(g)nomenon, that which comes
to be: 215,1; 232,16-32,
passim; 235,29; that which (a
thing) comes to be: 212,22-
213,23, *passim* (see nn. 293,
298)

gegonos, that which has
come to be: 215,1.9
gignôskein, know: 172,8; 176,23
gnôsis, knowledge: 174,32;
183,7.13; 186,5.17.31; 187,5
gnôstos, knowable: 184,34;
known: 212,9
gnôstikos, able to know: 175,21;
181,26.30; 182,29; 183,16.18;
184,21; 187,1; capable of
knowing: 184,18
glukus, sweet: 210,9
gnôrimos, known: 173,17.20;
obvious: 175,28; 218,14.33
ho gnôrimos, acquaintance:
227,14
oudamôs gnôrimôs, in a manner
quite unobvious: 219,1
gnôrimôteros, more familiar:
224,8
gnôrizein, know: 173,7.16;
181,14; 184,8; 188,18
gônia, angle: 176,27; 195,12
gramma, letter (of alphabet):
218,11; 234,7
grammê, line (geom): 195,5.8;
227,21-8, *passim*
kata grammên, along a line:
227,23; line to line: 227,27
graphein, write: 218,11; 224,19 (see
n. 393)
ameinon gegraphthai, be a
better text: 186,31; 233,26
graphetai en tisin, some manuscripts read: 194,3

haphê, contact: 232,15
haplos, simple: 206,28; 229,12
haplôs, simply: 179,5; 182,5;
206,26; 215,29; 227,20; without qualification: 175,30;
190,30.31; without expla-
nation: 218,34
haplousteros, simpler: 206,27
haptesthai, touch: 200,16,17; be in
contact: 232,1-10
harmonikos, harmonic
hê harmonikê, harmonics:
198,18.25
harmozesthai, fit together (notes):
198,19

harpagê, abduction: 186,9
haut-, reflexive pronoun
kath' hauto, *kath' hauta*, etc.,
essential, essentially: 176,18-
26, *passim*; 188,9.11; in (its,
their) own right: 178,4;
180,4.29; 182,14; 197,3;
210,30; by itself: 205,17
hêdonê, pleasure: 219,2
heis, one
hen ti epi pollôn, one thing over
many things: 217,2
arithmôi hen, one in number:
218,7-8
eidei hen, one in form: 216,13
hen kat' arithmon, numerically
one: 216,14
to hen, = unity, 216,21-217,25,
passim
to hen, One (Empedoclean principle): 219,31; 220,9.15
to hen, One (Platonic principle):
179,26; 203,25; 204,33-209,10,
passim; 223,9-228,25, *passim*;
alternative translation: Unity
hêgeisthai, believe: 185,29; consider: 191; 18; think: 196,2
hêgemonikôtatos, most suited to
lead: 184,21-2
hekateros, both
eis hekatera, on both sides (of a
case): 174,2
hekastos, each
to kath' hekaston, *ta kath'
hekasta*, particular, particulars: 178,24; 180,4-5;
204,2.28; 208,14; 209,32;
210,16; 211.21 (*to kath'
hekasta*); 233,12
hêlios, sun: 195,23; 198,6.7.9
henas, a one: 227,2.7
heneka, for the sake of
to hou heneka, that-for-the-sake-
of-which: 181,37; 182,27
henoun, unify: 216,8; (pass) become
one: 220,12
hepesthai, follow: 194,24; 195,30;
234,1
hermêneuein, express oneself:
235,19
heteros, different: 176,31

heteron ti, some other
thing: 223,23; 225,26.34
heuriskein, discover: 172,29; (passive) be found: 173,19
heuresis, discovery: 171,11;
172,2-24, *passim*; 173,21
hexês, next (adv): 176,1; 188,16;
199,25
to hexês, the next statement:
189,4; the next step: 192,6
hoi hexês, those (numbers) that
follow: 209,4
hikanos, sufficient: 221,12
hippos, horse: 197,10
histanai, make stand, stand
histasthai (mid), come to a halt:
174,19; 212,24; 221,28-35,
passim
statheis (pass ptc), made to intersect: 195,11
historein, give an account: 208,18;
relate: 209,9.13; 223,32;
recount: 224,15
historia, tale: 182,32
hodêgein, guide (v): 173,12
hoios, such as: 185,12; 208,13
oukh hoios, incapable: 220,32
hoion (adv), for example: 205,33
hoion te, be possible (can):
172,25.30
holos, whole
to holon, ta hola, the whole:
211,23; 221,12; 227,20.27
kata ta hola, in every respect:
201,6
holôs, at all: 179,1; 212,4; 229,2;
in general: 210,26; 233,1;
235,2; overall: 211,6
holoklerôs, in totality: 227,21
homoeidês, same in form: 192,32;
193,18; 234,18; of the same
form: 233,9; same in kind:
176,7
homoios, like: 173,1.18; 176,31;
213,19-20; 220,22
homoiôs, likewise: 179,10; in like
manner: 194,33; 231,2.4;
234,19
homoiousthai, be assimilated:
216,33
homologein, speak consistently:

219,16.20.23
homônumia, equivocal character:
207,2; 210,4
homônumos, equivocal: 224,26
homônumôs, equivocally: 226,8
horan, see: 204,5; survey: 175,5.6
pros to telos horan, have a view
to the end: 184,24
horatos, visible: 198,23.25
horos, boundary marker: 199,4;
definition: 185,10
horismos, definition: 176,21-2;
176,28; 183,31; 186,1-2;
193,22; 203,5-10, *passim*
horistikos, that defines:
193,26.29; 196,25 (but see n.
174); (science) of definition:
193,36
horistikoi logoi, definitory formulae: 205,23
horistikôs, by way of definition:
194,31-2
horistos, defined: 203,10; objects
of definition: 196,25 (cj)
horizein, define: 185,8; 193,28;
229,22-3.25
hôrismenos, definite: 179,6;
189,23.24.25; 233,16
houtos, demonstrative indicating
that which is nearer
aisthêseis para tautas, senses
distinct from the senses of this
world: 198,27
en toutois, in these (sensible)
bodies: 230,21
hudôr, water: 225,19; Water (Presocratic principle): 180,2
hugieia, health: 199,8-12, *passim*
hugieinos, healthful: 199,17
hugiês, valid (log): 181,6; true:
181,8 (see n. 76)
to hugies, sound point: 195,33
hugies lambanein, assume
rightly: 215,15
hugiôs, rightly: 194,27
mê hugiôs legesthai, be unsound:
199,26
hugiesteros, sounder: 173,25
hulê, matter: 177,28; 187,13;
203,23; 211,19-216,9, *passim*
hulikos, material (causes):

179,16; 180,20; 187,12;
(differences) 216,2; (elements)
220,32-3
hupagein, place under: 196,27
huparkhein, belong: 176,24.30
  huparkhon, thing that belongs:
    176,21.24; 185,5-6
  kath' hauto huparkhein, be
    essential property of: 195,17-
    18.25
  kath' hauto huparkhon, essen-
    tial property: 194,22.29.32;
    195,6.9.22
huphistanai, huphistasthai, exist:
  178,17; 197,33; subsist:
  180,14; 210,30; have existence: 236,14
  hupostasis, reality: 180,4.12;
    197,2; 199,20; 227,17-18;
    229,32; 230,21-34, *passim*;
    233,23; existence: 201,10;
    234,33
hupoballein, put (as subject):
  224,11
hupographê, description
  hoi di' hupographês logoi,
    descriptive accounts: 176,25
hupokeisthai, function as subject:
  179,33-180,1; 232,33
  genos hupokeisthai + dative,
    have genus as subject:
    189,36-7
  hupokeimenon, subject: 178,11;
    179,16; 189,37; 229,8-9;
    232,32
hupolambanein, suppose: 191,19;
  204,1; hold view(s): 172,4;
  223,32
hupomimnêskein, mention: 201,19;
  remind: 234,1; 235,1.6
hupostasis, see *huphestanai*
hupotithesthai, suppose: 177,29;
  178,6; 200,25; 216,20; 221,29-
  30; 234,27; assume:
  202,20.22.25; 203,29.30; 204,1
  hupothesis, hypothesis: 210,34;
    211,34; 212,1; 234,1
husteros, posterior: 176,33; 208,26-
  210,3, *passim*
  ta hustera analutika, the *Poster-*
    ior Analytics: 186,2

husteron (adv), later (i.e.
  now): 232,13
hê husteron euporia, the subsequent advance: 174,29

iatrikos, medical: 199,18
  hê iatrikê, medicine: 199,7-200,3,
    passim
idea, Idea (Platonic): 176,5.7;
  178,27; 180,22; 196,6.7.10;
  215,28; 216,15.30;
  217,20.21.23; 224,6; 225,24;
  233,6-235,5, *passim*
idein, survey: 175,6; see *horan*
idios, proper: 176,24; 191,27; 206,9
  idia hupostasis, a reality of their
    own: 199,20
  kat' idian hupostasis, a reality
    proper to themselves: 180,12
  idiâi, in an exclusive way: 207,1
isarithmos, equal in number:
  197,24; 235,4
isos, equal: 175,11.12; 176,27;
  185,33; 186,1; equivalent (in
  meaning): 172,15.32; 174,28;
  182,20; 185,24; 186,22
  isôs, equally: 184,20

kakia, evil: 221,6
kakos, evil: 220,27 (see *kheirôn*)
kalein, call: 175,7; 187,25; 211,8
kalos, noble: 182,17
  kalôs, well
  kalôs prostithenai, do well to
    add: 229,31
kanôn, ruler: 200,15
katadeesteros, deficient (relative
  to): 182,34
kataginesthai, concern oneself, be
  concerned with: 187,24-5;
  191,22; 192,19
katalegein, list (v tr): 177,6; 201,13
kataleipein, leave (v tr): 184,10;
  201,5-6
  ta kataleipomena, remainders
    (math): 175,12
katallêlos, consistent: 186,15
  to katallêlon, logical order:
    185,22
  katallêloteron, more consistent:
    172,13

property of circular motion:
212,17
kurios, proper
  kuriôs, in the proper sense:
176,21; 196,34; 203,31, *passim*
  kuriôteros: in a stricter sense:
187,11.12
  kuriôtatos, in the strictest sense:
185,29-30; in the most proper
sense: 190,22; supreme:
183,12; of the highest importance: 223,17

lambanein, assume: 181,6-7.15;
182,14; 185,4; 189,3; 190,30;
191,32; 194,24.32.35;
200,9-26, *passim*;
204,12.16.32; 207,35; 209,8;
take (intellectually): 192,29-
30; 193,36; 206,11; 217,2.34-5;
218,8-9; take (form): 211,25;
grasp (intellectually): 203,23;
grasp (form): 216,9; reach
(conclusion): 182,29; get (science): 203,12.13
lêpsis, grasp: 203,7
legein, say: 174,30; 196,11-12;
197,4.31; speak (of): 187,31-2;
195,6; 203,7-8; call: 197,6;
mean: 174,21; 175,8;
176,19.24; 195,7; 196,33
  dunatai legesthai, the meaning
may be: 184,4
  to legomenon, the meaning (of a
text): 176,19; 189,20-1;
192,12; 194,4
  lexis, text: 175,8; 185,22; 222,3;
224,17; phrase: 193,32
leipein, be lacking: 175,8; 193,32
lêpsis, see *lambanein*
leukos, white: 210,8
lexis, see *legein*
lithos, stone: 231,3.10
logos, discussion: 171,10; 179,32;
200,20; 222,27; formula:
176,2.3; 179,15; 183,30; 184,4;
185,7.9; 193,20; 197,19;
205,23; account: 176,25-6;
184,13; 201,17; reason (faculty): 201,7; 230.1; reasoning:
199,16; 200,3; 201,14; 210,19;

232,13; 234,20; argument, line
of argument: 182,38; 183,2;
196,24; 198,16; 205,3; 217,29;
222,18; 228,1; 231.11; status:
187,13; 200,27; ratio: 198,20;
229,4
  anankaios ho logos autôi, he
must speak: 176,22
  poieisthai logon, discuss: 179,2;
194,24; take account: 182,37;
produce a discussion: 222,27
  kata logon, in an orderly way:
173,13
  kat' oudena logon, without
reason: 174,26
logikos, rational: 205,18.30.31
logikotês, rationality: 205,33
logikos, verbal (see n. 34): 177,9;
235,9; 236,28
logikôteros, rather verbal:
206,12-3
logikôs, on a verbal level: 210,21
logikôs ekhein, be verbal: 218,17
loidoria, insult (n): 186,11
loipos, remaining, i.e. third (side of
a triangle): 176,27
luein, untie: 172,23-6, *passim*;
173,8; solve: 172,30; 173,27;
195,14; 236,28
lusis, solution: 172,14.17.25;
173,21

manotês, rarity: 178,9
manthanein, understand:
185,31.32
mathêmatikos, mathematical:
196,7; 198,33.35; 201,21;
233,17.29
  ta mathêmatika, the mathematicals (Platonic intermediates):
176,4-5.6; 196,8; 197,32-
201,25, *passim*; 233,5.7
  ta mathêmatika, the mathematicals (in Aristotelian sense):
201,1-9, *passim*
megas, great
  to mega, the Great (Platonic principle): 203,25-204,6; 228,13
  meizôn, greater, vs. *pleiôn*, more
numerous: 228,3
  A meizon, Alpha Meizon (*Metaph.*

1): 187,7
megistos, greatest: 183,13
megethos, magnitude: 200,1;
    201,27; 227,12-228,27,
    passim; contrasted with
    arithmos, 228,16-28
mêkos, length: 180,26; 195,9-10;
    200,24.26; 230,4.5
mellein, be in future
    mellonta deiknusthai, matters
        that are to be proven: 172,29
    ei mellei tis lusein, if one is to
        untie: 173,8
    mellôn legein, in preparation for
        his argument: 196,19
    ei melloien esesthai, if there are
        to be: 227,4
menein, remain: 216,9; 219,25;
    222,19; perdure: 220,9
mênutikos, that indicates: 197,13
meros, part: 191,12; 193,7.9; 200,28
    meristos, divisible into parts:
        232,29
mesos, mean (geom): 185,33.34;
    intermediate: 209,18 (but see
    n. 266)
    dia mesou, parenthetical: 189,7
    en mesôi, in between: 222,2
metabainein, shift (v): 236,20
metaballein, change (v intr):
    180,24; 186,6-7; 216,10
metabolê, change (n): 204,5
metalambanesthai, be taken:
    176,28
metapherein, infer: 195,2
metaxu, between: 176,5; 196,7
    metaxu, ta, intermediates: 197,31
metekhein, share: 199,39
meterkhesthai, move (v intr):
    197,31
methexis, participation: 197,2
metienai, proceed: 183,15; 200,36
metousia, participation: 216,31;
    233,32
metron, measure: 199,2
mignusthai, be mixed: 216,6
    to neikos mignumenon, the
        admixture of Strife: 220,9-10
mikros, small
    mikron ti, a small point:
        222,25.26

to mikron, the Small (Pla-
    tonic principle): 203,25-204,6,
    passim; 228,13
mimnêskesthai, attend to:
    182,27.35; mention: 187,18
mnêmoneuein, mention: 174,12.15;
    cite: 218,26
monakhôs, in one sense:
    176,2.12.14; in one manner
    only: 196,5
monas, unit: 224,33.34; 226,13-26,
    passim; 227,30; 231,16
    monadikos, unitary: 214,29
morion, part: 193,30; 194,6; 202,28;
    232,31; portion: 205,22
    to heteron morion, the other side:
        236,20
mousikos, musical, of music:
    190,5.6
    hê mousikê, music: 187,32
muthos, myth: 219,8.9
    dia muthôn, by way of myths:
        219,8.9
    muthikôs, in mythic form: 219,9

nama, fluid (see n. 351): 218,32-3
neikos, Strife (Empedoclean prin-
    ciple): 219,18-221,12, *passim*
nektar, nectar: 218,32; 219,3
noein, think, think of: 199,20.21;
    201,2.8.9; 220,21-7, *passim*
    noeisthai, be conceived of: 230,6;
        233,25
    noêtos, intelligible: 175,19;
        191,15; 193,12; 199,9.12;
        212,5.6
    nous, mind: 171,10; Mind (Preso-
        cratic principle): 180,2; sense
        (of a text): 234,2
nun, now
    to nun, the present instant:
        232,21-32, *passim*
    hoi nun, present day thinkers:
        218,19

oiesthai, think: 185,23.26
oikeios, proper: 175,5; 181,28.29;
    200,37; 201,2.24; 205,14.20;
    appropriate: 177,9
oikodomikos, of housebuilding
    hê oikodomikê, housebuilding:

183,30
oligôrein, neglect: 218,29
oligos, little
  met' oligon, a little further on:
    183,6
  pro oligou, a short while ago:
    180,7; a little earlier: 205,9.16
to on, see *einai*
onoma, word: 178,1; 197,16; (?)
  218,32-3 (see n. 351)
  onomazein, call: 178,1; name:
    204,1
  onomazesthai, receive a name:
    207,15.17
opheilein, ought: 174,8
optikos, optical
  hê optikê, optics: 198,17.24.25
organon, tool: 177,7
orthos, right (geom): 176,27
ouranos, heaven: 196,30-4, *passim*
ousia, substance: 171,9; 175,1.5.18;
  176,8; 187,21.22.23; 192,1;
  193,15; 206,1.30.31; 211,30;
  223,13.22; 224,22; 225,18.25;
  234,22.23; 236,9; essence:
  185,15; 205,24; 214,29.32;
  223,35-6; existence: 220,11
  en têi ousiâi, in the [category of]
    substance: 225,18
  ousiôdês, of the essence: 176,25

palaios, ancient
  hoi palaioi, the ancients: 196,17
pantêi, etc., see *pas*
para, distinct from: 175,28;
  176,13.14, *passim*; besides:
  192,3
  hê paragôgê para to lêphthênai,
    the fallacy is that (the axioms)
    are assumed: 190,30
  ta para phusin, things not found
    in nature: 178,28
paradeigma, example: 195,14; pattern (Platonic): 196,6
paragôgê, fallacy: 182,38; 190,29;
  231,11
paraiteisthai, decline (v): 179,12;
  201,13; 219,9
parakrouesthai, do violence to:
  219,10
paralambanesthai, be included:

176,22; 205,23
paraleipein, leave: 218,14; leave
  unresolved: 218,18.21
paramutheisthai, produce comfortable conviction: 222,29
parapan, at all: 215,6.7; whatsoever: 215,13
parapempein, dismiss: 222,24
paratithesthai, cite: 182,23.31-2;
  183,28.29; 195,4; mention:
  216,16; say: 225,10
parekhein, present (v): 179,28;
  180,17
  parekhesthai, present: 215,1; fur-
    nish: 201,30
paristasthai, support (v): 233,6
parorasthai, be overlooked: 172,8
pas, all
  pantêi, in every respect:
    227,19.30; 228,2; any way:
    176,28
  pantôs, at all: 194,28
  pantelôs, completely: 222,18
  pantapasin, utterly: 227,32; alto-
    gether: 230,24
pathos, attribute: 188,28.29;
  229,3(cj).13.14; 230,30;
  modification: 178,6
  pathêtos, subject to change: 223,5
  pathêtikos, receptive (principle):
    181,20.21; affective (motions):
    229,3 (but see n. 427)
  ta pathêtika, affective attributes:
    201,9-10
pauesthai, stop (v intr): 193,14;
  214,25
peirasthai, try: 229,4; 222,29
peithein, persuade: 218,29
peras, limit (n): 213,25-214,7,
  passim; 227,22.23.27
  peperasmenos, limited: 174,20;
    179,7-11, *passim*
periekhesthai, be included: 205,30
perilêpsis, comprehension: 211,2
peripherês, curved: 195,11; 200,13
peripherogrammos, curvilinear
  (plane figure): 195,18
peripoiein, effect (v): 199,18
perittos, odd (math): 176,29
phainesthai, appear: 178,15;
  181,27; 201,30; 210,11

phainomenon agathon,
apparent good: 175,13
phanai
phêsi, he (Aristotle) says:
175,3.23.27; 177,19.22.26.32;
178,13
phasi, they (Platonists) say:
197,12; 199,1
phateon, one should say: 176,13;
should be said: 184,10
phaneros, evident: 202,31
pherein, bear
pistin pherein, confirm: 199,28
philia, Friendship (Presocratic
principle): 180,2
philia, Friendship (Empedoclean
principle): 219,17-221,11,
passim; 224,9
philosophia, philosophy: 174,1;
181,18; 191,12; 193,10
kata philosophian zêtêseis, philosophical inquiries: 174,3-4
philosophos, philosopher: 175,4;
177,9; 191,1.3.9.10
phônê, sound: 177,31; 202,11-12;
speech: 218,10
phortikos, crude: 228,1
phroimiazein, preface (v)
ta pephroimiasmena, prefatory
remarks: 174,5-22, *passim*
phthanein, be (previously)
phthasanta keisthai, which had
earlier been set down: 199,4
phthartos, perishable: 179,23.24;
199,34; 212,13-19, *passim*;
218,23
phtheiresthai, perish: 199,29-200,6,
passim; 213,35
phthora, perishing: 219,18-36,
passim; 222,13; 231,27-
232,27, *passim*
phuein, be by nature: 221,12.14
phusis, nature: 177,27; 178,28;
179,33; 181,37; 182,5; 189,14-
20, *passim*; 192,19; 196,33;
200,37; 201,2-24, *passim*;
212,14; 213,11.19; 220,15;
223,11.12; 225,31; 230,30;
232,11; 233,23
ousiôn phusis, grade of substances: 176,8

phusikos, natural: 193,12;
195,23; 199,22
hoi phusikoi, the natural philosophers: 178,5; 180,2; 202,19.24;
224,6
phusiologos, natural scientist:
219,16
ta phusika, natural things:
195,25; works of nature:
211,32
meta ta phusika, metaphysics:
171,6
hê phusikê, natural philosophy:
181,17; 195,20
hê phusikê akroasis, the *Physics*:
223,29
phulattein, retain: 220,36
piptein, fall
hupo deixin piptein, be able to be
exhibited: 229,10
hupo ekthesin kai deixin piptein,
be subject to exhibition and
proof: 236,8.11
pistis, certitude
pistin pherein, confirm: 199,28
pistôsis, confirmation; *eis pis-
tôsin*, to confirm: 230,8
pistousthai, confirm: 174,17-18;
197,8
pithanos, plausible: 218,27; 222,28
kata to pithanon, on the level of
plausibility: 236,27
plasmatôdes, contrived: 206,21
platos, breadth: 200,26; 227,28;
230,4.5
kata platos, breadth to breadth:
227,24
pleiôn, more (than one): 174,9;
175,18
pleion, more numerous, vs.
meizôn, larger: 228,3
epi pleon, more extensively:
205,17.19; 208,1
pleonektein, seek to share: 220,28
(cj, see n. 362)
pleonektounta têi prosthêkêi,
with benefit of the addition:
197,18
plêthos, multiplicity: 207,35; plurality: 226,26
pleura, side: 176,27; 185,35

201,21; commonplace argument: 229,19

trephesthai, be nourished: 219,5.6

trias, (the number) three: 209,3

trigônon, triangle: 176,26; 180,26-7

trikhêi, in three dimensions: 229,15

trophê, nourishment: 219,5

tropos, manner: 188,17; 197,3; 202,31; 216,6; 235,8.11; form (log): 181,6; type (of cause): 183,21; mode (of prior): 209,35

tunkhanein, happen: 188,18; 195,10; attain: 182,18-19

tukhôn (ptc): matter of chance: 202,2; chance thing: 189,3; 190,3

tuphlos, blind: 173,9

zêtein, inquire: 173,9; 174,32; 193,22; 210,28

zêteisthai, be object of inquiry: 177,10

zêtoumenon, object of inquiry: 171,12; 173,11.25

telos tou zêtoumenou, end of the inquiry: 173,17-18

telos ekhei to zêtoumenon, the inquiry has come to a [successful] end: 173,16

zêtesis, inquiry: 173,13; 174,4; 223,15.17.20

zôion, animal: 198,28.29.30; 199,12; 205,30.31; 210,6

Subject Index

Three sorts of items appear in this index: the names of the thinkers mentioned by Alexander in his commentary on *Metaphysics* 3; Alexander's references to the works of Aristotle; and entries bearing on the principal philosophical issues discussed in the aporiae. *Metaphysics* 3 is mainly dialectical and aporetic, and Alexander's commentary reflects, by and large, the book's inconclusive character. This index may serve as a guide to where in the commentary various subjects are discussed; but it cannot, in general, tell the reader what Aristotle or Alexander thinks about those subjects; and readers desiring to trace a word or concept through the commentary will find more help in the Greek-English Index. Aristotle and Alexander did not number the aporiae; here they are numbered in the order in which they are discussed in chapters 2-6 of *Metaphysics* 3.

abstraction, *aphairesis*: mathematicals known by abstraction: 199,19-20; 200,1-2
actuality, *energeia*:
  aporia (14) whether principles are in actuality or potentiality: 180,13-15; 235,9-32
  case against principles in actuality: 235,11-24
  case against principles in potentiality: 235,24-32
Alexander of Aphrodisias:
  speaking in first person: 192,7; 204,18; 212,18
  explicit evaluations of Aristotle: 172,13-16; 181,5-19; 182,38-183,11; 206,12-13; 210,20-1; 212,12; 214,12-18; 218,17; 229,31; 231,11-20; 235,9; 236,26-9
Anaximenes: air as subject for One, Being: 224,12

aporia, *aporia*:
  necessity of facing: 171,11-173,27
  sources of: 172,2-9
  difficulty of working through: 180,30-3
Aristippus: criticism of mathematics: 182,32-8
Aristotle, predecessors, global references: 218,20-1; 230,8-13
Aristotle, references to works:
  An. Post.: 186,2; 194,27; 204,13-14
  Cat.: 209,36; 224,26; 233,20-1(?); 236,6-7
  DA 1: 174,11-12
  EN 1: 209,13-14
  GC 1 (?): 216,7-8
  Metaph. 1: 174,16.31; 176,8-9; 179,33; 184,15-16; 187,7; 196,13.20.31; 197,3.22; 201,19; 233,8-9; 235,5-6
  Metaph. 2: 174,18.25-6; 179,12-13; 201,18; 213,14-15.33;

Appendix

The Commentators*

The 15,000 pages of the Ancient Greek Commentaries on Aristotle are the largest corpus of Ancient Greek philosophy that has not been translated into English or other modern European languages. The standard edition (*Commentaria in Aristotelem Graeca*, or *CAG*) was produced by Hermann Diels as general editor under the auspices of the Prussian Academy in Berlin. Arrangements have now been made to translate at least a large proportion of this corpus, along with some other Greek and Latin commentaries not included in the Berlin edition, and some closely related non-commentary works by the commentators.

The works are not just commentaries on Aristotle, although they are invaluable in that capacity too. One of the ways of doing philosophy between A.D. 200 and 600, when the most important items were produced, was by writing commentaries. The works therefore represent the thought of the Peripatetic and Neoplatonist schools, as well as expounding Aristotle. Furthermore, they embed fragments from all periods of Ancient Greek philosophical thought: this is how many of the Presocratic fragments were assembled, for example. Thus they provide a panorama of every period of Ancient Greek philosophy.

The philosophy of the period from A.D. 200 to 600 has not yet been intensively explored by philosophers in English-speaking countries, yet it is full of interest for physics, metaphysics, logic, psychology, ethics and religion. The contrast with the study of the Presocratics is striking. Initially the incomplete Presocratic fragments might well have seemed less promising, but their interest is now widely known, thanks to the philological and philosophical effort that has been concentrated upon them. The incomparably vaster corpus which preserved so many of those fragments offers at least as much interest, but is still relatively little known.

The commentaries represent a missing link in the history of philosophy: the Latin-speaking Middle Ages obtained their knowledge of Aristotle at least partly through the medium of the commentaries. Without an appreciation of this, mediaeval interpretations of Aristotle will not be understood. Again, the ancient commentaries are the unsuspected source of ideas which have been thought, wrongly, to originate in the later mediaeval

* Reprinted from the Editor's General Introduction to the series in Christian Wildberg, *Philoponus Against Aristotle on the Eternity of the World*, London and Ithaca N.Y., 1987.

period. It has been supposed, for example, that Bonaventure in the thirteenth century invented the ingenious arguments based on the concept of infinity which attempt to prove the Christian view that the universe had a beginning. In fact, Bonaventure is merely repeating arguments devised by the commentator Philoponus 700 years earlier and preserved in the meantime by the Arabs. Bonaventure even uses Philoponus' original examples. Again, the introduction of impetus theory into dynamics, which has been called a scientific revolution, has been held to be an independent invention of the Latin West, even if it was earlier discovered by the Arabs or their predecessors. But recent work has traced a plausible route by which it could have passed from Philoponus, via the Arabs, to the West.

The new availability of the commentaries in the sixteenth century, thanks to printing and to fresh Latin translations, helped to fuel the Renaissance break from Aristotelian science. For the commentators record not only Aristotle's theories, but also rival ones, while Philoponus as a Christian devises rival theories of his own and accordingly is mentioned in Galileo's early works more frequently than Plato.[1]

It is not only for their philosophy that the works are of interest. Historians will find information about the history of schools, their methods of teaching and writing and the practices of an oral tradition.[2] Linguists will find the indexes and translations an aid for studying the development of word meanings, almost wholly uncharted in Liddell and Scott's *Lexicon*, and for checking shifts in grammatical usage.

Given the wide range of interests to which the volumes will appeal, the aim is to produce readable translations, and to avoid so far as possible presupposing any knowledge of Greek. Footnotes will explain points of meaning, give cross-references to other works, and suggest alternative interpretations of the text where the translator does not have a clear preference. The introduction to each volume will include an explanation why the work was chosen for translation: none will be chosen simply because it is there. Two of the Greek texts are currently being re-edited –

---

[1] See Fritz Zimmermann, 'Philoponus' impetus theory in the Arabic tradition'; Charles Schmitt, 'Philoponus' commentary on Aristotle's *Physics* in the sixteenth century', and Richard Sorabji, 'John Philoponus', in Richard Sorabji (ed.), *Philoponus and the Rejection of Aristotelian Science* (London and Ithaca, N.Y. 1987).

[2] See e.g. Karl Praechter, 'Die griechischen Aristoteleskommentare', *Byzantinische Zeitschrift* 18 (1909), 516-38 (translated into English in R. Sorabji (ed.), *Aristotle Transformed: the ancient commentators and their influence* (London and Ithaca, N.Y. 1990)); M. Plezia, *de Commentariis Isagogicis* (Cracow 1947); M. Richard, 'Apo Phônês', *Byzantion* 20 (1950), 191-222; É. Evrard, *L'Ecole d'Olympiodore et la composition du commentaire à la physique de Jean Philopon*, Diss. (Liège 1957); L.G. Westerink, *Anonymous Prolegomena to Platonic Philosophy* (Amsterdam 1962) (new revised edition, translated into French, Collection Budé; part of the revised introduction, in English, is included in *Aristotle Transformed*); A.-J. Festugière, 'Modes de composition des commentaires de Proclus', *Museum Helveticum* 20 (1963), 77-100, repr. in his *Études* (1971), 551-74; P. Hadot, 'Les divisions des parties de la philosophie dans l'antiquité', *Museum Helveticum* 36 (1979), 201-23; I. Hadot, 'La division néoplatonicienne des écrits d'Aristote', in J. Wiesner (ed.), *Aristoteles Werk und Wirkung* (Paul Moraux gewidmet), vol. 2 (Berlin 1986); I. Hadot, 'Les introductions aux commentaires exégétiques chez les auteurs néoplatoniciens et les auteurs chrétiens', in M. Tardieu (ed.), *Les règles de l'interprétation* (Paris 1987), 99-119. These topics are treated, and a bibliography supplied, in *Aristotle Transformed*.

those of Simplicius *in Physica* and *in de Caelo* – and new readings will be exploited by translators as they become available. Each volume will also contain a list of proposed emendations to the standard text. Indexes will be of more uniform extent as between volumes than is the case with the Berlin edition, and there will be three of them: an English-Greek glossary, a Greek-English index, and a subject index.

The commentaries fall into three main groups. The first group is by authors in the Aristotelian tradition up to the fourth century A.D. This includes the earliest extant commentary, that by Aspasius in the first half of the second century A.D. on the *Nicomachean Ethics*. The anonymous commentary on Books 2, 3, 4 and 5 of the *Nicomachean Ethics*, in *CAG* vol. 20, is derived from Adrastus, a generation later.[3] The commentaries by Alexander of Aphrodisias (appointed to his chair between A.D. 198 and 209) represent the fullest flowering of the Aristotelian tradition. To his successors Alexander was The Commentator *par excellence*. To give but one example (not from a commentary) of his skill at defending and elaborating Aristotle's views, one might refer to his defence of Aristotle's claim that space is finite against the objection that an edge of space is conceptually problematic.[4] Themistius (*fl.* late 340s to 384 or 385) saw himself as the inventor of paraphrase, wrongly thinking that the job of commentary was completed.[5] In fact, the Neoplatonists were to introduce new dimensions into commentary. Themistius' own relation to the Neoplatonist as opposed to the Aristotelian tradition is a matter of controversy,[6] but it would be agreed that his commentaries show far less bias than the full-blown Neoplatonist ones. They are also far more informative than the designation 'paraphrase' might suggest, and it has been estimated that Philoponus' *Physics* commentary draws silently on Themistius six hundred times.[7] The pseudo-Alexandrian commentary on *Metaphysics* 6–14, of unknown authorship, has been placed by some in the same group of commentaries as being earlier than the fifth century.[8]

[3] Anthony Kenny, *The Aristotelian Ethics* (Oxford 1978), 37, n.3; Paul Moraux, *Der Aristotelismus bei den Griechen*, vol. 2 (Berlin 1984), 323-30.

[4] Alexander, *Quaestiones* 3.12, discussed in my *Matter, Space and Motion* (London and Ithaca, N.Y. 1988). For Alexander see R.W. Sharples, 'Alexander of Aphrodisias: scholasticism and innovation', in W. Haase (ed.), *Aufstieg und Niedergang der römischen Welt*, part 2 *Principat*, vol. 36.2, *Philosophie und Wissenschaften* (1987).

[5] Themistius *in An. Post.* 1,2-12. See H.J. Blumenthal, 'Photius on Themistius (Cod.74): did Themistius write commentaries on Aristotle?', *Hermes* 107 (1979), 168-82.

[6] For different views, see H.J. Blumenthal, 'Themistius, the last Peripatetic commentator on Aristotle?', in Glen W. Bowersock, Walter Burkert, Michael C.J. Putnam, *Arktouros*, Hellenic Studies Presented to Bernard M.W. Knox (Berlin and N.Y., 1979), 391-400; E.P. Mahoney, 'Themistius and the agent intellect in James of Viterbo and other thirteenth-century philosophers: (Saint Thomas Aquinas, Siger of Brabant and Henry Bate)', *Augustiniana* 23 (1973), 422-67, at 428-31; id., 'Neoplatonism, the Greek commentators and Renaissance Aristotelianism', in D.J. O'Meara (ed.), *Neoplatonism and Christian Thought* (Albany N.Y. 1982), 169-77 and 264-82, esp. n. 1, 264-6; Robert Todd, introduction to translation of Themistius *in DA* 3.4-8, in *Two Greek Aristotelian Commentators on the Intellect*, trans. Frederick M. Schroeder and Robert B. Todd (Toronto 1990).

[7] H. Vitelli, *CAG* 17, p. 992, s.v. Themistius.

[8] The similarities to Syrianus (died *c*.437) have suggested to some that it predates Syrianus (most recently Leonardo Tarán, review of Paul Moraux, *Der Aristotelismus*,

By far the largest group of extant commentaries is that of the Neoplatonists up to the sixth century A.D. Nearly all the major Neoplatonists, apart from Plotinus (the founder of Neoplatonism), wrote commentaries on Aristotle, although those of Iamblichus (*c.* 250 – *c.* 325) survive only in fragments, and those of three Athenians, Plutarchus (died 432), his pupil Proclus (410 – 485) and the Athenian Damascius (*c.* 462 – after 538), are lost.[9] As a result of these losses, most of the extant Neoplatonist commentaries come from the late fifth and the sixth centuries and a good proportion from Alexandria. There are commentaries by Plotinus' disciple and editor Porphyry (232 – 309), by Iamblichus' pupil Dexippus (*c.* 330), by Proclus' teacher Syrianus (died *c.* 437), by Proclus' pupil Ammonius (435/445 – 517/526), by Ammonius' three pupils Philoponus (*c.* 490 to 570s), Simplicius (wrote after 532, probably after 538) and Asclepius (sixth century), by Ammonius' next but one successor Olympiodorus (495/505 – after 565), by Elias (*fl.* 541?), by David (second half of the sixth century, or beginning of the seventh) and by Stephanus (took the chair in Constantinople *c.* 610). Further, a commentary on the *Nicomachean Ethics* has been ascribed to Heliodorus of Prusa, an unknown pre-fourteenth-century figure, and there is a commentary by Simplicius' colleague Priscian of Lydia on Aristotle's successor Theophrastus. Of these commentators some of the last were Christians (Philoponus, Elias, David and Stephanus), but they were Christians writing in the Neoplatonist tradition, as was also Boethius who produced a number of commentaries in Latin before his death in 525 or 526.

The third group comes from a much later period in Byzantium. The Berlin edition includes only three out of more than a dozen commentators described in Hunger's *Byzantinisches Handbuch*.[10] The two most important are Eustratius (1050/1060 – *c.* 1120), and Michael of Ephesus. It has been suggested that these two belong to a circle organised by the princess Anna Comnena in the twelfth century, and accordingly the completion of Michael's commentaries has been redated from 1040 to 1138.[11] His commentaries include areas where gaps had been left. Not all of these gap-fillers are extant, but we have commentaries on the neglected biological works, on the *Sophistici Elenchi*, and a small fragment of one on the *Politics*. The lost *Rhetoric* commentary had a few antecedents, but the *Rhetoric* too had been comparatively neglected. Another product of this

---

vol. 1, in *Gnomon* 46 (1981), 721-50 at 750), to others that it draws on him (most recently P. Thillet, in the Budé edition of Alexander *de Fato*, p. lvii). Praechter ascribed it to Michael of Ephesus (eleventh or twelfth century), in his review of *CAG* 22.2, in *Göttingische Gelehrte Anzeiger* 168 (1906), 861-907.

[9] The Iamblichus fragments are collected in Greek by Bent Dalsgaard Larsen, *Jamblique de Chalcis, Exégète et Philosophe* (Aarhus 1972), vol.2. Most are taken from Simplicius, and will accordingly be translated in due course. The evidence on Damascius' commentaries is given in L.G. Westerink, *The Greek Commentaries on Plato's Phaedo*, vol.2., Damascius (Amsterdam 1977), 11-12; on Proclus' in L.G. Westerink, *Anonymous Prolegomena to Platonic Philosophy* (Amsterdam 1962), xii, n.22; on Plutarchus' in H.M. Blumenthal, 'Neoplatonic elements in the de Anima commentaries', *Phronesis* 21 (1976), 75.

[10] Herbert Hunger, *Die hochsprachliche profane Literatur der Byzantiner*, vol.1 (= *Byzantinisches Handbuch*, part 5, vol.1) (Munich 1978), 25-41. See also B.N. Tatakis, *La Philosophie Byzantine* (Paris 1949).

[11] R. Browning, 'An unpublished funeral oration on Anna Comnena', *Proceedings of the Cambridge Philological Society* n.s. 8 (1962), 1-12, esp. 6-7.

period may have been the composite commentary on the *Nicomachean Ethics* (*CAG* 20) by various hands, including Eustratius and Michael, along with some earlier commentators, and an improvisation for Book 7. Whereas Michael follows Alexander and the conventional Aristotelian tradition, Eustratius' commentary introduces Platonist, Christian and anti-Islamic elements.[12]

The composite commentary was to be translated into Latin in the next century by Robert Grosseteste in England. But Latin translations of various logical commentaries were made from the Greek still earlier by James of Venice (*fl. c.* 1130), a contemporary of Michael of Ephesus, who may have known him in Constantinople. And later in that century other commentaries and works by commentators were being translated from Arabic versions by Gerard of Cremona (died 1187).[13] So the twelfth century resumed the transmission which had been interrupted at Boethius' death in the sixth century.

The Neoplatonist commentaries of the main group were initiated by Porphyry. His master Plotinus had discussed Aristotle, but in a very independent way, devoting three whole treatises (*Enneads* 6.1–3) to attacking Aristotle's classification of the things in the universe into categories. These categories took no account of Plato's world of Ideas, were inferior to Plato's classifications in the *Sophist* and could anyhow be collapsed, some of them into others. Porphyry replied that Aristotle's categories could apply perfectly well to the world of intelligibles and he took them as in general defensible.[14] He wrote two commentaries on the *Categories*, one lost, and an introduction to it, the *Isagôgê*, as well as commentaries, now lost, on a number of other Aristotelian works. This proved decisive in making Aristotle a necessary subject for Neoplatonist lectures and commentary. Proclus, who was an exceptionally quick student, is said to have taken two years over his Aristotle studies, which were called

[12] R. Browning, op. cit. H.D.P. Mercken, *The Greek Commentaries of the Nicomachean Ethics of Aristotle in the Latin Translation of Grosseteste, Corpus Latinum Commentariorum in Aristotelem Graecorum* VI 1 (Leiden 1973), ch.1, 'The compilation of Greek commentaries on Aristotle's Nicomachean Ethics'. Sten Ebbesen, 'Anonymi Aurelianensis I Commentarium in *Sophisticos Elenchos*', *Cahiers de l'Institut Moyen Age Grecque et Latin* 34 (1979), 'Boethius, Jacobus Veneticus, Michael Ephesius and "Alexander"', pp. v-xiii; id., *Commentators and Commentaries on Aristotle's Sophistici Elenchi*, 3 parts, *Corpus Latinum Commentariorum in Aristotelem Graecorum*, vol. 7 (Leiden 1981); A. Preus, *Aristotle and Michael of Ephesus on the Movement and Progression of Animals* (Hildesheim 1981), introduction.

[13] For Grosseteste, see Mercken as in n. 12. For James of Venice, see Ebbesen as in n. 12, and L. Minio-Paluello, 'Jacobus Veneticus Grecus', *Traditio* 8 (1952), 265-304; id., 'Giacomo Veneto e l'Aristotelismo Latino', in Pertusi (ed.), *Venezia e l'Oriente fra tardo Medioevo e Rinascimento* (Florence 1966), 53-74, both reprinted in his *Opuscula* (1972). For Gerard of Cremona, see M. Steinschneider, *Die europäischen Übersetzungen aus dem arabischen bis Mitte des 17. Jahrhunderts* (repr. Graz 1956); E. Gilson, *History of Christian Philosophy in the Middle Ages* (London 1955), 235-6 and more generally 181-246. For the translators in general, see Bernard G. Dod, 'Aristoteles Latinus', in N. Kretzmann, A. Kenny, J. Pinborg (eds). *The Cambridge History of Latin Medieval Philosophy* (Cambridge 1982).

[14] See P. Hadot, 'L'harmonie des philosophies de Plotin et d'Aristote selon Porphyre dans le commentaire de Dexippe sur les Catégories', in *Plotino e il neoplatonismo in Oriente e in Occidente* (Rome 1974), 31-47; A.C. Lloyd, 'Neoplatonic logic and Aristotelian logic', *Phronesis* 1 (1955-6), 58-79 and 146-60.

the Lesser Mysteries, and which preceded the Greater Mysteries of Plato.[15] By the time of Ammonius, the commentaries reflect a teaching curriculum which begins with Porphyry's *Isagôgê* and Aristotle's *Categories*, and is explicitly said to have as its final goal a (mystical) ascent to the supreme Neoplatonist deity, the One.[16] The curriculum would have progressed from Aristotle to Plato, and would have culminated in Plato's *Timaeus* and *Parmenides*. The latter was read as being about the One, and both works were established in this place in the curriculum at least by the time of Iamblichus, if not earlier.[17]

Before Porphyry, it had been undecided how far a Platonist should accept Aristotle's scheme of categories. But now the proposition began to gain force that there was a harmony between Plato and Aristotle on most things.[18] Not for the only time in the history of philosophy, a perfectly crazy proposition proved philosophically fruitful. The views of Plato and of Aristotle had both to be transmuted into a new Neoplatonist philosophy in order to exhibit the supposed harmony. Iamblichus denied that Aristotle contradicted Plato on the theory of Ideas.[19] This was too much for Syrianus and his pupil Proclus. While accepting harmony in many areas,[20] they could see that there was disagreement on this issue and also on the issue of whether God was causally responsible for the existence of the ordered physical cosmos, which Aristotle denied. But even on these issues, Proclus' pupil Ammonius was to claim harmony, and, though the debate was not clear cut,[21] his claim was on the whole to prevail. Aristotle, he maintained, accepted Plato's Ideas,[22] at least in the form of principles (*logoi*) in the divine intellect, and these principles were in turn causally responsible for the beginningless existence of the physical universe. Ammonius wrote a whole book to show that

[15] Marinus, *Life of Proclus* ch.13, 157,41 (Boissonade).

[16] The introductions to the *Isagôgê* by Ammonius, Elias and David, and to the *Categories* by Ammonius, Simplicius, Philoponus, Olympiodorus and Elias are discussed by L.G. Westerink, *Anonymous Prolegomena* and I. Hadot, 'Les Introductions', see n. 2. above.

[17] Proclus *in Alcibiadem 1* p.11 (Creuzer); Westerink, *Anonymous Prolegomena*, ch. 26, 12f. For the Neoplatonist curriculum see Westerink, Festugière, P. Hadot and I. Hadot in n. 2.

[18] See e.g. P. Hadot (1974), as in n. 14 above; H.J. Blumenthal, 'Neoplatonic elements in the de Anima commentaries', *Phronesis* 21 (1976), 64-87; H.A. Davidson, 'The principle that a finite body can contain only finite power', in S. Stein and R. Loewe (eds), *Studies in Jewish Religious and Intellectual History presented to A. Altmann* (Alabama 1979), 75-92; Carlos Steel, 'Proclus et Aristote', Proceedings of the Congrès Proclus held in Paris 1985, J. Pépin and H.D. Saffrey (eds), *Proclus, lecteur et interprète des anciens* (Paris 1987), 213-25; Koenraad Verrycken, *God en Wereld in de Wijsbegeerte van Ioannes Philoponus*, Ph.D. Diss. (Louvain 1985).

[19] Iamblichus ap. Elian *in Cat.* 123,1-3.

[20] Syrianus *in Metaph.* 80,4-7; Proclus *in Tim.* 1.6,21-7,16.

[21] Asclepius sometimes accepts Syrianus' interpretation (*in Metaph.* 433,9-436,6); which is, however, qualified, since Syrianus thinks Aristotle is really committed willy-nilly to much of Plato's view (*in Metaph.* 117,25-118,11; ap. Asclepium *in Metaph.* 433,16; 450,22); Philoponus repents of his early claim that Plato is not the target of Aristotle's attack, and accepts that Plato is rightly attacked for treating ideas as independent entities outside the divine Intellect (*in DA* 37,18-31; *in Phys.* 225,4-226,11; *contra Procl.* 26,24-32,13; *in An. Post.* 242,14–243,25).

[22] Asclepius *in Metaph* from the voice of (i.e. from the lectures of) Ammonius 69,17-21; 71,28; cf. Zacharias *Ammonius, Patrologia Graeca* vol. 85, col. 952 (Colonna).

Aristotle's God was thus an efficient cause, and though the book is lost, some of its principal arguments are preserved by Simplicius.[23] This tradition helped to make it possible for Aquinas to claim Aristotle's God as a Creator, albeit not in the sense of giving the universe a beginning, but in the sense of being causally responsible for its beginningless existence.[24] Thus what started as a desire to harmonise Aristotle with Plato finished by making Aristotle safe for Christianity. In Simplicius, who goes further than anyone,[25] it is a formally stated duty of the commentator to display the harmony of Plato and Aristotle in most things.[26] Philoponus, who with his independent mind had thought better of his earlier belief in harmony, is castigated by Simplicius for neglecting this duty.[27]

The idea of harmony was extended beyond Plato and Aristotle to Plato and the Presocratics. Plato's pupils Speusippus and Xenocrates saw Plato as being in the Pythagorean tradition.[28] From the third to first centuries B.C., pseudo-Pythagorean writings present Platonic and Aristotelian doctrines as if they were the ideas of Pythagoras and his pupils,[29] and these forgeries were later taken by the Neoplatonists as genuine. Plotinus saw the Presocratics as precursors of his own views,[30] but Iamblichus went far beyond him by writing ten volumes on Pythagorean philosophy.[31] Thereafter Proclus sought to unify the whole of Greek philosophy by presenting it as a continuous clarification of divine revelation,[32] and Simplicius argued for the same general unity in order to rebut Christian charges of contradictions in pagan philosophy.[33]

Later Neoplatonist commentaries tend to reflect their origin in a teaching curriculum:[34] from the time of Philoponus, the discussion is often divided up into lectures, which are subdivided into studies of doctrine and of text. A general account of Aristotle's philosophy is prefixed to the *Categories* commentaries and divided, according to a formula of Proclus,[35] into ten questions. It is here that commentators explain the eventual purpose of studying Aristotle (ascent to the One) and state (if they do) the requirement of displaying the harmony of Plato and Aristotle. After the ten-point introduction to Aristotle, the *Categories* is given a six-point introduction, whose antecedents go back earlier than Neoplatonism, and which requires

[23] Simplicius *in Phys.* 1361,11-1363,12. See H.A. Davidson; Carlos Steel; Koenraad Verrycken in n.18 above.

[24] See Richard Sorabji, *Matter, Space and Motion* (London and Ithaca N.Y. 1988), ch. 15.

[25] See e.g. H.J. Blumenthal in n. 18 above.

[26] Simplicius *in Cat.* 7,23-32.

[27] Simplicius *in Cael.* 84,11-14; 159,2-9. On Philoponus' *volte face* see n. 21 above.

[28] See e.g. Walter Burkert, *Weisheit und Wissenschaft* (Nürnberg 1962), translated as *Lore and Science in Ancient Pythagoreanism* (Cambridge Mass. 1972), 83-96.

[29] See Holger Thesleff, *An Introduction to the Pythagorean writings of the Hellenistic Period* (Åbo 1961); Thomas Alexander Szlezák, *Pseudo-Archytas über die Kategorien*, Peripatoi vol. 4 (Berlin and New York 1972).

[30] Plotinus e.g. 4.8.1; 5.1.8 (10-27); 5.1.9.

[31] See Dominic O'Meara, *Pythagoras Revived: Mathematics and Philosophy in late Antiquity* (Oxford 1989).

[32] See Christian Guérard, 'Parménide d'Elée selon les Néoplatoniciens', forthcoming.

[33] Simplicius *in Phys.* 28,32-29,5; 640,12-18. Such thinkers as Epicurus and the Sceptics, however, were not subject to harmonisation.

[34] See the literature in n. 2 above.   [35] ap. Elian *in Cat.* 107,24-6.

the commentator to find a unitary theme or scope (*skopos*) for the treatise. The arrangements for late commentaries on Plato are similar. Since the Plato commentaries form part of a single curriculum they should be studied alongside those on Aristotle. Here the situation is easier, not only because the extant corpus is very much smaller, but also because it has been comparatively well served by French and English translators.[36]

Given the theological motive of the curriculum and the pressure to harmonise Plato with Aristotle, it can be seen how these commentaries are a major source for Neoplatonist ideas. This in turn means that it is not safe to extract from them the fragments of the Presocratics, or of other authors, without making allowance for the Neoplatonist background against which the fragments were originally selected for discussion. For different reasons, analogous warnings apply to fragments preserved by the pre-Neoplatonist commentator Alexander.[37] It will be another advantage of the present translations that they will make it easier to check the distorting effect of a commentator's background.

Although the Neoplatonist commentators conflate the views of Aristotle with those of Neoplatonism, Philoponus alludes to a certain convention when he quotes Plutarchus expressing disapproval of Alexander for expounding his own philosophical doctrines in a commentary on Aristotle.[38] But this does not stop Philoponus from later inserting into his own commentaries on the *Physics* and *Meteorology* his arguments in favour of the Christian view of Creation. Of course, the commentators also wrote independent works of their own, in which their views are expressed independently of the exegesis of Aristotle. Some of these independent works will be included in the present series of translations.

The distorting Neoplatonist context does not prevent the commentaries from being incomparable guides to Aristotle. The introductions to Aristotle's philosophy insist that commentators must have a minutely detailed knowledge of the entire Aristotelian corpus, and this they certainly have. Commentators are also enjoined neither to accept nor reject what Aristotle says too readily, but to consider it in depth and without partiality. The commentaries draw one's attention to hundreds of phrases, sentences and ideas in Aristotle, which one could easily have passed over, however often one read him. The scholar who makes the right allowance for the distorting context will learn far more about Aristotle than he would be likely to on his own.

The relations of Neoplatonist commentators to the Christians were subtle. Porphyry wrote a treatise explicitly against the Christians in 15 books, but an order to burn it was issued in 448, and later Neoplatonists

---

[36] English: Calcidius *in Tim.* (parts by van Winden; den Boeft); Iamblichus fragments (Dillon); Proclus *in Tim.* (Thomas Taylor); Proclus *in Parm.* (Dillon); Proclus *in Parm.*, end of 7th book, from the Latin (Klibansky, Labowsky, Anscombe); Proclus *in Alcib. 1* (O'Neill); Olympiodorus and Damascius *in Phaedonem* (Westerink); Damascius *in Philebum* (Westerink); *Anonymous Prolegomena to Platonic Philosophy* (Westerink). See also extracts in Thomas Taylor, *The Works of Plato*, 5 vols. (1804). French: Proclus *in Tim.* and *in Rempublicam* (Festugière); *in Parm.* (Chaignet); Anon. *in Parm.* (P. Hadot); Damascius *in Parm.* (Chaignet).

[37] For Alexander's treatment of the Stoics, see Robert B. Todd, *Alexander of Aphrodisias on Stoic Physics* (Leiden 1976), 24-9.

[38] Philoponus *in DA* 21,20-3.

were more circumspect. Among the last commentators in the main group, we have noted several Christians. Of these the most important were Boethius and Philoponus. It was Boethius' programme to transmit Greek learning to Latin-speakers. By the time of his premature death by execution, he had provided Latin translations of Aristotle's logical works, together with commentaries in Latin but in the Neoplatonist style on Porphyry's *Isagôgê* and on Aristotle's *Categories* and *de Interpretatione*, and interpretations of the *Prior* and *Posterior Analytics, Topics* and *Sophistici Elenchi*. The interruption of his work meant that knowledge of Aristotle among Latin-speakers was confined for many centuries to the logical works. Philoponus is important both for his proofs of the Creation and for his progressive replacement of Aristotelian science with rival theories, which were taken up at first by the Arabs and came fully into their own in the West only in the sixteenth century.

Recent work has rejected the idea that in Alexandria the Neoplatonists compromised with Christian monotheism by collapsing the distinction between their two highest deities, the One and the Intellect. Simplicius (who left Alexandria for Athens) and the Alexandrians Ammonius and Asclepius appear to have acknowledged their beliefs quite openly, as later did the Alexandrian Olympiodorus, despite the presence of Christian students in their classes.[39]

The teaching of Simplicius in Athens and that of the whole pagan Neoplatonist school there was stopped by the Christian Emperor Justinian in 529. This was the very year in which the Christian Philoponus in Alexandria issued his proofs of Creation against the earlier Athenian Neoplatonist Proclus. Archaeological evidence has been offered that, after their temporary stay in Ctesiphon (in present-day Iraq), the Athenian Neoplatonists did not return to their house in Athens, and further evidence has been offered that Simplicius went to Ḥarrān (Carrhae), in present-day Turkey near the Iraq border.[40] Wherever he went, his commentaries are a treasure house of information about the preceding thousand years of Greek philosophy, information which he painstakingly recorded after the closure in Athens, and which would otherwise have been lost. He had every reason to feel bitter about Christianity, and in fact he sees it and Philoponus, its representative, as irreverent. They deny the divinity of the heavens and prefer the physical relics of dead martyrs.[41] His own commentaries by

[39] For Simplicius, see I. Hadot, *Le Problème du Néoplatonisme Alexandrin: Hiéroclès et Simplicius* (Paris 1978); for Ammonius and Asclepius, Koenraad Verrycken, *God en Wereld in de Wijsbegeerte van Ioannes Philoponus*, Ph.D. Diss. (Louvain 1985); for Olympiodorus, L.G. Westerink, *Anonymous Prolegomena to Platonic Philosophy* (Amsterdam 1962).

[40] Alison Frantz, 'Pagan philosophers in Christian Athens', *Proceedings of the American Philosophical Society* 119 (1975), 29-38; M. Tardieu, 'Témoins orientaux du *Premier Alcibiade* à Ḥarrān et à Nag 'Hammādi', *Journal Asiatique* 274 (1986); id., 'Les calendriers en usage à Ḥarrān d'après les sources arabes et le commentaire de Simplicius à la *Physique* d'Aristote', in I. Hadot (ed.), *Simplicius, sa vie, son oeuvre, sa survie* (Berlin 1987), 40-57; id., *Coutumes nautiques mésopotamiennes chez Simplicius*, in preparation. The opposing view that Simplicius returned to Athens is most fully argued by Alan Cameron, 'The last days of the Academy at Athens', *Proceedings of the Cambridge Philological Society* 195, n.s. 15 (1969), 7-29.

[41] Simplicius *in Cael.* 26,4-7; 70,16-18; 90,1-18; 370,29-371,4. See on his whole attitude Philippe Hoffmann, 'Simplicius' polemics', in Richard Sorabji (ed.), *Philoponus and the Rejection of Aristotelian Science* (London and Ithaca, N.Y. 1987).

contrast culminate in devout prayers.

Two collections of articles by various hands have been published, to make the work of the commentators better known. The first is devoted to Philoponus;[42] the second is about the commentators in general, and goes into greater detail on some of the issues briefly mentioned here.[43]

[42] Richard Sorabji (ed.), *Philoponus and the Rejection of Aristotelian Science* (London and Ithaca, N.Y. 1987).

[43] Richard Sorabji (ed.), *Aristotle Transformed: the ancient commentators and their influence* (London and Ithaca, N.Y. 1990). The lists of texts and previous translations of the commentaries included in Wildberg, *Philoponus Against Aristotle on the Eternity of the World* (pp.12ff.) are not included here. The list of translations should be augmented by: F.L.S. Bridgman, Heliodorus (?) in *Ethica Nicomachea*, London 1807.

I am grateful for comments to Henry Blumenthal, Victor Caston, I. Hadot, Paul Mercken, Alain Segonds, Robert Sharples, Robert Todd, L.G. Westerink and Christian Wildberg.